Making a Living
in
Spain

A Survival Handbook

by
Anne Hall

SURVIVAL BOOKS • LONDON • ENGLAND

First published 2005

Survival Books Limited,
26 York Street, London W1U 6PZ, United Kingdom
☎ +44 (0)20-7788 7644, 📠 +44 (0)870-762 3212
✉ info@survivalbooks.net
💻 www.survivalbooks.net
To order books, please refer to page 323.

British Library Cataloguing in Publication Data.
A CIP record for this book is available
from the British Library.
ISBN 1 901130 83 5

Printed and bound in Finland by WS Bookwell Ltd

Acknowledgements

Iwould like to thank all those who contributed to the publication of this book, family and friends and in particular Joanna Styles (friend and fellow Survival Books writer) for her support, advice and encouragement, David Hampshire for his guidance and Joe and Kerry Laredo for their tireless work editing, proofreading and desktop publishing. I would also like to thank everyone who provided photographs and Jim Watson for his wonderful illustrations, cartoons, maps and cover design. Finally, thanks must go to the countless people who provided me with information and advice of all kinds, with particular thanks to those who have allowed me to include their experiences in the book. Their time, effort and openness about their own efforts to make a living in Spain are much appreciated.

Titles by Survival Books

Alien's Guides
Britain; France

The Best Places To Buy A Home
France; Spain

Buying A Home
Abroad; Cyprus; Florida;
France; Greece; Ireland; Italy;
Portugal; South Africa; Spain;
Buying, Selling & Letting
Property (UK)

**Foreigners Abroad: Triumphs
& Disasters**
France; Spain

Lifeline Regional Guides
Costa Blanca; Costa del Sol;
Dordogne/Lot; Normandy;
Poitou-Charentes

Living And Working
Abroad; America;
Australia; Britain; Canada;
The European Union;
The Far East; France; Germany;
The Gulf States & Saudi Arabia;
Holland, Belgium & Luxembourg;
Ireland; Italy; London;
New Zealand; Spain;
Switzerland

Making A Living
France; Spain

Other Titles
Renovating & Maintaining
Your French Home;
Retiring Abroad

Order forms are on page 323.

WHAT READERS & REVIEWERS

When you buy a model plane for your child, a video recorder, or some new computer gizmo, you get with it a leaflet or booklet pleading 'Read Me First', or bearing large friendly letters or bold type saying 'IMPORTANT – follow the instructions carefully'. This book should be similarly supplied to all those entering France with anything more durable than a 5-day return ticket. It is worth reading even if you are just visiting briefly, or if you have lived here for years and feel totally knowledgeable and secure. But if you need to find out how France works then it is indispensable. Native French people probably have a less thorough understanding of how their country functions. – Where it is most essential, the book is most up to the minute.

LIVING FRANCE

Rarely has a 'survival guide' contained such useful advice. This book dispels doubts for first-time travellers, yet is also useful for seasoned globetrotters – In a word, if you're planning to move to the USA or go there for a long-term stay, then buy this book both for general reading and as a ready-reference.

AMERICAN CITIZENS ABROAD

It is everything you always wanted to ask but didn't for fear of the contemptuous put down – The best English-language guide – Its pages are stuffed with practical information on everyday subjects and are designed to complement the traditional guidebook.

SWISS NEWS

A complete revelation to me – I found it both enlightening and interesting, not to mention amusing.

CAROLE CLARK

Let's say it at once. David Hampshire's *Living and Working in France* is the best handbook ever produced for visitors and foreign residents in this country; indeed, my discussion with locals showed that it has much to teach even those born and bred in l'Hexagone. – It is Hampshire's meticulous detail which lifts his work way beyond the range of other books with similar titles. Often you think of a supplementary question and search for the answer in vain. With Hampshire this is rarely the case. – He writes with great clarity (and gives French equivalents of all key terms), a touch of humour and a ready eye for the odd (and often illuminating) fact. – This book is absolutely indispensable.

THE RIVIERA REPORTER

A mine of information – I may have avoided some embarrassments and frights if I had read it prior to my first Swiss encounters – Deserves an honoured place on any newcomer's bookshelf.

ENGLISH TEACHERS ASSOCIATION, SWITZERLAND

HAVE SAID ABOUT SURVIVAL BOOKS

What a great work, wealth of useful information, well-balanced wording and accuracy in details. My compliments!

THOMAS MÜLLER

This handbook has all the practical information one needs to set up home in the UK – The sheer volume of information is almost daunting – Highly recommended for anyone moving to the UK.

AMERICAN CITIZENS ABROAD

A very good book which has answered so many questions and even some I hadn't thought of – I would certainly recommend it.

BRIAN FAIRMAN

We would like to congratulate you on this work: it is really super! We hand it out to our expatriates and they read it with great interest and pleasure.

ICI (SWITZERLAND) AG

Covers just about all the things you want to know on the subject – In answer to the desert island question about the one how-to book on France, this book would be it – Almost 500 pages of solid accurate reading – This book is about enjoyment as much as survival.

THE RECORDER

It's so funny – I love it and definitely need a copy of my own – Thanks very much for having written such a humorous and helpful book.

HEIDI GUILIANI

A must for all foreigners coming to Switzerland.

ANTOINETTE O'DONOGHUE

A comprehensive guide to all things French, written in a highly readable and amusing style, for anyone planning to live, work or retire in France.

THE TIMES

A concise, thorough account of the DOs and DON'Ts for a foreigner in Switzerland – Crammed with useful information and lightened with humorous quips which make the facts more readable.

AMERICAN CITIZENS ABROAD

Covers every conceivable question that may be asked concerning everyday life – I know of no other book that could take the place of this one.

FRANCE IN PRINT

Hats off to *Living and Working in Switzerland*!

RONNIE ALMEIDA

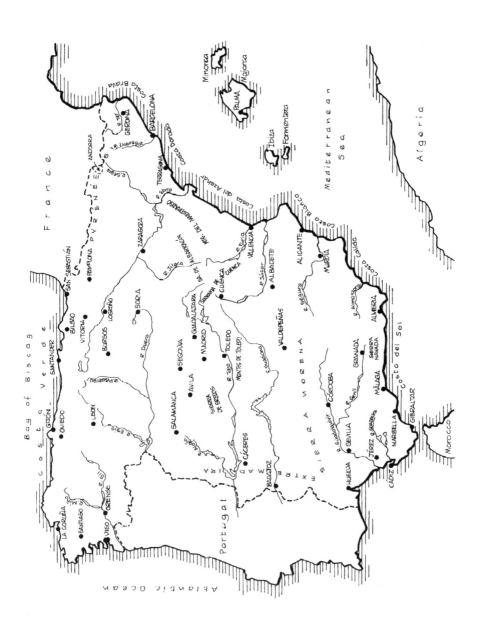

CONTENTS

Part One

Part Two

THE AUTHOR

A nne Hall was born in the UK and began her working life at the BBC in London. Before having her children, she worked chiefly in broadcasting and television production, both for the BBC and for independent production companies. She studied English literature as a mature student at the University of London and began her freelance writing career after a family move to the Costa del Sol, Spain in 2002. She writes for UK publications and English-language publications in Spain. *Making a Living in Spain* is her first Survival Books publication. Anne is married with two children.

Important Note

Spain is a large country with myriad faces and many ethnic groups, religions and customs. Although ostensibly the same throughout the country, many laws, rules and regulations, especially those associated with doing business, are open to local interpretation and are occasionally even formulated on the spot. Laws and regulations are changing at a considerable rate as Spain continues to enjoy healthy economic growth.

I cannot recommend too strongly that you check with an official and reliable source (not always the same) before making any major decisions or undertaking an irreversible course of action. However, don't believe everything you're told or have read, even – dare I say it? – in this book! Always check and double check things for yourself.

To help you obtain further information and verify data with official sources, useful addresses and references to other sources of information have been included in all chapters and in **Appendices A to C**. Important points have been emphasised throughout the book **in bold print**, some of which it would be expensive or foolish to disregard. **Ignore them at your peril or cost.** Unless specifically stated, the reference to any company, organisation, product or publication in this book doesn't constitute an endorsement or recommendation.

AUTHOR'S NOTES

- Frequent references are made throughout this book to the European Union (EU), which comprises 25 countries, and to the European Economic Area (EEA), which comprises the EU countries plus Iceland, Liechtenstein and Norway.

- Whenever references are made to the Spanish language, this means Castilian, spoken as a first or second language throughout Spain.

- Spanish place names (shown in brackets below) are often changed when written in English. In many cases this means just dropping an accent, e.g. Cadiz (Cádiz), Cordoba (Córdoba), Malaga (Málaga) and San Sesbastian (San Sesbastián), while other changes are more pronounced, e.g. Andalusia (Andalucía), Alicante (Alacant), Majorca (Mallorca), Seville (Sevilla) and Zaragossa (Zaragoza).

- **Prices quoted should be taken as estimates only**, although they were mostly correct when going to print and fortunately don't usually change overnight in Spain. Most prices in Spain are quoted inclusive of value added tax (*IVA incluido*), which is the method used in this book (unless otherwise indicated, i.e. *mas IVA*).

- His/he/him (etc.) also mean her/she/her (no offence ladies!). This is done simply to make life easier for both the reader and, in particular, the author, and isn't intended to be sexist.

- The Spanish translation of key words and phrases is shown in brackets in *italics*.

- Warnings and important points are shown in **bold** type.

- All spelling is (or should be) British and not American English.

- All times are shown using am (*ante meridiem*) for before noon and pm (*post meridiem*) for after noon. All times are local, so check the time difference when making international telephone calls.

- The following symbols are used in this book: ☎ (telephone), 🗐 (fax), 💻 (internet) and ✉ (email).

- Lists of useful addresses, further reading material and useful websites are contained in **Appendices A, B** and **C** respectively. Imperial/metric conversion tables are included in **Appendix D**. Maps of Spain and the main transport networks are contained in **Appendix E** and a map showing the major cities and geographical features is on page 6. Tables of scheduled airline services between Spain and the UK/Ireland and a list of airlines are in **Appendix F**.

INTRODUCTION

Spain continues to hold a fascination for millions of tourists every year, many of whom decide to buy holiday homes or retire to Spain. The last few years have seen a significant change in expatriate demographics, with a growing number of younger people, many with families, selling up in their home countries and coming to Spain in search of a new life. The average age of those moving here is closer to 45 than 65 and more immigrants than ever want to make a living in Spain, rather than spend their time on the beach or golf course.

The purpose of *Making a Living in Spain* is to provide you with the information necessary to help you to do just that. One of the most common mistakes people make when coming to work or start a business in Spain is to assume that they can continue working in the way they did in their home country, especially if they had a successful business. **Don't assume anything!** Spain is a large and immensely varied country, with 17 autonomous communities, some of which have their own regional languages. Each area has its own culture and, inevitably, its own way of doing business, and the one thing you can be sure of is that it won't be the same as in your home country! You will be far more successful if you learn to adapt and be flexible than if you try to fight the system.

Making a Living in Spain contains practical advice to help you find work in Spain, whether you're seeking a job, wish to be self-employed or plan to start your own business, as well as the experiences of people from all walks of life who have already taken the plunge and are successfully making a living in Spain. They explain how they've overcome the notorious Spanish bureaucracy and achieved (more or less!) what they set out to do. Their hard work, perseverance and sense of humour should inspire you to follow in their footsteps.

A love affair with Spain is all very well, but if you want to do business there you cannot afford to view the country through rose-tinted glasses, but must take a long, hard look at the realities of Spanish life give it your long-term commitment. It may be less romantic, but you're more likely to succeed if you accept that life in Spain, as in any country, has its bad days as well as its good. Making a living in Spain will change your life for ever and, if you approach it in the right way, can open your mind, broaden your horizons, improve your language skills and hopefully make you some money along the way!

¡Mucha suerte!   **Anne Hall**
                                                                    March 2005

1.

WHY WORK IN SPAIN?

If you've only ever visited Spain on holiday, it can be difficult to be clear-headed about your decision to live and work in the country. The big cities are vibrant, colourful places and you can't help being seduced by the relaxed lifestyle and, of course, in the south of the country at least, those endless sunny days. Perhaps that's why you began to think about settling in Spain in the first place. **It may sound obvious, but holidays and earning a living are two completely different things and confusing the two is a fundamental mistake many people make when they come to work in Spain.**

SEEING PAST THE SUNSHINE

It isn't easy to stay focused when you're surrounded by holiday-makers enjoying a long, lazy lunch and your own, seemingly endless, stream of visitors keep urging you to join them on the beach. You will have to be very strong-willed not to take the day off or shut up shop and join them. In this sense, Spain is one of the most difficult places to work (at least in the tourist areas) but, unless you have large financial reserves, you cannot afford to play at earning a living, especially in a foreign country. You must be professional, hard-working, determined to keep bouncing back after the inevitable knocks, and willing to leave the sunbathing for the weekends!

The people who tend to make a success of making a living in Spain have usually done exhaustive research and spent a lot of time in the country (other than on holiday). Begin your research by thinking hard about why you've chosen Spain to work in, rather than any other country. Can you speak any Spanish? This book looks in detail at language learning options both in your home country and in Spain because, even if you only plan to live and work in the expatriate community, **you must be able to speak at least basic Spanish**. How well do you know the area you're planning to settle in? Buy yourself a large map of Spain and read as much as you can about the areas you're interested in (such as *The Best Places to Buy a Home in Spain* – see page 323). Find out about Spain's economy in general and especially the economy of your chosen area. This book contains economic guides to the regions of Spain that attract the most foreigners. How well do you know the Spanish people and understand their history and culture? It's important to have a little background knowledge before you launch yourself into their world.

Most importantly, are you prepared to forget everything you've learned in your own country and begin again with none of the support networks you used to take for granted? Are you strong enough to deal with feeling like the new boy in school not just for a few months, but for longer than you can imagine? Finally, take a long hard look at Spain's unemployment figures, which are still the highest in Europe at over 11 per cent, compared with UK figures of around 4.5 per cent, for example.

All this may seem daunting, but these are the questions it's vital to research and think about before you make any other decisions. Make yourself answer them honestly at an early stage and you will save yourself time, money and endless heartache in an unfamiliar country. If after that you're still feeling strong and determined to try to make a living in Spain, then you can start to consider how exactly you're going to do so. There's no doubt that it's a long and difficult road; as you struggle to make your way, you will hear plenty of hair-raising stories about people who have lost everything. Learn from them, but don't allow yourself to be thrown off balance by their misfortune. There are many foreigners who have successful businesses and good jobs in Spain. They're usually the ones who have done, and continue to do, their homework and who are willing to adapt and keep an open mind. Above all, they're prepared to work long and hard to create their own 'luck', rather than sit in a bar talking enviously about other people's 'luck'.

THE SPANISH ECONOMY

The end of the Franco regime in 1975 and the creation of the Spanish Constitution in 1978 heralded a new era for Spain's economy. It has experienced intensive growth and development during the last 25 years, making Spain one of Europe's greatest success stories. The country has progressed in leaps and bounds from a mainly rural economy to a dynamic, developed member of the European Union (EU) with a strong services and industry sector. According to Spain's Ministry of Economy, average annual economic growth in 2003 stood at 2.4 per cent, four times as fast as the rest of the EU, and there are predictions that by the end of 2005 the growth rate will have reached 3.3 per cent.

Part of the reason for this rapid growth is strong domestic demand thanks to an increasingly open economy and a higher standard of living. Spain has a population of around 43 million people with an estimated annual per capita income of €20,800. That doesn't include the millions of visitors (around 80 million in 2003) who come to Spain every year. All of this makes the country an attractive market for overseas companies and investors, which of course boosts the economy even further.

Spain's high unemployment figures are the other side of the story, official figures standing at over 11 per cent in 2004, with only a slight reduction predicted in the near future. The government has managed to control inflation – just over 2 per cent in 2004 – and long-term interest rates, which have come down from 10 per cent to 4.2 per cent during the last ten years. Yet unemployment remains among the highest in Europe, and the real percentage is almost certainly much higher than the official figure. This is partly because many unemployed people don't register with the National Employment Service (*Instituto Naciónal de Empleo/INEM*) during the required four-week period before statistics are collected (or at all!) and so aren't included in the figures. The other reason is the huge 'black' economy which exists in Spain, not just among the Spanish but also within the expatriate communities. A study in 2003 by the Institute of Tax Studies showed that at least 20 per cent of the workforce was working illegally despite the government's hope that the introduction of the euro would dramatically reduce illegal working.

Growth Areas

There are growth areas in the Spanish economy which may be relevant to you if you want to make a living here, whether by finding a job or by starting your own business. The boom areas are tourism (more specifically, residential tourism), construction and property services, and –a relatively recent major growth area – information technology. These are summarised below. For details of opportunities in the areas of Spain most popular with foreigners, see **Chapter 2**.

Tourism

Tourism is Spain's largest industry, accounting for 10 per cent of employment in the country. It offers a wealth of opportunities, whether you're simply looking for a summer job or you want to open a bar or restaurant (see **Chapter 7**). In 2003, more than 52 million tourists visited Spain – not just the Costas but also the big cities, particularly Madrid and Barcelona.

One important development in tourism is that, although Spain has traditionally catered to the cheaper, package-holiday end of the market, it's now making an enormous effort to attract the more up-market traveller and to that end has created the impressively named Comprehensive Plan for Quality in Spanish Tourism (*Plan Integral de Calidad de Turismo Español 2000-2006*). Both the private and the public sector are involved in this upgrade and, with the help of EU funds and

€150 million from the Spanish Official Credit Institute, the government aims to improve current tourist facilities and create new and more diverse facilities. Areas designated for particular promotion include sports holidays (see **Chapter 14**), cultural and business tourism, health tourism (which generates business worth more than €600 million), and rural tourism – favoured by Spaniards but becoming increasingly popular with foreigners.

Residential tourism is now a significant part of the Spanish economy and one which isn't affected by seasonal highs and lows. A residential tourist is someone who owns a home here but spends less than six months of the year in Spain. According to the World Tourism Organisation, there are 3.8 million second homes in Spain and during the next five years as many as 1.7 million Europeans are expected to add to this figure. Not surprisingly, the coastal areas are the focus of this growing business. Sixty per cent of visitors to the province of Malaga in 2003 chose private residences over hotels for their stay and for the first time residential tourism figures topped hotel occupancy figures. This kind of tourist needs to spend far more money than a hotel guest, boosting the economy further, and there are obvious ramifications for the construction and property industries.

Construction & Property

Alongside buoyant consumer spending, the construction and property industries are both helping to keep the Spanish economy healthy. The demand for housing among Spaniards and foreigners shows no signs of abating so whether you're a jobbing builder or a property developer, Spain offers more opportunities than most European countries. There has been continuous growth in employment in the construction industry in recent years, and latest figures put it at 11.8 per cent of the total working population. Residential construction accounts for a third of all construction business, which means plenty of potential work for estate agents and property management and letting companies.

Information Technology

The world technological revolution didn't reach Spain until the mid-'80s, since when it has enjoyed fairly consistent growth, although in the last few years it has suffered a slight downturn. According to the Spanish Association of Technology and Information Companies, Spain is still around 12 years behind the EU average, so there's a lot of catching up to do which is vital for future economic development in Spain. The problem is that growth in this sector is outpacing the availability of qualified, skilled IT professionals, so IT graduates are very much in demand, particularly in Madrid and Barcelona, where many of the jobs don't require an IT degree. A useful internet portal for IT-related jobs in Spain is 💻 www.computrabajo.es, which is only in Spanish. 💻 www.manpower.co.uk is an English-language site with information (under 'X-Border Connections') about jobs available abroad, including IT jobs in Spain. Another useful website is 💻 www.hayspersonnel.es, also available in English, which has an extensive IT section including surveys on the sector and average salaries.

EARNINGS

It's often difficult to find out what a reasonable wage is for a particular job, as salaries aren't generally included in advertisements. Salaries for the more senior positions compare favourably with those in other western countries. If you use a recruitment agency to obtain your job, they should be able to advise you on salary levels or you should ask someone who is familiar with the job market in Spain.

COST OF LIVING

One of the first things you will need to know is how much it's going to cost to live in Spain. Many foreigners have fond memories of the '70s and the '80s, when Spain was a cheap place to live compared with the rest of Europe. This is no longer the case, as Spain is 'catching up' fast. It's true that the cost of living is cheaper in Spain than in the UK, for example, but you must bear in mind that Spaniards earn less than their counterparts in northern Europe, and that will apply to you too when you begin earning money there. At the end of 2004, the minimum wage was just €460.50 per month or €5,526 per annum for full-time workers. When considering earnings, you must also take into account Spanish taxes, which may be higher than those in your previous country of residence (see **Chapter 5**).

It's difficult to be specific about the cost of living because, as in other countries, prices vary from area to area. In the big cities, such as Madrid and Barcelona, the cost of housing is high compared with other living costs, accounting for around half of the average monthly income. Coastal areas are going through yet another boom, especially areas slightly inland from the coast, and property prices in many areas are certainly not the bargain they once were, due to the increasing number of foreigners buying homes. A rule of thumb is that living costs, with the exception of property, are generally around a third cheaper in Spain than in the UK. There are several useful websites that cover this in more detail and give you typical shopping basket prices to compare; these include 💻 www.idealspain.com and 💻 www.spain-info.com.

PERMITS & VISAS

Before making any plans to live and work in Spain, you must ensure that you have the necessary identity card or passport (with a visa if necessary) and, if you're planning to stay long-term, the appropriate documentation to obtain a residence and/or work permit. There are different requirements for different nationalities and circumstances, as detailed below.

Whether you're a European Union (EU) citizen or a non-EU citizen, you must have *Número de Identificación de Extranjero (NIE)*, which identifies you to the tax authorities. Obtaining an *NIE* is relatively easy (see page 72).

Immigration is a complex and ever-changing subject and the information in this chapter is intended only as a general guide. You shouldn't base any decisions or actions on the information contained herein without confirming it with an official and reliable source, such as a Spanish embassy or consulate.

European Union Citizens

Nationals of all European Union (EU) countries, their family members and dependents are entitled to free movement throughout the EU and may therefore live, work, start a business or study in Spain without restriction – in theory. Armed with just your passport or identity document, you can stay in Spain for up to six months, looking for work or doing market research for your business.

As an EU citizen, once you find a job or start your own business, you don't need a work permit or a residence permit provided you have an employment contract, are registered as self-employed or are the owner of a Spanish company. If you fall into any of these categories, you're in the Spanish system and are treated in the same way as a Spaniard. If you haven't found work or started a business, you must apply for a residence card once you've been in Spain for more than 90 days. However, most Foreign Residents' Departments advise that you apply for one whatever your situation. Spaniards and foreigners alike must carry some form of photo identification at all times in Spain, and present it on demand to the police or the authorities. Your residence card is effectively an identity card and means that you don't have to carry your passport. Moreover, obtaining residence means that you enjoy some tax advantages over non-residents.

Residence Permit

If you decide to apply for a residence permit (*residencia*), it's advisable to use the services of a good *gestor* (see page 89). Even if you have the time and the language skills, you will still need someone who knows the system to help you get things done. The process usually takes several months, whether you do it yourself or through a *gestor*, so be prepared for a long wait and carry your passport in the meantime. **Ask for a list of the necessary documents in advance**, because if you don't present what's required you will simply be sent away and told to return when you have everything. Even if you follow the list religiously, you may find that things have changed by the time you get to submit your application. Requirements also vary from area to area and may even depend on the mood of the official processing applications! Always make several copies of any original documents. Below is a guide (only!) to the documents that are usually required.

- Several copies of your completed application form, which you can either obtain from the provincial police station where you make your application or download from the Ministry of the Interior's website (🖥 www.mir.es);
- Evidence that you've paid the application fee in advance. (When you obtain the application form, you should also be given a paying-in slip for your bank to stamp as proof of payment.)
- Your passport and a photocopy. This must be a full, valid passport.
- Proof of residence, which can be your *escritura*, if you've bought a property, a rental contract or a utilities bill in your name;
- Proof of income in the form of bank statements;
- A medical certificate;
- Details of medical insurance, if you aren't entitled to Spanish social security cover. Some offices insist that your health cover is with a recognised Spanish health insurance company with offices in Spain.
- At least four passport-size photographs, preferably more. You can never have enough!

- Evidence that you meet the requirements to carry out your profession or operate your business in Spain. This could be proof of membership of a relevant professional college (*colegio*) and your validated qualifications (see page 30).
- Marriage and/or divorce certificates if applicable.

Once your application has been approved, you should receive a temporary residence card, which is valid for two months and renewable until your full *residencia* is issued. Once this is ready, you must go to the police station and have fingerprints taken for inclusion on the card and police records. A full residence card lasts for up to five years and is automatically renewable; you can apply for a temporary card if your stay is going to be relatively short.

Non-EU Citizens

Life is rather more complicated if you aren't a citizen of an EU country. You can stay in Spain for up to 90 days but, unlike an EU national, you may not arrive as a visitor and then decide to stay on. If you enter as a visitor, the authorities are likely to want to see evidence of a booked return ticket, so **if your intention is to live and work in Spain you must obtain a visa before you leave your home country**. You should apply to the Spanish embassy or consulate closest to where you live for a residence visa (*visado de residencia*), which you will need when you apply for a work permit or residence card in Spain.

There are two websites which give full information about the requirements. One is the Spanish Ministry of Employment and Social Affairs Immigration site (🖥 www.extranjeros.mir.es), which is in English and French as well as Spanish. If you go to the section entitled 'Orientation for Immigrants', you will find detailed information about applying for visas and work permits. The other site (🖥 www.spain business.com) is operated by Spain's commercial offices in the US and contains a wealth of information about doing business in Spain in general but also has a section on visas, work and residence permits.

Visas

There are several different types of visa, so make sure you obtain the right one, according to your employment plans, as you cannot change the type of visa without returning to your home country first. The categories are for salaried employees, investors, business people, those being re-located by multi-national companies, students, teachers and retired people.

Below is a guide to items required to apply for a visa. It isn't a definitive list, and **you must check with a Spanish embassy or consulate**.

- A full, valid passport with at least six months' validity plus a photocopy of the pages showing your details;

- At least three recent, colour, passport-size photographs. Always have plenty of spare photographs.

- Several completed application forms (the number varies);

- A certificate from the police authorities in your country, confirming that you have no criminal record. This is valid only for three months, so don't request it too early or you will have to reapply.

- A medical certificate from a doctor in your home country – also only valid for three months.

Depending on the reason you want to stay in Spain, there are further requirements that must be met, including the following.

- If you already have a job in Spain, you must provide evidence that you've been offered a job and that your employer has registered the fact with the labour authorities.

- If you plan to be self-employed, you must prove that your qualifications are acceptable to practise your profession in Spain and that you've filed a Work Authorisation application with the Ministry of Labour.

- Starting a business is a very expensive way for a non-EU citizen to make a living. You must provide details of your financial situation and, most importantly, must prove that you have sufficient funds to invest in your business, which in 2004 was €120,000. The regulations are strict but, in view of the high unemployment in Spain, if you plan to employ several Spaniards in your business, your application is likely to be favourably regarded by the authorities.

- If you aren't eligible for healthcare under the Spanish social security system, you must also provide proof that you have private health insurance.

Your visa application should take around six to eight weeks to be approved, although it could be a lot longer. The visa is subject to the authorities granting you a work permit (see below).

Work Permits

Obtaining a work permit is a long and complicated process and it's well worth seeking advice from a lawyer who is familiar with the procedure. **Since the EU was enlarged to 25 countries, it has become even more difficult for non-EU citizens to obtain a work permit.**

If you already have a job in Spain, you should send a copy of your visa application, as soon as it's in the system, along with a copy of your passport and medical certificate, to your prospective employer in Spain, who will then inform the labour authorities that the process has been started. The Spanish embassy or consulate that has responsibility for your visa application also informs the relevant labour authority office in Spain, which must be satisfied that the job in question has been advertised to Spanish and EU citizens. **Only when it has been demonstrated that no Spanish or EU citizen is available to do the job will a work permit be granted.** If your job is a temporary or seasonal one, you will be given a Class A permit, which is valid for a maximum of nine months and not renewable. If you're an employee, you will initially be granted a Class B permit, which is valid for one year and limits you to a specific employer and location. When that is renewed, it will carry the same restrictions but will last for two years. Finally a Class C permit allows you to work for any employer in any part of Spain, but not to be self-employed, for up to two years.

If you're planning to be self-employed or start your own business, you need a Class D permit, which restricts you to a specific activity and area and lasts for one year. **You will need a considerable amount of good professional help to obtain a Class D permit.** As with an employee permit, you can renew it and obtain a two-year permit and finally, when this has expired, you may be granted a Class E permit, which allows any kind of activity in any part of Spain for up to two years.

When you present your application for a Class D permit, it must be accompanied by all the documents relating to your proposed business activity. These include some or all of the following, but **check with your embassy or consulate or the relevant labour authorities before submitting your application**:

- Your qualifications, properly validated by the relevant college (see page 30);
- A valid passport and a copy;
- As many recent passport size photographs as you can carry;
- A completed application form and several copies;

- Written details of the business activity you plan to carry out, known as a *memoria de actividades*;

- Your Deed of Incorporation (see page 97) if you've already formed a trading company;

- Proof of registration with the Spanish tax authorities for business tax (*Impuesto de Actividades Economias* – see page 132). Although you won't have to pay this tax unless your profits are over a certain amount, you must still register and obtain a code number (*epigrafe*).

- Proof of registration of your business and yourself with Spanish Social Security as a self-employed worker (*trabajador autónomo* – see page 79);

- If relevant, you must also show you have an opening licence (*licencia de apertura*) and a food handler's licence (*carnet de manipulador de alimentos*).

All these documents must be translated into Spanish, by an official translator approved by your embassy or consulate. If you can manage to wade through all this bureaucracy, you're obviously made of stern stuff and are likely to succeed pretty well in making your living in Spain!

Once the labour authorities have granted you a work permit, they notify the Ministry of the Interior, which issues your residence permit, and the Spanish embassy or consulate where you made your visa application. The embassy or consulate will then contact you and ask you to collect your visa in person. Your work and residence permits, which should be issued for the same duration, can be collected from the relevant office of the Ministry for the Interior in Spain.

Your visa will be stamped in your passport and **it's vital to get a date stamp in your passport when you first enter Spain,** as this defines your visa validity. If you enter Spain from another EU country, it's easy to forget to do this, as passports aren't generally stamped or scrutinised within the EU. **It's your responsibility to ensure that your passport is correctly stamped. Failure to do so can result in your deportation**.

QUALIFICATIONS & EXPERIENCE

If you're a professional wanting to find similar work in Spain, you must first find out whether your qualifications are recognised in Spain. Your trade or professional association in your home country may be able to help you, or you can contact the education department of the Spanish Embassy, where staff can often begin the process for you. In theory, if you're an EU citizen, your qualifications should be recognised by Spain, as an EU member state, but this isn't always the case and recognition varies from country to country.

You can find information in English about your specific qualification is the European Union website (🖳 http://europa.eu.int), which is a valuable research tool if you're planning a move to Spain. It's easy to navigate and has living and working fact sheets for each EU country, covering every conceivable aspect of working within Europe. It provides not only official information on the recognition of qualifications, but also information specific to Spain, as well as a list of all the paperwork you will need to get your qualifications validated by the Spanish Ministry of Education. The relevant section is called 'Dialogue with Citizens' and there's a more personalised advice service, called the 'Citizens' Signpost Service'.

Even if your profession is regulated in Spain, you won't be able to practise there until your qualification has been officially recognised, which can take several months, so you should get the process started as early as possible. First, check whether your profession comes under what is called a Sectoral Directive (*Directiva Sectorial*), which it should do if your training was regulated by statute, statutory instrument or a professional college in your home country and involved at least three years of degree-level study plus job-based training. In 2004, the professions that were recognised as such were general doctors, medical specialists, nurses, midwives, dentists, veterinarians, pharmacists and architects. If you're a member of any of these professions, your qualifications are automatically recognised in EU member states, but you must still get them validated (see below).

If your profession isn't included in the above list, your qualifications won't automatically be recognised and you must apply for recognition before you can start the validation process. The relevant procedure is called the General System of Recognition (*Sistema General de Reconocimiento*). The professions included in this system include lawyers, accountants, engineers, teachers, opticians and physiotherapists. Recognition for each profession is granted by the relevant 'competent authority'. Your local Spanish embassy or consulate can advise you which authority to apply to.

For professions regulated under this system, the paperwork required is more comprehensive than for those regulated under the Sectoral Directive. This is because the Spanish authorities need to find out whether the duration and content of your training is similar to that required for the same profession in Spain. If there isn't much difference, the relevant authority should accept your qualifications as they stand. However, if there's a significant difference, you may be required to take an exam or undergo a period of re-training within your chosen profession in Spain before your qualifications are accepted.

To start the recognition process, you must provide certified photocopies of all your qualifications, along with proof of nationality of a member state, plus a summary of all the examinations and studies undertaken to gain your qualification. Again, this must be accompanied by an official translation in Spanish of all the required paperwork. Finally, make sure that you have available plenty of passport-size photographs available – Spanish bureaucrats seem to eat them for breakfast!

There are two ways of obtaining a definitive list of recognised qualifications under both the Sectoral and the General Systems of recognition. If your Spanish is up to it, consult the website for the Ministry of Education, Culture and Sport (🖥 www.mec.es); go to 'Educación', then to 'Títulos' and click on 'Reconocimiento de títulos regulados por directivas de la Unión Europea a efectos profesionales'. On the left of that page are 'Directivas sectoriales' and 'Sistema General de Reconocimiento', which give the lists in Spanish. If you want information in English, go into the EU website (🖥 http://europa.eu.int/eures), choose 'en' for English and click on 'Living and Working', choose 'Spain', then 'Living and Working Conditions' and finally, under 'Working Conditions', 'Recognition of Diplomas and Qualifications'. On the right of this page there's a link back to the MECS site.

You can obtain further information on the relevant procedures from the European Union website (see above) and, if you live in the UK, from the Department for Education and Skills – specifically a page entitled 'Europe, Open for Professions' on 🖥 www.dfes.gov.uk/europeopen. The National Academic Recognition Centre (NARIC), ☎ 0870-990 4088, 🖥 www.naric.org.uk, is the official source of information and advice about comparability of qualifications, but they generally advise on whether European qualifications are recognised in the UK. If you want to know if your UK qualifications are acceptable in Spain, you must approach NARIC's Spanish section, ☎ 915 065 593, where an English speaker should be available to help you.

Validation

To have your qualifications validated by the Spanish authorities, you must apply in the first instance to The Ministry for Education, Sport and

Culture in the area where you want to work. The process confers official approval of your qualifications (*convalidación y homologación de títulos*). You must provide the following:

- Certified photocopies of your academic and professional qualifications;

- An official translation into Spanish of your academic and professional qualifications;

- A certified photocopy of any document that confirms your EU nationality.

Spanish civil servants **never** accept photocopies of official documents unless they've been certified by a 'competent authority', i.e. a Spanish government official, including Spanish embassy or consulate staff, or by a notary (*notario*) – a person authorised to draw up and certify legal and official documents. Notaries are listed in the yellow pages (*páginas amarillas*), but to get things done at a notary's office you usually need a fairly advanced command of the language, so if your abilities don't stretch that far, take a Spanish speaker along with you. Alternatively, you can employ the services of a *gestor*, a kind of middleman between you and Spanish bureaucracy (see page 89), who can help you with both the Spanish and the paperwork.

LANGUAGE

If you're planning to work in Spain, or set up your own business there, **the first and most important thing to consider is your ability to speak Spanish**. If you speak little or no Spanish, you would be well advised to put your plans on hold for at least a year and sign up for a Spanish course. This may seem an unnecessarily cautious approach, but almost all of those interviewed during the research for this book were in agreement on this point. Many people choose to come to Spain, especially the coastal areas, because they think they can get away without learning even the basics of the language. "Everyone speaks English", they assume. "I'm no good at languages and anyway, I'm far too busy." If those thoughts have crossed your mind, think again and ask yourself how serious you **really** are about earning your living in Spain.

Whichever path you take, you will immediately be at a major disadvantage if you cannot communicate in Spanish. Although English is widely spoken and understood in resort areas, you will find that the majority of Spanish businesses don't use English as a working language.

Even if you plan to work solely within the expatriate community, don't forget that you will still have to interact with Spanish people at some point. Small businesses may have Spanish suppliers, and then there's Spanish officialdom to deal with whatever you do – and you certainly won't find many civil servants willing to speak English. Surely, if you've been pioneering enough to come and work here in the first place, you can cross that final frontier and learn the language?

Learning Spanish will not only improve your business opportunities and widen your social horizons; just think how vulnerable you will be if you always have to rely on someone else to negotiate on your behalf. You will never really be in control – a sitting target for anyone who wants to take advantage of you and relieve you of your hard-earned capital. **Don't give them the opportunity!**

So, before you do anything else, research your language-learning options thoroughly and decide on the fastest and most effective way for you to learn, both in your home country and, just as importantly, once you arrive in Spain. If you're in an area where you have to speak Spanish all day and every day, you will certainly improve very quickly – you will have to. But if you're going to be living and working where there is a large expatriate community, you will have to make an effort to study and practise.

A good place to start, and a resource you can continue to use wherever you are, is the impressive languages section of the BBC website (🖳 www.bbc.co.uk/languages/spanish), which is both comprehensive and informative. You can test your ability to find out which level is best for you and learn Spanish online at your own pace. The site also contains news and features about Spain, to help you get a feel for the country and its people, and there's a fascinating section entitled 'Spanish for Work'. Here, you can find out what it's like working in a Spanish business environment and get help with specialist language practice for a variety of business situations. Particularly valuable are the experiences of those who have already taken the plunge and the expert tips from those who have been in the world of work in Spain for some time.

If you're serious about learning Spanish, The Cervantes Institute is another organisation that you should investigate. Like the BBC, it can help you both in your home country and when you arrive in Spain. The Instituto Cervantes was set up in 1991 to promote Spanish language teaching throughout the world. With more than 40 branches in four continents, it offers much more than just Spanish lessons, with an extensive cultural programme and well stocked libraries. The Instituto Cervantes has two branches in the UK, in London and Manchester, branches across Europe and two in the US, in New York and Chicago. Whatever your level of Spanish, it will have a course suitable for you. If you aren't close to any of its centres, staff can tell you about courses in other areas that are accredited by the institute. Rest assured that any qualifications are awarded on behalf of the Spanish Ministry of Education, Culture and Sport and are therefore officially recognised in Spain. If you cannot attend classes, the institute's website (💻 www. cervantes.es) has a 'virtual' Spanish Classroom (AVE), which allows you to check your level and study online and, of course, continue with your studies once you get to Spain.

Finally, if you're resident in the UK, don't forget your Local Education Authority, which will have lists of Spanish courses in your area. Your nearest further education college is a useful point of contact because you can usually find a Spanish student who is studying English as a foreign language and arrange free Spanish conversation practice with a native speaker in return for your help with his English.

Make no mistake, learning a foreign language is difficult, and Spanish is no exception, especially if you're over 25 and have other demands on your time, such as a job and a family. There will be times when you love it and find it rewarding and times when you just want to forget all about it, but if you want to earn your living in Spain, as opposed to retiring in the sun, **speaking and understanding Spanish is a vital first qualification**.

Regional Languages

If you plan to settle in an area where regional languages are spoken, you will have an extra language problem to consider. When a foreigner refers to Spanish, they are referring to the Castilian (*castellano*) language, which began to be used as the language of official government as far back as the 13th century. Castilian is the main Spanish language and is spoken by 65 per cent of Spaniards as their first and only language. However, the use of Castilian Spanish as the primary language didn't eradicate the other languages spoken in Spain, although they were banned when the country was under the rule of Franco, and you should be aware that the autonomous regions of the Basque Country, Catalonia and Galicia all have their own official languages – Basque (also know as *euskera*), Catalan (*catalán*) and Galician (*gallego*) respectively. If you're thinking of living and working in any of these areas you would be well advised to gain at least a working knowledge of the local language as well as Castilian Spanish.

Official communications from the authorities are often in the local language and Spanish red tape will become even more insurmountable if civil servants insist on speaking to you in their regional language. If you have school-age children and are considering a move to one of the above areas, think particularly carefully about subjecting yourself and your family to this added complication. The regional language will taught in schools alongside Castilian and you may even find that in some areas Castilian is treated as a second language in schools and all lessons are taught in Catalan. In Catalonia, for example, Castilian is treated as a 'minority language'! The Catalan government is very strict about enforcing its language in all areas of daily life. Almost everyone in Catalonia **can** speak Castilian and will usually do so, especially with non-Catalans, but some refuse to or even pretend not to understand when you speak to them in Spanish.

Barcelona, which is popular with expatriates from all over the world, is part of Catalonia, and Catalan is the official language there and is spoken by around 7 million people. The Costa Brava area is also part of Catalonia, where you may have the same kind of language problems.

The two other official regional languages, Galician and Basque, are less likely to affect expatriates, but you should be aware that Galician is spoken exclusively by 40 per cent of the population of that region and Basque by around half a million inhabitants of the Basque country, mainly in rural areas.

Whereas Catalan and Galician have some similarities with Spanish, Basque isn't a Latin-based language and in fact bears no relation to any other European language and is incomprehensible to anyone but a native speaker. Only learn it if you have to!

Dialects

Never make the mistake of thinking of or referring to any regional language as a dialect. Since Franco's death in 1975 they have enjoyed increasing status and are an inseparable part of the greater autonomy enjoyed by the 17 regions of Spain. There are, however, some other areas of Spain where dialects of Castilian – as opposed to distinct regional languages – are spoken, and these too can make your life more complicated in language terms. In the autonomous community of Valencia, a dialect of Catalan called Valencian (*valenciano* in Spanish, *valencià* in Valencian) is spoken by some locals and at the end of 2004, there was something of a political tussle over whether Valencian should be regarded as a regional language. Locals on the Balearic Islands also speak dialects of Catalan – a different one on each island!

Further information about which languages are spoken in which parts of Spain is contained in **Chapter 2**.

WORK CULTURE

If you're going to work or do business in Spain, you must try to forget how things are done in your home country. Many expatriates, especially those from the UK and the US, completely underestimate the dramatic differences in culture between the Spanish and northern Europeans, which are naturally reflected in the business and work environment. Whether it's the length of the working day, the way business meetings are conducted, or the less formal approach to business that Spaniards prefer, working in Spain can involve a fairly steep learning curve for a foreigner.

"Spain is a people place; you've got to have a personal relationship with someone before anything happens." This statement by Adela Gooch, *The Economist*'s Spanish Correspondent, sums up the Spanish work culture. Spaniards favour personal contact in business, preferring to get to know and trust someone well before they commit themselves. Consequently, everything happens much more slowly than in northern Europe or the US but, if you learn to relax and keep a sense of humour, you will find it a far more enjoyable process. For example, doing business over lunch or dinner is much more common than in the UK or US, where long lunches are very much a thing of the past.

Once a Spaniard has confidence in you, he won't expect you to confirm everything in writing and in triplicate. Even if you do, he probably won't read it. If you write a letter or email that requires a reply, it's always a good idea to follow it up with a telephone call. The Spanish are notoriously bad at committing anything to paper, but this is for the simple reason that they would much rather talk to you, on the telephone or, preferably, face to face.

Time Differences

For northern Europeans and Americans, the Spanish concept of time can be very frustrating, especially when you're trying to do business. However, don't be fooled by that old *mañana* cliché. The Spanish work extremely hard; they just do so in different ways.

Foreigners usually encounter this cultural difference when they arrive early or on time for a meeting, only to be kept waiting 15 or 30 minutes. When the person you're meeting eventually turns up, he will appear totally unconcerned and certainly won't apologise. Whatever you do, don't interpret this as rudeness; it's considered perfectly normal to arrive a little late for meetings in Spain. As a foreigner, you should arrive on time (but never early, as this irritates Spaniards, especially if they're running late after a previous meeting), ensuring that you have something to do while waiting.

To avoid frustration, it's best not to attempt to do too much in one day, especially if you're dealing with civil servants (they're the worst timekeepers), and relax and accept that you may not 'achieve' as much in a day as you would in your home country. You've come to Spain for a different lifestyle and this is all part of it.

If you're used to working or doing business in the UK or the US, you will also notice that everything happens much later in the day. Don't expect breakfast meetings; meetings that start before 8.30am are generally frowned upon, lunch doesn't start until between 2 and 3pm and you might well find yourself doing business over dinner – an event which doesn't start until around 10pm and may go on until the early hours of the morning.

If you're working in an office, the length of your working day will depend on the kind of business it is, but office or trading hours are usually from 9am to 1.30pm, followed by a long lunch break, work starting again around 4.30pm and continuing until between 7 and 8pm. All these times vary somewhat from area to area but the general pattern is the norm in Spain, where many people still go home for lunch and a siesta with their families. Some businesses are open from 9am until 3pm and then don't re-open in the afternoon, especially during the long hot summers. It's always best to check, as no two businesses are the same. Working hours are changing and the siesta is certainly less common than it was, especially in areas where there's a lot of international business, but for many Spaniards it's still an important part of their day and one they won't relinquish in a hurry.

Attitudes to Foreigners

With the number of foreigners resident in Spain rising every year – it has quadrupled since 1996 – Spaniards have had to come to terms with working alongside or doing business with foreigners. Attitudes towards foreigners are generally positive, although many Spaniards are bemused by the influx of *extranjeros* or *guiris*. Only a few are antagonistic.

Language is the key to your acceptance and integration in the workplace. Obviously, it's **always** better if you can communicate with any Spanish colleagues or business associates in their own language, even in areas where English is widely spoken. Apart from any possible communication problems, they will appreciate and respect the effort you've made. Don't forget that the majority of Spanish businesses don't use English as a working language, so think hard about how effective you can be either in a job or in your own business if you can't speak Spanish. Turn the situation on its head and imagine your reaction if a foreigner arrived in your home country and expected to set up and run a business without being able to communicate in your language. Needless to say, Spaniards will be far happier to tolerate your excruciatingly bad Spanish than they will a superior attitude and no effort on your part to engage in even basic pleasantries. See also **Language** on page 31.

Women in the Workplace

In the last ten years, more women than ever before have entered the Spanish workforce and they now amount to 42 per cent of all workers. According to a report by the Spanish Economic and Social Council, there has also been an increase in younger, better qualified women, especially in technical and professional areas, where they now make up more than 50 per cent of workers. Things have changed dramatically for women over the last 25 years and their position in the workforce reflects their improved position in Spanish society. However, their official unemployment rate is still almost twice as high as men's at over 15 per cent, and the proportion of women in low-paid and temporary employment and working part-time is higher than men, which means that their average salary is around 20 per cent lower than men's.

If you're a woman looking for a job in Spain or you want to start a business, the good news is that legally there should be no discrimination against you on the grounds of sex. However, Spain does have a far more macho culture than many northern European countries or the US, and some men might resent having to work for a female boss. As in many countries, the law may say one thing, but the reality is often quite different. The government is working hard to change attitudes and it encourages job creation for women by rewarding employers with social security rebates if they hire women. There are also new measures to encourage female entrepreneurship through state grants, which are issued by the Dirección General de la Mujer, the government department responsible for supporting women in all areas of their lives, including work and starting a business. Most town halls (*ayuntamiento*) have a department that caters for women's needs at a local level. Prime Minister José Luis Rodríguez Zapatero's socialist government, elected in March 2004, has promised to 'eradicate machismo' and, as half of his Cabinet is female, there's every chance that women's roles will continue to improve.

Dress

When you're working or doing business in Spain, it's advisable to dress formally and conservatively. Spanish men and women are usually very well groomed and wear good quality clothes; they will be impressed if you do the same. If you want to be taken seriously, don't even consider going to a meeting wearing anything that remotely resembles 'beachwear', especially shorts and sandals, even in very hot weather.

Forms of Address

Even if you don't speak much Spanish, it's advisable to brush up on how to greet and address people politely. Normally, when you meet in a business setting, it's polite to shake hands (both at the beginning and at the end of the meeting) and address men as *Señor*, married and mature women as *Señora* and young or unmarried women as *Señorita*.

For foreigners, there seem to be two main confusions over how to address Spanish people. The first is whether to use the informal word for 'you', which is *tu*, or the more formal, *usted*. You should **always** use *usted* to begin with, especially in meetings, after which your Spanish colleagues may switch to the more informal *tu*, in which case you may do likewise.

The second area of confusion is that the Spanish have two surnames, the first being the first surname of their father and the second the first surname of their mother. This is not as confusing as it sounds but to make sure you get it right you should address them either by both surnames, although this isn't always necessary, or by just their first surname. So, for example, *Juan Garcia Martinez* can be safely addressed as such, or as *Juan Garcia* or *Señor Garcia* (but **not** *Juan Martinez* or *Señor Martinez*).

2.

CHOOSING THE AREA

You may already have decided on the area of Spain you want to work in, you may have a shortlist of possible locations or you may have little idea of where the best place for you to live will be. In any case, you should consider the alternatives, taking into account the local language (see page 31) as well as the cost of living, the infrastructure and the labour market.

According to figures from the Spanish government's Institute of Statistics in 2004, there were 2.7 million (legal) foreigners living in Spain, which amounts to just over 6 per cent of the total population. The number has increased four-fold since 1996 and the most popular regions (in alphabetical order) are the Balearic Islands; the Canary Islands; Catalonia, including the province of Barcelona; Madrid; Malaga, where the Costa del Sol is situated; and Valencia, which includes the Costa Blanca.

A large proportion of the foreign population, especially in the cities of Madrid and Barcelona, are from South America and Morocco, but in the coastal provinces of Malaga and Alicante nationals of the UK and Germany make up the largest percentage of foreign residents. More immigrants than ever are arriving to make a living rather than to retire and spend their time on the beach or the golf course, and a large proportion of them, especially those from the European Union (EU), work in the service industries. This chapter looks at each of these 'hot spots' in detail and offers economic and more general information about each area, along with an idea of the cost of both residential and commercial property.

BALEARIC ISLANDS

The Balearic Islands are located off the east coast of Spain and consist of three main islands, Majorca, Minorca and Ibiza, as well as several smaller ones, although the majority of foreign residents (mainly from Germany and the UK) settle on one of these three islands. At the end of 2003 there were around 126,000 foreigners out of a total population of just  under 950,000 people living on the Balearic Islands. They're one of Europe's top tourist destinations, popular for their endless sun, magnificent landscapes and impressive coastlines.

Majorca is the largest and most popular island with tourists, Minorca, a much quieter island, the next largest, and Ibiza, the last word in hip nightlife and a meeting point for Europe's jet set, the smallest of the three main islands. Unsurprisingly, tourism is the most important industry on the Balearic Islands and, directly or indirectly, it has a huge effect on employment and the economy of the area, although agriculture, mainly olives and citrus fruits, still plays an important role. Employment figures here are among the healthiest in Spain, although they have recently taken a dip due to a weakened German economy, resulting in fewer German visitors.

Business and job opportunities are naturally linked to tourism and services, including expatriate services. Like all coastal areas that are popular with foreign residents, there are plenty of seasonal and part-time opportunities in the service industries, especially in catering, but your search will be easier if you can speak Spanish and German, especially as a large proportion of tourists and foreign residents are German nationals. It's difficult to find information in English about starting a company on the Balearics, but the islands do work hard to promote small and medium size businesses and have a *Ventanilla Unica Empresarial* (see page 86). The Chamber of Commerce website (🖥 www. cambresbalears.com) is in Spanish only but has links to plenty of other useful sites, including that of the Federation of Small and Medium Size Businesses on the islands (🖥 www.pimem.es), which is in English.

Language

Although the Balearics have a large proportion of foreign residents and German and English are widely spoken in resort areas, if you plan to live and work there, you must learn the local language, which presents a complicated problem. To begin with, the islands have two official languages, Spanish and Catalan, and the regional government's policy is to ensure that Catalan is spoken in everyday life; the state school system, for example, is bilingual. To make matters worse, a different dialect of Catalan is spoken on each of the islands: *mallorquín* on Majorca, *menorquín* on Minorca and *ibicenco* on Ibiza. The good news is that, if you can understand one, you can understand the others! Of course it isn't essential to learn Catalan but, if you think your future could be on one of the islands, it will help you enormously if you have a working knowledge of the language as well as Spanish.

Property

The Balearic Islands have a healthy property market. Prices have risen steadily over the last few years and property is among the most expensive in Spain. Tourism began in Majorca in the '60s and development in some resorts, e.g. Magaluf, spiralled out of control and resulted in some ugly buildings. To prevent the same thing happening on the rest of the island, strict building controls were introduced and happily the character of the rest of the island has been retained. In the south-west, in areas like Santa Ponsa, a studio apartment near the beach costs around €100,000 and a three-bedroom apartment around €200,00, although you can add another €200,000 to those prices if you want a beach-front property. Modern two-bedroom duplexes start at around €200,000 and detached villas cost from €800,000 but are generally €2 or 3 million euros depending on location and luxury quota. The old town of Palma has retained its Spanish flavour and is a chic and stylish location where a two-bedroom apartment will cost almost €300,000 and a four-bedroom apartment around €400,000.

The island of Ibiza is on a par with Majorca in terms of property prices, reflecting the wealth of residents and visitors to the islands. Cheaper property can be found on the quieter island of Minorca, where there are apartment blocks in the tourist resorts to the west of the island and luxury villas on the outskirts of the resorts. Apartments cost from €150,000 and you can find quite a large villa for around €320,000.

Rented Accommodation

As with other popular holiday resort areas, the rental market on the Balearic Islands is very healthy, although mainly for short-term lets (less than six months). Long-term rentals are harder to find at short notice and rental costs are high all year round but especially in the high season. Two-bedroom apartments start at €1,000 per month but may rise to €2,000 or more in the high season, and a four-bedroom villa costs around €6,000 per month.

Commercial Property

In Palma, commercial space costs around €55 per square metre per month, but in the tourist areas you will generally have to work hard to find suitable empty space to rent, as most property is sold as a 'going concern'.

CANARY ISLANDS

A group of seven inhabited islands in the Atlantic, around 100km (60mi) off the north-west coast of Africa. Although they're over 1,000km

(700mi) from the Spanish mainland, they've belonged to Spain for over 500 years and now form the autonomous region of *Canarias*. The region is separated into two provinces, confusingly named after the capital cities of Gran Canaria and Tenerife: Las Palmas de Gran Canaria, which is the eastern province and consists of the islands of Gran Canaria,  Fuerteventura and Lanzarote; and Santa Cruz de Tenerife, which is the greener of the two provinces and consists of the islands of Tenerife, La Gomera, El Hierro and La Palma.

The Canary Islands are a firm favourite with both tourists and foreign residents. In 2003 they were home to almost 180,000 foreign residents, mainly English and German, out of a total population of around 1.9 million. There are two main reasons for the popularity of the Canary Islands: their year round spring-like climate, which doesn't generally drop below 18°C even in winter and averages a pleasant 24°C in summer; and certain tax incentives for investors, which are detailed below.

Tenerife is by far the most popular island with tourists, due to its excellent year round climate and spectacular scenery. It's highly developed and very noisy in some resort areas in the south and gets crowded with holidaymakers during the high season, which is from November to February. If you're going to live on Tenerife permanently, you must consider whether you want to live in the midst of a tourist hot spot.

Like other Spanish resort areas, the Canary Islands have experienced an increase in demand for construction skills and related services, and the development of tourism has meant increased public investment in the infrastructure of the islands. The overwhelming economic force is tourism, with an annual 'floating' population of more than 10 million visitors. The growing dependence on tourism means that traditionally strong economic sectors, such as agriculture (mainly bananas and grapes), are on the decline and currently account only for a very small percentage of jobs. Employment levels are quite high, but jobs and business opportunities are almost exclusively in the tourism and services sectors, particularly catering. The main tourist season runs from November to February and during this time the islands are inundated with tourists so part-time or temporary work in shops and bars is relatively easy to find.

If you want to start your own business on the Canary Islands, there are some very favourable low taxation schemes to encourage economic development and diversify their manufacturing and service sectors. Although the Canary Islands is part of Spain and so mainland tax regulations apply, companies that operate there qualify for special tax incentives known as the *régimen económica y fiscal* (*REF*). One of these is that there's no VAT; instead there's a sales tax which has a general rate of 4.5 per cent and a zero rate for certain basic products and services. There's also a low taxation scheme known as *zona especial canaria* (*ZEC*), which has been authorised by the EU. If you're planning to start a company involved in manufacturing or a commercial or service activity (but not financial services) on the Islands, you can register for *ZEC*. However, at least one of the managers of the company must be resident on the Canary Islands and you must invest at least €100,000 and create at least five jobs. Further information can be found on 🖥 www.zec.org, which is in English as well as Spanish.

The Canary Islands governments are keen to promote small business and help is available through their Chambers of Commerce (🖥 www. camaralp.es for Las Palmas and 🖥 www.itcanarias.org/empresas/ camaratf for Santa Cruz de Tenerife). Although the sites are in Spanish only, they offer a tremendous amount of information. Information in English can be found on the website of the Canary Islands Business Information System (🖥 www.siecan.org), which also has useful links. The system is supported by all seven island authorities and offers a considerable amount of help to those wishing to set up small and medium size businesses on the islands.

Language

If you want to succeed in the Canaries, especially with your own business, language is the key. Although English and German are widely spoken, you're strongly advised to speak Spanish and, if possible, German if you want to have the edge. Most local businessmen don't speak other languages fluently, although they may have a smattering of English and German.

Property

Tenerife

The capital of Tenerife is Santa Cruz de Tenerife, which is a lively, cosmopolitan city with plenty of culture, but it tends not to be popular with foreign buyers. On the northern coast, Puerto de la Cruz is popular all year round, as it has excellent congress facilities. A one-bedroom apartment here costs around €190,000 and a five-bedroom villa around €425,000. Two areas that are popular with foreign residents because of their outstanding natural beauty and tranquillity are the Orotava Valley and Los Gigantes on the west coast. A two-bedroom apartment close to Los Gigantes costs around €130,000 and a four-bedroom villa around €330,000; the Orotava Valley is more expensive, a three-bedroom chalet costing from €350,000 and a four-bedroom villa around €750,000.

Much further south, but still on the west coast are the resort areas of Las Americanas and Los Cristianos. These are lively, noisy tourist areas, aimed mainly at younger people with lots of apartment blocks, bars and clubs. If this is for you, a three-bedroom apartment will cost you around €180,000 and a four-bedroom duplex around €350,000. Further round the coast is the Costa de Silencio, which has no beach but two resort areas, including Chayofa – popular with families because of the nearby international schools. Ironically, however, the Costa de Silencio can be rather noisy, as it's a little too close for comfort to Reina Sofia airport. A two-bedroom apartment there costs in the region of €200,000 and a three-bedroom villa around €550,000.

Rented Accommodation: As with the other resort areas, Tenerife's rental market is thriving, but mainly for short-term and holiday lets. Longer lets are more difficult to find, so start searching well in advance, using a reputable estate agent who deals in long-term rentals. Typical rental costs are around €650 per month for a one-bedroom apartment, around €950 for a two-bedroom apartment and around €1,500 for a three-bedroom townhouse or small villa.

Commercial Property: There's little shop or office space available in Santa Cruz de Tenerife. If you're fortunate enough to find a property, you should pay around €10 per square metre per month. Warehouse space costs around €3 per square metre per month.

Fuerteventura & Lanzarote

Fuerteventura, the second-largest of the islands, is under-developed in comparison with Tenerife and Gran Canaria, although that's beginning to change. The island's long, white, sandy beaches are unspoilt and considered the best in the Canary Islands. Property on the island is cheaper than on Tenerife because land isn't as expensive, although foreigners are now showing more interest in the island and several developments are under construction. Nevertheless, it's still possible to find a one-bedroom apartment for around €65,000, a two-bedroom apartment for around €100,000 and a three-bedroom villa for just over €200,000.

Rented Accommodation: Rented accommodation is difficult to find, especially for long-term lets, which are in short supply. Short-term lets have improved over the last few years, with monthly rentals at around €500 for a two-bedroom apartment and €600 for a three-bedroom apartment.

Gran Canaria

Despite its name, Gran Canaria isn't the largest of the islands but comes in third behind Tenerife and Fuerteventura. However, its capital, Las Palmas, is the largest town in the Canary Islands and is the capital of the region. The island is divided into two parts, the south, which is famous for its long beaches and (unfortunately) its huge, modern, over-developed resorts. If you're planning to live on Gran Canaria, you might prefer one of the resorts further to the west, which are far more attractive and certainly much quieter. The northern coast is considered the most beautiful part of the island with its dramatic, rugged scenery. You can find a two-bedroom apartment in Puerto Rico on the south coast for around €150,000 or a three-bedroom house in Maspalomas for around €300,000. In San Isidro in the north, a three-bedroom house with good views will cost around €320,000.

Rented Accommodation: Long-term lets on Gran Canaria are hard to find and are expensive when you do find them. Most of the thriving rental market consists of short-term and holiday lets, so start your search as early as possible. You will have to pay around €700 per month for a one-bedroom apartment, €1,000 for a two-bedroom apartment and around €2,000 for a larger villa.

Commercial Property: Office and shop space is around €10 per square metre per month.

Lanzarote

The fourth-largest island in the group, Lanzarote has been more restrained in its development than the three biggest islands, although this is beginning to change. New construction is supposed to keep to traditional island architectural styles, but the popularity of Lanzarote over the last ten years means that there are some enormous new coastal developments. The property market is very healthy, although further building is opposed by locals and so may be limited. Property prices are a little higher than on Fuerteventura, one-bedroom apartments starting at around €70,000, a townhouse costing around €200,000 and a villa around €300,000.

Rented Accommodation: The holiday rental market is particularly healthy, which is good news for property investors, but as on the other islands, long-term lets are hard to find and rents are expensive. Monthly rentals for a two-bedroom apartment start at around €700 and for a three-bedroom apartment at around €900.

Commercial Property: As in many other coastal and tourist locations, empty commercial space isn't easy to find, and agents prefer to sell businesses as going concerns. If you can find an empty retail unit in the centre of Puerta del Carmen – the main tourist resort, popular with expatriates – you should pay around €11 per square metre per month. In the capital, Arrecife, which is also the island's commercial centre, prices are less than half this.

CATALONIA & BARCELONA

Catalonia (*Cataluña* in Catalan), and especially its capital Barcelona, which competes with Madrid for the top spot as cultural and business centre, is the second most popular area in Spain for foreign residents, especially those from other EU countries and the United States. Catalonia as a whole has a population of 6.7 million, of which some 543,000 are  foreign residents. Almost two thirds of the Catalan population lives in Barcelona, which has a relentlessly 'cool' image and is famous for being one of Europe's liveliest cities with a compelling cosmopolitan and cultural atmosphere. It also manages to be one of the top European business cities.

Many major international and Spanish companies have head offices in Barcelona, especially those in the car manufacturing industry. One car industry boss called it the perfect working environment, with an ideal combination of "Latin joviality and central European efficiency". Design is also a major industry in Catalonia, with more than 8,000 professionals working in almost every area of design including graphic design, product design, interior design and textile and fashion design. Catalonia is home to a vast number of design schools, whose graduates are highly regarded in the industry. The car and design industries come together in Barcelona: Mercedes, Renault and Volvo are just a few of the companies that have their central design office there.

This area of Spain is extremely well tuned in to the needs of promoting business, both large and small, and there are several organisations that will give you detailed information about setting up a business or working in the region. Information on the whole region is provided by Catalonia's investment promotion agency, CIDEM, whose comprehensive website (🖥 www.catalonia.com) is in English as well as Spanish and Catalan. Although CIDEM is geared to larger companies, the site has some excellent general information, including details about the different legal business entities in Spain, taxation, employment, location and financial assistance for newly created companies.

Language

If you're considering working or starting a business in Catalonia, including Barcelona, language is an especially important issue, as the region has its own official language, Catalan (*catalán*), which is spoken by around 7 million people (see page 31). You should be aware that in Catalonia government officials may use only the local language and that forms and official paperwork may only be available in Catalan. As an example of how strictly this linguistic restriction is imposed, in October 2004 the Catalan government fined the Spanish postal service €30,000 for not printing all its labels and stamps in Catalan. Chapter 13 contains the experiences of two women setting up businesses in Barcelona who felt they missed out on financing opportunities because they couldn't communicate in effectively in Catalan. **Make sure you at least have a working knowledge of Catalan, along with pretty fluent Castilian Spanish.** Almost everyone in Catalonia **can** speak Castilian Spanish and will usually do so, especially with non-Catalans, but a few refuse to or even pretend not to understand when you speak to them in Spanish.

Barcelona

Like Madrid, Barcelona has recently invested in science and technology with three new science parks focused on biotechnology and the pharmaceutical industry. Six of the top ten pharmaceutical companies in the world now have operations in Catalonia and the Government of

Catalonia has helped with the creation of 20 new biotechnology companies through its Entrepreneurship programme.

One of the best sources of all kinds of useful information about Barcelona is a website (🖳 www.barcelona-online.com) sponsored by one of the major Spanish language teaching schools in Spain, International House. The site has an extensive list of useful links covering topics such as business, new technology, trade fairs, as well as to other more general sites. Details of jobs available can be found on the general site 🖳 www.infojobs.com and, for jobs in Barcelona, 🖳 www.servijob.com, which contains the classified jobs advertisements from Barcelona's main daily newspaper, *La Vanguardia*.

Other sites worth a visit are those of the Barcelona Chamber of Commerce (🖳 www.cambrabcn.es), which is in English as well as Catalan, and Barcelona Activa (🖳 www.barcelonanetactiva.com), whose home page only is available in English. The latter is run by the local authority (Ayuntament de Barcelona); once you're registered, you can obtain help and guidance with all the necessary procedures to set up your business from start to finish (provided your Spanish is up to it). Test your entrepreneurial skills with their questionnaire, get advice on your business plan and then go on to legally incorporate your business. The authority gives advice on all business entities but is keen to promote the new form of company incorporation, *Sociedad Limitada Nueva Empressa* (*SLNE* – see page 94), which it claims can be completed within 48 hours.

Business Networking Groups

If you're thinking of starting a business in Barcelona, make sure you take advantage of the city's excellent business networking groups, in which you can discuss ideas, make presentations of your business plans and meet professionals who can help you turn your ideas into something tangible. Meetings are attended by budding entrepreneurs of all nationalities and are a good opportunity to make business contacts. Groups include the following, which meet monthly unless otherwise stated:

● The Barcelona Women's Network (🖳 www.bcnwomensnetwork.com), which is for women only, was started as a means of making social contacts but has recently initiated a business networking session. The group has published a book called *Gateway to Barcelona*, which contains some useful contacts.

- The British Chamber of Commerce in Barcelona (💻 www.british chamberspain.com) runs a networking group with a mixture of members, who tend to be over 40; you need to be a good mixer as there's no formal talk and feedback session.

- The Business Lunch (💻 www.thebizlunch.com) is slightly more formal, with a lunch and a brief talk by a member.

- Business Networking Barcelona (BNB, 💻 www.business-networking-barcelona.com) meets weekly and is the most active of the networking groups. It's run by an English lawyer, and members meet to chat and listen; each gives a brief talk in Spanish, before one member gives a longer presentation.

- The Entrepreneurs Network in Barcelona (ENBarcelona, 💻 www.en-barcelona.org) is a non-profit-making organisation which encourages its members – prospective entrepreneurs – to share resources, ideas and information. Monthly meetings are free, and the informal talks may be in English or Spanish.

- Eurocircle (💻 www.eurocircle.com) is a mixed group, which all nationalities and professions are encouraged to join. The founder is a Finnish woman but the group has its roots in New York and started operating in Barcelona two years ago. It's a great place to make contacts but is better for socialising than doing business.

- The International Women's Club of Barcelona (💻 www.iwc barcelona.com), another all-women group, is a very influential and well connected organisation, which is primarily for making social contacts but is also a useful source of information and will provide good contacts if you're a woman new to the city.

Property

Property prices in Barcelona are amongst the highest in the country, reflecting the city's wealth, and come a close second to those of Madrid. Prices rose by more than 17 per cent between 2002 and 2003 and the rate of increase shows no sign of dropping. There are, however, substantial price differences between the various areas, which include the following:

- **Old City** – The old city (*ciutat vella*) is quite a small area right in the middle of Barcelona. It's a favourite with tourists, students and young professionals, as it's a lively and sometimes noisy area that has some of the best museums in the city, as well as interesting artisan workshops, bars and restaurants and unusual shops. It's made up of four districts: Barceloneta, Ribera (which includes the Born – currently the chicest spot in Barcelona), the Gothic Quarter, and the Raval. The Barceloneta and Born areas of the old city are particularly popular with foreigners and property there is highly sought-after by expatriate young professionals from EU countries, as it's close to both the beach and the main attractions of the city. Property in the old city tends to be limited to apartments and loft conversions, which are becoming increasingly popular. In the Barceloneta and Born areas, prices start at around €160,000 for studios and one-bedroom apartments and around €280,000 for a three-bedroom apartment (note that these are **starting** prices). Larger, more luxurious apartments have price tags of several hundred thousand euros up to well over €1 million. There are hardly any family houses to be found in the old city and those who want more space tend to live in the suburbs, within easy travelling distance of the city.

- **Gràcia** – The Gràcia area used to be a village on the outskirts of Barcelona but has become one of its central residential districts. The atmosphere is similar to that of the old city in the sense that many of its residents are young. There are plenty of bars and restaurants, and the area has a lively feel. However, it's more residential than the old city and doesn't have its petty crime problems. The property for sale here is also mainly apartments, ranging from around €200,000 to up to €1 million.

- **High Area** – The high area of Barcelona, Sarrià and the larger Zona Alta area, is the most elegant expensive and a favourite with expatriates and their families who want to live close to the centre but not too close. Barcelona's business centre is only a ten-minute car drive away, there are plenty of good international schools and the motorway is accessible at nearby Pedralbes. A three- or four-bedroom apartment in the area costs around €500,000, while a larger family home is likely to be upwards of €1 million.

- **San Cugat** – The suburb of San Cugat, which is also popular with families, is well connected to the city centre by train and is a quieter place to live. It's possible to find larger apartments and townhouses here, although prices are high, a three-bedroom apartment costing around €450,000 and a four-bedroom family house on a new development from around €900,000 to over €1 million.

- **Castelldefels & Sitges** – Castelldefels and Sitges are both popular coastal resorts about half an hour to the south of the city. Castelldefels has the best international schools outside Barcelona. Prices in these areas are fairly high, two- and three-bedroom flats costing from around €350,000 and four- and five-bedroom chalets around €800,000.

Rented Accommodation: As in all large cities, rented accommodation in Barcelona is hard to find and expensive when you do find it. Rents in the old town start at around €700 per month for a one-bedroom apartment, while in the desirable Sarrià area, you must pay around €2,000 per month for a larger apartment or small family home, although prices can be much higher depending on the location. Most rented accommodation is let unfurnished.

Commercial Property: There are a large number of multinational companies that have offices in Barcelona, which means that its office market is sensitive to economic fluctuations throughout the world. Office rents in Barcelona rose slightly in the second quarter of 2004, although that was thought to be due to a large sale of office stock for hotel and residential use, which was expected to increase demand. In the central business district, office rentals are around €27 per square metre per month, although rents in the suburbs are significantly lower, around €16 per square metre per month. Warehouse space costs much the same as in Madrid: around €7 per square metre per month. Retail units also follow the Madrid pattern, shops in the main commercial area costing around €126 per square metre per month.

MADRID

It isn't surprising that Madrid is one of the most attractive areas of Spain for those foreigners who want to make a living in the country. Figures in 2004 showed that the total number of foreign residents in the region was around 590,000, that's 10 per cent of the population. It has a thriving economy, one that is growing at a rate faster than that of Spain as  a whole, and 73 per cent of foreign investment in Spain goes to Madrid. Easily accessible by both road and air from the rest of Europe, the United States and Latin America, Madrid has extensive employment opportunities in information technology, the service industries, construction and teaching English as a foreign language. One of Europe's great cities, Madrid also offers an excellent quality of life with a never-ending supply of culture and history in its many art galleries and museums. The city has been called the capital of joy and contentment and its inhabitants, known as *Madrileños*, have a reputation for staying up late and enjoying life to the full. Make sure you have plenty of energy if you choose Madrid as your preferred area to make a living in Spain!

If you think Madrid could be the area for you, the first thing you should do is to learn Spanish. Despite its popularity as a tourist destination, there is very little English spoken there, so try the language learning options listed on page 31 or have a look on the internet for Spanish courses in Madrid – there's certainly no shortage of them. You will find that your fluency improves quickly once arrive in Madrid, as you will be expected to speak Spanish almost all the time. There are plenty of opportunities for teaching English as a foreign language in Madrid, especially if you're a graduate and have done a TEFL course. See page 212 for more information about teaching English in Spain.

The high tech sector in Madrid is growing particularly fast and there has been a lot of recent investment in four new Science and Technology Parks, which have been built on the outskirts of the city. There is a chronic shortage of IT skills in Spain in general, but especially in Madrid, so if you're a graduate with IT skills and can speak Spanish, you should have no trouble finding work. One employment agency survey showed that out of 11,000 jobs on offer in Madrid, more than 32 per cent were IT-related and many of them didn't require a university degree. The following websites specialise in IT jobs:

- 💻 **www.infojobs.net** – In Spanish only but has a good choice of jobs, listed in categories, and shows you what's available in each area of the country;

- 💻 **www.jobpilot.com** – An excellent site in English, with good information on Spain in general, an interesting Expat Corner and a comprehensive international job search section.

If you want to set up a business in Madrid, the Madrid Chamber of Commerce is an excellent starting point. The Chamber is keen to support small businesses, promote industry and help Madrid companies to move into foreign markets. Its website (💻 www.camara madrid.es) is available in English and gives full information about services to promote business and the economy of Madrid. Chamber staff will help with your business plan and give you information about government grants, and they have the right contacts to help you get one! They also offer a women's business support programme and, if you're looking for a job, you can submit your CV to them and they will make it available to prospective employers. The website also contains more general, but useful, information about forming a company, franchising, foreign trade and tourism.

Property

Madrid is the capital city and consequently property purchase and rental prices are among the highest in Spain. *Madrileños* spend almost half their monthly income on housing. In central Madrid most of the properties are older apartment blocks with no parking facilities and so many expatriates choose to live in larger apartments or houses in the suburbs. Chamartín, to the north, is within easy reach of the centre and to the north-west of the city you will find newly constructed modern urbanisations with good quality apartments, houses and villas. La Moraleja in the north-east corner of the city is the most exclusive area with the highest prices for both purchase and rentals.

In the centre of Madrid, a studio flat costs around €175,000, two-bedroom apartments costing from around €250,000. Larger apartments cost up to around €1 million depending on the number of bedrooms and amount of living space. A modest three-bedroom family home costs at least €450,000 and more substantial properties can easily be well over €1 million, some as high as €3 million.

Rented Accommodation

Rented accommodation is hard to come by in Madrid and rents are generally high compared with other areas of Spain. Monthly rents start at around €900 for a small apartment and around €1,500 for a three-bedroom apartment.

Commercial Property

Office rental costs have always been high in Madrid because of lack of available space. However, things are changing rapidly as big businesses begin to move to the outskirts of the city. A vast 'corporate campus' 17km (10mi) outside Madrid opened in December 2004, housing the staff of Santander Central Hispano Bank. Lack of affordable, modern space and the logistics of moving around in the city's business district have started an exodus which is set to continue as motorway access and public transport to business areas outside the city start to improve. This in turn will ease the crowded office market and, in theory at least, bring prices down. Prices in 2004 were around €30 per square metre per month in the city centre, falling to €20 per square metre in the suburbs.

Retail units in Madrid are divided between those located in the main commercial areas of the city, where rents are astronomical (around €180 per square metre per month), and retail units in commercial parks or shopping centres. Shopping centres are becoming more and more popular and, of course, affect nearby retail trade. The prices for units in these centres are a fraction of the cost of those in the city, around €14 per square metre per month. Warehouse space costs around €7 per square metre per month.

MALAGA & COSTA DEL SOL

Malaga province, and the Costa del Sol in particular, is the most popular area with foreign residents, especially those from the UK. Malaga is one of the eight provinces of Andalusia, which covers an enormous area stretching across the southernmost part of Spain. This is the part of Spain that is home to all things archetypically Spanish – flamenco music and dancing, bull-fighting and sherry – but this vast and beautiful region has much more to offer and is rich in history and culture, the legacy of thousands of years of invading peoples. Almost 21 per cent of the foreign population of Andalusia can be found in Malaga and growing numbers are coming to work and set up businesses. Traditionally, foreigners came to Malaga to retire, play golf, relax and enjoy more than 300 days of sunshine per year. However, figures released by the Spanish Interior Ministry show that, increasingly, immigrants are professionals in their 30s and 40s with young families.

Things were not always so prosperous for Andalusia. Until relatively recently, its economy was based around agriculture and it was one of the poorest areas of Spain, with high unemployment levels. It still has one of the highest unemployment levels in Spain at around 18 per cent, but things are changing fast. The service sector, which of course includes tourism, now dominates employment and business opportunities in Andalusia. Only the construction industry comes anywhere near to it in importance. Malaga province has the largest number of small businesses (between one and nine employees) – just over 22 per cent of the Andalusian total. The enormous tourism industry obviously offers plenty of seasonal job possibilities but, if you plan to make a living here permanently, you should look to work in a sector that will offer a year round income.

Don't forget that if you want to live and work here, especially if you have children, a good infrastructure is vitally important and you may find that in some areas it isn't as good as you imagined. This is because until relatively recently large parts of the coast were open countryside or used for farming. The situation is changing fast, but it's something you should check carefully, along with availability of telephone lines and ADSL connection, especially if you plan to work from home. In coastal areas, communications are generally good, but if you plan to move further inland, it's often difficult to get a fixed telephone line and relying on a mobile telephone when there's little or no signal can make it almost impossible to do business from home.

At the less developed eastern end of the coast in particular, services and amenities aren't as good as they are at the western end and there isn't such a good choice of international schools. The city of Malaga is a short drive away, but the main coast road that runs from Malaga to Nerja is often at a standstill in rush hours – and in Spain that's four times a day, as many people go home for their siesta and return to work later. The other thing to remember if you choose this area is that fewer tourists means less English spoken, so you will have to make sure your Spanish is up to scratch.

Skilled building workers are much in demand in most parts of the Costa del Sol due to the ever-expanding construction industry. There are plenty of jobs in property, but also lots of competition. Sales and marketing offer plenty of opportunities, as does that old favourite for native English-speakers, teaching English as a foreign language. This is by no means a definitive list and, as with the Costa Blanca, the increasing numbers of expatriates who settle on the coast also require specialised services, so you may still be able to find a lucrative gap in the market. However, don't forget that catering solely to the expatriate population can be very limiting; consider how you might diversify your business if necessary.

A growing number of foreigners are setting up businesses in Malaga. In fact, Malaga has one of the highest rates of self-employment and entrepreneurship in the country. Tourism, hotels and catering are favourite areas among foreigners. There's a wealth of information and advice for those wanting to set up small businesses in the region but most of it is in Spanish. Only parts of the Chamber of Commerce's website (🖥 www.camaramalaga.es) are in English. There are a number of Spanish organisations whose sole purpose is to advise and support small businesses. Malaga is the home of the Andalusia Technology Park, which is the base for the Andalusian Centre for Entrepreneurs (Centros Andaluces Emprendadores/CADE), which advises and supports budding entrepreneurs. The demand for business advice from foreigners has meant that the Andalusian Government has asked CADE to run an initiative called Multi-Cultural Entrepreneurs, which gives general advice as well as information about grants and subsidies. However, even though this initiative is aimed specifically at foreigners, CADE's website (🖥 www.juntadeAndalusia.es/servicioandaluzdeempleo/cade) is only in Spanish.

There's some information in English about the Technology Park in Malaga on 🖥 www.pta.es, which explains what kind of businesses are based there and how you can become part of it.

A relatively new website is 🖥 www.freshdirectory.com, which contains all kinds of useful information for English-speaking businesses on the Costa del Sol. This includes extensive, detailed information about living and working in Spain. At the end of 2004, many pages were complete, but others were in the process of being compiled. When finished, it hopes to be 'a Survival Bible for newcomers to the Costa del Sol, existing residents and tourists alike, as well as a valuable business and marketing tool.'

Language

In language terms, Malaga is full of surprises. As the above information about business organisations confirms, although English is widely spoken, there are important areas that you may miss out on if you can't speak Spanish. Just when you thought everyone spoke English, you will get caught out, perhaps with a vital service for your business or a contact who can might have been able to help you get that all important grant or bank loan. If you want to make the most of your opportunities, even on the Costa del Sol, it will pay dividends for you to learn Spanish and preferably one other language – German especially. You will jump straight to the front of the jobs queue with your superior language skills and will find that running a small business, even one for expatriates, is infinitely easier if you can communicate with suppliers and those infamous bureaucrats in their own language. Many expatriates live and work in Spain for years without speaking more than a few words of Spanish, but your chances of success will increase a hundred-fold if you can learn the language and integrate, even just a little, into Spanish society.

Property

Malaga City

Malaga city is the capital both of the province and of the Costa del Sol, but the city itself has few foreign residents. This is beginning to change as foreigners discover the delights of a city with plenty of culture and an authentic Spanish feel. There's much more to Malaga than meets the eye and it's a world away from some of the heavily developed tourist spots along coast. The city been working hard to improve its image and is proud to finally have its own Picasso Museum in the old quarter, an area which is currently being restored. Property in Malaga city is usually cheaper than on the Costa del Sol, a two-bedroom apartment costing around €120,000. To the east are some of the city's most exclusive and expensive areas, where a two-bedroom apartment costs from €240,000 and three-bedroom villas start at €600,000.

Rented Accommodation: There's no significant holiday rental market in Malaga city, which means that longer lets are generally easier to find. However, the city itself is fast becoming a desirable place for foreigners, especially those who speak Spanish. Rentals available tend to be apartments, with a few duplexes and chalets. A one-bedroom apartment costs around €500 per month, a three-bedroom flat €800, and a four-bedroom duplex €1,200 per month.

Commercial Property: According to property consultants CB Richard Ellis, office space in the main business area of Malaga city costs between €11 and €14 per square metre per month; on the outskirts of the city, costs are between €9 and €11. Retail space in the main commercial areas costs between €40 and €60 per square metre per month, and retail premises in Malaga's most prestigious shopping street, Calle Larios, cost around €80 per square metre per month. On the outskirts of the city, rents go down to between €12 and €20; units in shopping centres cost between €25 and €50 per square metre per month and industrial or warehouse space can be had between €3 and €6 per square metre per month.

Costa del Sol

The property market on the Costa del Sol has been booming for some years. According to Hamptons International, despite a noticeable drop in demand at the end of 2003, the early part of 2004 saw renewed interest, especially among UK buyers. There has been an increase in demand for good quality townhouses and small villas by those who want to live there permanently and the international schools in the area have long waiting lists.

The Costa del Sol (apart from the city of Malaga) divides roughly into three parts. The western end encompasses the areas from Sotogrande to Marbella. Sotogrande, just inside the province of Cádiz, is an exclusive area, a luxury development covering around 5,000 acres which was started in the mid-'60s. All the property is very expensive here, a two-bedroom apartment costing around €400,000, a three-bedroom townhouse around €600,000 and larger villas from €1 million. East of Sotogrande are Estepona and the famous resort of Marbella, both of which have excellent services and amenities but also property prices that reflect this. Estepona is less expensive, the average price of a two-bedroom flat being around €325,000, compared with around €500,000 in Marbella. A three-bedroom townhouse costs around €400,000 in Estepona and €550,000 in Marbella and a four-bedroom villa in Estepona should cost around €850,000; in Marbella you will be looking at prices well over €2 million!

Prices are lower in the central part of the Costa del Sol, which includes Fuengirola and Torremolinos. Some of these areas are heavily developed, although there are still some tranquil havens left and, if you venture even a couple of streets back from the coast, you will find 'real' Spanish life going on around you. Fuengirola has undergone something of a facelift recently and is much improved. A two-bedroom apartment in this area will cost just over €200,000 and a three-bedroom villa around €700,000.

The less developed eastern end of the coast stretches from Malaga to Nerja and is less crowded with tourists, with a more genuine Spanish feel to it. An enormous number of holiday homes are being built in Nerja and some figures suggest that over half of them are occupied only for a few weeks per year. Despite this, the town seems to retain its Spanish charm, especially the old part of the town. Prices in Nerja start at around €200,000 for a two-bedroom apartment, €300,000 for a three-bedroom townhouse and €500,000 for a three-bedroom villa.

Rented Accommodation: Like the Costa Blanca, the Costa del Sol has a thriving rental market, but it's almost all short-term holiday lets. However, the glut of properties means that some owners are having difficulty finding people to rent. Consequently there's a greater selection of properties available than on the Costa Blanca and at lower prices. As you might expect, Marbella rental prices are very high, especially close to Puerto Banús. Unless you have a limitless supply of money, it's advisable to look for somewhere within easy driving distance of Marbella, rather than right in the centre; it will be much cheaper and considerably less crowded, especially in the summer months. The lowest prices in Marbella are around €800 per month for a one-bedroom apartment and €3,000 per month for a three-bedroom apartment, but just 15 minutes out of Marbella, e.g. in Elvira, you can find a three-bedroom house for around €1,500 per month. On the other hand, a large, luxurious villa close to Puerto Banús could set you back around €10,000 per month!

Commercial Property: On the Costa del Sol, in common with many other tourist locations, many agents want to sell businesses as 'going concerns' rather than empty commercial property, and you should therefore check exactly what an agent is offering you. Does the price include a business? Is it freehold or leasehold (see page 91)? As a guide to prices, expect to pay around €160,000 for a leasehold property of around 45m² in Mijas Costa (between Malaga and Marbella) and around €250,000 for a similar-size freehold property in Marbella.

VALENCIA & COSTA BLANCA

The Valencia region (*La Comunidad Valenciana*) includes the provinces of Alicante on the Costa Blanca, Castellón and Valencia. It's the third-most popular destination for foreign residents. Latest figures show that of a total population of around 4.5 million there are just under 415,000 foreigners living there, mainly in the city of Valencia, the capital of  the region, and on the Costa Blanca. Valencia is Spain's third-largest city, home to one of the largest universities in the country and a major tourist attraction thanks to its rich cultural heritage and its reputation for the best paella in Spain. It has also become a favourite business destination for international exhibitions and conferences. Valencia is proud to have been chosen to host the America's Cup yacht racing competition in 2007 and this will undoubtedly boost the economy and bring jobs to the region.

Business and employment possibilities in this area tend to be predominantly in the service industries, in hotel and catering and property-related services. This is especially true of Alicante province and the Costa Blanca area, although textiles, shoes and construction materials also contribute to the prosperity of the region. The city of Valencia is well set up for business tourism and many trade fairs and conventions are held there. Construction, especially in coastal areas, continues to flourish as demand for property continues unabated. Costa Blanca tourism and residential tourism are big business and continue to grow, so if you can speak fluent Spanish and preferably also German, you will quickly find a job in this sector. If you just want part-time work or work experience to get a feel for the area, there are usually plenty of opportunities for seasonal part-time work in shops and bars. The ever-growing expatriate population on the Costa Blanca also means that there's an increasing demand for all kinds of English-speaking services, such as gardening, childcare and nursing care for the elderly.

Neither the Valencian Regional Government nor the Alicante Regional Government is quite as tuned in to the promotion of small businesses as the governments of Madrid and Barcelona. The website for the Valencian Regional Government is available in English, but it's almost impossible to navigate and the same is true of the Alicante government website. Instead, try the website for all the Chambers of Commerce in the Valencian community (🖥 www.comextcv.com), which has a link to an English version, and go to the area you're interested in. The favourite location for immigrants from the EU (predominantly English and German nationals) in this area of Spain is Alicante province and its Chamber can be found at 🖥 www.camar alicante.com (in Spanish only), where there's information about services for setting up a business.

Language

This is another area where language considerations are important. In the city of Valencia a dialect of Catalan, *valenciano*, is widely spoken. Some claim that it should be an official language alongside Catalan. Many of Valencia's inhabitants, *Valencianos*, are bilingual, as instruction in Catalan is compulsory in all schools (a hot political potato in Spain). As in Barcelona, everyone can speak Castilian Spanish, but the people are fiercely proud of their area and their language and it may help your integration with the locals if you can learn at least the basics of *valenciano.*

Property

Valencia City

Since the announcement that Valencia will host the 2007 America's Cup, property prices in and around the city have been rising dramatically. Unlike Madrid and Barcelona, Valencia has always had plenty of property available at reasonable prices. These are usually older apartments, costing around €70,000 for a two- or three-bedroom property. If you prefer a house, you must look a little outside the city, where property is also reasonably priced, a three-bedroom house costing around €270,000. The city and the Spanish government are committed to improving the city's transport system and its marina facilities as well as its infrastructure in general to cope with a projected 10 million visitors between now and the start of the America's Cup. Good news for those planning to live there, but make sure you buy well in advance of 2007!

Rented Accommodation: This is also readily available in the city, although you should try to avoid the start of a university term, when the market gets rather overloaded with students. You can usually find a three-bedroom apartment for around €700 per month.

Commercial Property: The office market in Valencia is not as developed as in Madrid and Barcelona and, although there's increasing demand for modern office space, most of what's available is in the historic city centre and in short supply. However, the business district is beginning to expand outwards from its traditional borders, and technology parks, business parks and shopping centres are starting to appear on the outskirts of the city. For a good location in the city, you can expect to pay around €14 per square metre per month and on the outskirts around €10 per square metre per month.

Costa Blanca

The Costa Blanca, part of the Valencian Community and in the province of Alicante, is one of the most popular areas of Spain with foreign buyers. However, you should bear in mind that the criteria for an ideal property may be different if you're planning to live there on a permanent basis from those for a holiday home you use for a just few weeks a year. Something which didn't seem too much of a problem when you were on holiday may affect your quality of life to quite a degree if you have to live with it on a daily basis. Think about access to main roads and public transport, the surrounding infrastructure and the availability of good schools if you have school-age children.

Average prices on the Alicante coast rose by more than 16 per cent in 2003, according to the *Costa Blanca News*. The Valencian Institute of Economic Research believes that after 2007 half of all new properties built on the Costa Blanca will be bought by foreigners, and growing numbers of those will be younger workers. With the Costa Blanca property market so buoyant and so much choice available, it's hard to know where to start, but whether you want a small studio flat or an enormous villa, it's bound to be there somewhere!

Prices are generally lower than on the Costa del Sol and you will find the cheapest properties in Torrevieja and Benidorm, in the south, where there has been massive expansion in recent years. Some are already over-developed but construction seems to continue unabated, although more recently it has shown a tendency towards lower-density, far better designed properties. In this part of the Costa Blanca, one-bedroom studio apartments start at around €65,000 and a three-bedroom house costs around €160,000.

The more expensive Costa Blanca property is to be found in the north, e.g. in Altea, Moraira and Javea, which have a large expatriate community. In these areas development is more restrained and a little more of 'real Spain' remains. However, you can still buy a two-bedroom apartment from around €110,000; a three-bedroom house in the residential Altea Hills costs around €350,000 and just over €500,000 will buy you a palatial villa with five or six bedrooms.

Rented Accommodation: As the Costa Blanca is a popular holiday destination, there's no shortage of property to rent, but unfortunately there's a sting in the tail. It's extremely difficult to find a long-term let on the Costa Blanca, where they're usually for a period of less than six months so that landlords can get the highest return on their investment and make the most of high season demand. Many simply don't want to offer long-term lets, as Spanish law favours the tenant rather than the landlord. Outside the high season (i.e. from October to May) you may pay only around €150 per week for a one-bedroom apartment and €300 per week for a house or a villa. However, in high season rents rise to around €250 per week and €450 to €500 per week respectively.

Commercial Property: On the Costa Blanca, in common with many of the other coastal areas in Spain, commercial agents tend to offer businesses for sale, rather than simply premises. Ordinary *locales* in prime tourist areas can cost anything from around €12 to about €30 per square metre per month. Contact a reputable commercial agent with your requirements.

3.

EMPLOYMENT & SELF-EMPLOYMENT

One of the most important decisions to be taken when contemplating making a living in Spain is whether you're happy working for an employer or whether you would prefer the freedom of being self-employed. As an employee, you enjoy far more job security, and in Spain that's a substantial benefit. As a self-employed person, your freedom brings with it certain risks and the monthly financial burden of paying your entire social security contributions, rather than having a large percentage of them paid by your employer. This book is principally concerned with self-employment and running a business in Spain but – just as when planning to buy a home it pays to rent first – it may well be to your advantage to take a temporary job in a similar business to the one you're intending to run, in order to gain some work experience, improve your Spanish and make contacts without any of the risk, expense and responsibility associated with setting up on your own. The first part of this chapter therefore deals briefly with finding employment in Spain; further details can be found in *Living and Working in Spain* (see page 323).

FINDING A JOB

Finding a job in Spain is certainly a lot easier than it used to be, but unemployment here is still the highest in Europe despite a strong economic recovery in recent years. Unless you have specialist skills that are in particular demand and can speak fluent Spanish – particularly if you're a non-EU national (see **Permits & Visas** on page 23) – don't expect to find a job straight away or even within a relatively short period. **The two golden rules are: bring as much money as possible – enough to support yourself for at least a year – and do plenty of research before you commit yourself**.

If you want to work in Spain, it's imperative that you don't make any spur-of-the-moment decisions. Research should start from the moment the first idea trickles into your head and be a continuous and exhaustive process that becomes second nature to you. You will always be a foreigner (*extranjero* or *guiri*) in Spain and, as such, you won't be competing on equal terms with Spaniards. Many expatriates find it especially difficult to break into the job market because a large proportion of vacancies are filled through personal recommendations or internally within a company. You will have to be very determined indeed to overcome this hurdle.

When job-hunting, it's advisable to make use of all the available services (detailed below) and follow up every lead you can. Before you can begin your search, however, you must learn Spanish, update your curriculum vitae (CV) and obtain an *NIE* (see below).

Language

It goes without saying that it's a huge bonus if you have at least a working knowledge of Spanish (see page 31). If not, your employment possibilities are immediately restricted. In fact, you will have difficulty getting anywhere with either the government employment service or a private recruitment agency if you cannot speak fluent Spanish. It's estimated that around 60 per cent of English-speaking job applicants on the Costa del Sol don't speak any Spanish, so you will immediately put yourself in the top 40 per cent if you do. If you don't speak any Spanish, your experience will be the deciding factor and it may be possible to find a job with an English-speaking company operating in Spain. To obtain a job with a Spanish company, however, you will be expected to be fluent in both written and spoken Spanish. Most agencies say that, if you're experienced in your field and speak English and Spanish (and possibly one other European language) fluently, you can usually get a job within a few days.

Curriculum Vitae

Make sure that your CV (résumé) is up to date, translated into Spanish and in a style recognised by Spanish employers. It should be short (one or two pages), easy to read and geared towards the post you're applying for. It should have all the usual personal details, details of education and training, details of other qualifications you feel are relevant, such as languages, followed by details of work experience (in chronological order) and finally things not directly related to work which might be relevant.

Your covering letter (*carta de presentación*) should be approximately three paragraphs. The first should refer either to the advertisement for the post or to the company and why you want to work for it. The second should be about yourself and how your qualifications are appropriate, and the third should ask if you can call to arrange a meeting or, if it's a specific post, be included in the selection process.

The Spanish recruitment agency, Adecco, has particularly good advice on preferred forms of CV and covering letter on its website (🖳 www.adecco.es), although the information is only in Spanish. Go to the section called *Candidato*, then *Guia de Empleo*, where you will find a section entitled *Documentación Escrita*. This has sections explaining what should be included in the CV and covering letter.

Foreigner's Identification Number

You should make it a priority to obtain a foreigner's identification number (*Número de Identificación de Extranjero/NIE*). This is a number that identifies you to the Spanish tax authorities and is necessary for all kinds of transactions and legal procedures in Spain.

It's possible to obtain an *NIE* by going to any national police station and completing an application form. You must present your passport, proof of residence (which can be your rental contract with your landlord or, if you own a property, the purchase contract) and – inevitably! – lots of passport-size photographs. In areas where there's significant number of foreign residents, there are often advisers and interpreters at the police station who can help you.

If you don't feel confident in tackling the process yourself, you can obtain an *NIE* with the help of an agent known as a *gestor* (see page 89), who is a kind of middleman between you and the State and should be able to speed up the process on your behalf. He will know where to go, whom to see and the right queue to stand in to get what you want. You will be charged for his services, but obtaining an *NIE* number is a relatively straightforward process and should cost only around €40. Depending on whether you use a *gestor* or not, and how lucky you are, it should take between two and four weeks to obtain an *NIE*.

Government Employment Service

If your Spanish is fluent, you can sign on at the nearest government employment office (Instituto Naciónal de Empleo/INEM). There are INEM offices in many cities and in all provincial capitals, and their services are theoretically available to all. Note, however, that they're usually unhelpful to foreign jobseekers unless they speak fluent Spanish (or even Catalan in some parts of Spain!), have already been employed in Spain or are unemployed and receiving unemployment benefit. Being a government department, INEM isn't service-oriented and the quality of service and co-operation varies according to the region, the office and the person handling your case. Note also that the INEM deals mainly with skilled industrial and service personnel, as well as unskilled jobs in areas such as retailing, catering and construction.

Private Recruitment Agencies

The most popular private recruitment agencies in Spain are Adecco (🖳 www.adecco.com), Flexiplan (🖳 www.flexiplan.com), Manpower (🖳 www.manpower.es), and Select (🖳 www.select.es), although these tend to be for temporary work and you will need to speak fairly fluent Spanish to make the most of their services (and their websites). Adecco's site has a particularly good information section. There are also agencies that specialise in particular fields, such as banking, hotel and catering staff and computer personnel.

In some coastal areas, private agencies catering specifically for English-speakers are beginning to appear. These include Jobtoasterspain SL (🖳 www.jobtoasterspain.com), Recruit Spain (🖳 www.recruit spain.com), which is a member of the UK Recruitment and Employment Federation, and Wemploy SL (🖳 www.wemploy.com). These are a good place to start your job-hunting if you wish to work in one of these areas. Most of them offer an online service, whereby you can find out about job opportunities in Spain without leaving home and post your CV online, making it available to prospective employers. Often, for a small fee, the agency will help you to revise your CV, define your skills and look at your possible career development. However, once you've narrowed down the areas you're interested in, you will need to spend some time in Spain, researching possibilities and getting a feel for the area where you think you want to live and work. The internet is a wonderful research tool, but there's no substitute for being in Spain and visiting the agencies in person. This demonstrates your commitment and allows them to interview you face to face; most of the agencies won't accept telephone interviews, except occasionally for very senior positions.

EURES

The European Union has an employment service network called EURES (🖳 http://europa.eu.int/eures). The website has a job-search database in English that's updated daily by the employment services in all member countries. It contains information about the format of a European CV and allows you to post your CV free of charge in the 'CV Search' section. If you want to apply for a job in Spain through EURES, you will need an *NIE* (see above). Finding a job this way can be a very long-winded process, so make sure that it isn't your only option. Graduates can obtain country-specific information about working in Spain via the website of the Association of Graduate Careers Advisory

Services (AGCAS, 💻 www.prospects.ac.uk). This contains general information about the job market for graduates and advises which degrees are most likely to secure a job, along with details of language requirements and postgraduate study.

Newspapers

Over a hundred daily newspapers are published in Spain and these are a good place to look for job advertisements. Some of the most important are *El País*, *El Mundo* and *Diario 16* in Madrid and *El Periódico* and *La Vanguardia* in Barcelona. All of them have daily sections with job offers but the Sunday editions contain the largest number of job advertisements. Recruitment companies and head-hunters often place advertisements in these newspapers for senior positions, but you must be an outstanding candidate in terms of your experience and language ability. *El Mercado de Trabajo* is a specialist jobseekers' newspaper, which sometimes carries advertisements in English. If you want to place a 'situation wanted' advertisement in a Spanish newspaper, Publicitas Ltd (💻 www.publicitas.com/uk) will recommend the most appropriate publication and arrange for the text to be translated into Spanish; Publicitas charges a fee in addition to the cost of the advertising space.

There are also plenty of expatriate publications in major cities and coastal areas, all of which carry advertisements in English. *The Broadsheet* (💻 www.tbs.com), which is a Madrid-based magazine, used to be free of charge and the country's only English-language magazine with national distribution. In 2004, it began to charge a subscription fee and its distribution outside the big cities has since become unreliable. However, if you can get hold of a copy, it has some useful information, including classifieds and a directory of English-speaking services in Madrid. Its website (💻 www.tbs.com) has information about distribution points, which includes some outlets in the UK. The *Sur in English* (💻 www.surinenglish.com) newspaper covers Malaga and the Costa del Sol area; the east coast is covered by *The Costa Blanca News* (💻 www.costablanca-news.com). Both have extensive 'situations vacant' sections.

You can find details of all publications in Spain in the European volume of *Benn's Media Directory*, which is updated annually. It's only available in print form and is expensive, but in the UK a copy is available at most public libraries and the relevant pages can be photocopied. In the US, it's available from Grey House Publishing.

Internet

The internet is an increasingly popular job-hunting tool and there are dozens of websites that have lists of permanent, part-time and temporary positions as well as a number of sites where you can post your CV. Sites often provide useful information about living and working in Spain, although you should check all the information carefully, as some are better informed (and more up-to-date) than others. English-language sites include 💻 www.expatica.com, which is one of the best, 💻 www.eurojobs.com and 💻 www.jobpilot.es, which has a good Expat Corner. Spanish sites include 💻 www.empleo.com, 💻 www. monster.es and 💻 www.trabajo.es.

Job Applications

If you're applying for a job in writing, address it to the personnel director (*el director de personal* or *la directora*) and enclose the following:

- A short covering letter (in Spanish) explaining briefly your suitability for the post;
- Your CV (see page 71), translated into Spanish;
- Copies of references and relevant qualifications, also translated into Spanish;
- A recent photograph of yourself.

Spanish companies are **very** slow at responding to letters and emails and they respond far more positively to personal contact, so you should steel yourself for a follow-up phone call – in fluent Spanish, of course. If you get to the interview stage, you will be expected to dress formally and be honest about your experience and your level of Spanish and any other languages. Your claims will always be checked!

EMPLOYMENT CONTRACTS

Once you've found a job, you will have the same rights and responsibilities as a Spanish worker, **provided you have a legal employment contract**. Spanish workers are well protected by trade union agreements and as an employee you should enjoy good working conditions. Your contract (*contrato de trabajo*) should contain, as a minimum, your details and that of your employer; your job title and description, detailing your duties; your salary and any benefits;

working hours, benefits and holidays; and, most importantly, what type of contract it is and its duration. It's important to check the length of your contract, as an increasing number of employers are offering consecutive short-term contracts (*contrato temporal*) rather than indefinite, fixed employment contracts (*contrato indefinido/fijo*). This is because of the high cost of laying off staff in Spain, and some employers take on staff on temporary contracts during peak periods and fire them just before their contracts expire, thereby saving a fortune in dismissal and redundancy payments.

There are certain circumstances when temporary contracts are permissible and legal: for example, for training purposes; to complete a specific, short-term project; for the temporary replacement of permanent employees, e.g. those on sickness or maternity leave; and to cover a busy period. This last reason is the one that employers may use to employ seasonal staff. If you're offered a short-term contract for any of these reasons, remember that your contract must still be in writing, stating the reason for your temporary employment. Training and work experience contracts should last a minimum of six months and a maximum of two years and can be extended twice within the two-year period. If you're contracted for a specific project, you may be employed for the length of that project. If you're replacing permanent workers, your contract simply covers the period of their absence. If you have a short-term contract to cover a heavy workload, your employer can hire you for a maximum of six months within a 12-month period; however, he **cannot** keep renewing it indefinitely throughout the year.

Even if you're offered a permanent contract, your employer may still want to start with a short-term, probationary contract to see how you get on. This is acceptable provided it's for an agreed period and is described in writing as a probationary contract before you start work. The duration will depend on your status; collective agreements specify the duration of probationary periods for each category of worker.

By law, all contracts must be written in Spanish, so if your Spanish isn't up to it (and you would have to be pretty skilled in the language to get to grips with some of the legal jargon), make sure you get a contract translated and that you understand every word before signing it. Once both parties have signed the contract, two copies should be sent by the employer to the appropriate INEM office, where they're stamped and returned; you're given one copy for your records. Apart from any employment rights that this gives you, you will usually need a copy of your employment contract when renting or buying property. Your employer will then make tax and social security payments on your behalf.

Your Rights

You enjoy many rights as a worker in Spain and they begin with a minimum wage (*salario mínimo interprofesional*), which for the second half of 2004 was €460.50 per month for an unskilled worker. Although most employees earn more than this, it's used as a guide when employers and trade unions negotiate salaries for particular jobs and professions. Whatever your salary, you will find that, like most Spanish employees, you receive 14 'monthly' payments during the year. This very welcome extra money (*paga extraordinaria*) is usually paid twice a year: at Christmas and just before the long summer holiday in August. The standard working week in Spain is 40 hours, although this varies from job to job.

Make sure that you're clear about how your working hours are distributed, which should be detailed in your contract. Many businesses in Spain close for several hours in the afternoon for a siesta and re-open late in the afternoon and continue into the early evening. This will obviously depend on the company. The long siesta isn't as common as it used to be and international companies may operate differently depending on their business needs.

Under Spanish employment law it's never compulsory to do overtime and you shouldn't be expected to work more than 80 hours' overtime per year. Overtime rates must not be less than 175 per cent of your normal hourly rate; or you can take time off in lieu, but you must make sure that this is written into your contract. You're also entitled to a minimum of one and a half days' off per week (including Sundays) plus public holidays. There are 14 public holidays per year in Spain, two of which are local holidays. Weekends and public holidays are taken very seriously and few people expect to work on these days unless it's mandatory and has previously been agreed and stated in their contract. The Spanish work hard but their overriding philosophy is that they work to live, not live to work. This can be a source of much frustration at first but, once you stop fighting it and learn to adapt, it's a philosophy that works surprisingly well and certainly keeps the stress levels down.

SELF-EMPLOYMENT

Many foreigners come to Spain to escape the daily grind of a nine-to-five job and throw off the millstone of being answerable to a boss. If you want more freedom but still need to make a living, registering as self-employed could be the answer. It means that you can work when you like and for whom you like, whether as a tradesman, in a profession or as a small businessman, operating as a sole trader. Most importantly, it means that you can start your new venture on a small scale until you see how much demand there is for your services. The disadvantage is that self-employment, especially as a sole trader, carries certain risks and you will have none of the extensive protection that an employed person enjoys. You may also need to work all hours of the day and night to get your business going – and keep it going. So, before you take the plunge, look carefully at the cost implications in terms of tax and social security and also consider your personal liability if you operate as a self-employed sole trader.

In Spain, being self-employed is known as working on 'your own account' (*cuenta propria*) because you are, literally, on your own in the sense that you don't have the support of an employer, especially when it comes to paying social security contributions! A self-employed person is an 'autonomous worker' (*trabajador autónomo*). Many people who start small businesses in Spain operate as sole traders and opt for self-employed taxation. This is a good way to begin, especially if you don't have much capital and aren't sure how the business will go. However, you should remember that you won't have the protection of a limited liability company if your business fails and you will be personally liable if anyone sues you or your company. If you want to work this way to begin with, you'd be advised to take out insurance cover to protect yourself.

European Union Citizens

You can register as self-employed if you're a national of an EU country; the registration process is explained below. One of the first things you should do, even before you arrive in Spain, is to find out whether your profession is regulated in Spain and whether your current qualifications are recognised by the authorities (see page 28).

If you're already in Spain and your Spanish is reasonably good, you can go to your local Spanish employment office (INEM), where there should be a representative of the National Academic Recognition Centre (NARIC) to advise you about recognition and the validation process. If you aren't in Spain, you can contact NARIC Spain via its website (🖳 wwwn.mec.es/mecd/titulos); follow the link to *Centros y Puntos de Información*, where, in the Madrid section, there's an email link (*consultas electronicas*). Bear in mind, however, that Spanish government departments are particularly bad at responding to emails and you're better advised to contact them by telephone (☎ 915 065 593), where someone should be able to help you in English.

Once you've set the validation process in motion, you can register as self-employed. The process is the same for Spaniards and foreigners alike and entails registering for social security, tax and VAT (*IVA*).

Social Security

As a self-employed person, you're obliged to pay all your social security contributions, as opposed to an employer paying a large percentage on your behalf (see page 138). In 2004, the monthly minimum contribution was €225.11. **This is the minimum amount you must pay every month, irrespective of your earnings, even if they amount to nil.**

Income Tax & VAT

You must pay 20 per cent income tax on all your earnings, irrespective of how much or how little you earn (see page 130). Once a year, usually in June, you're required to make a tax declaration for the previous calendar year's earnings (January to December) and pay the full amount in cash (see page 128). You must also charge VAT (currently at 16 per cent) on your services. VAT is paid quarterly (in January, April, July and October). **Make sure that your earnings will cover all these costs and leave sufficient for your living expenses.**

Registration Process

If your Spanish isn't fluent, hire the services of a *gestor* (see page 89) to deal with the formalities of registration on your behalf. It's possible to do this yourself, but you must have plenty of time (and patience), along with fluent Spanish. The procedure is as follows:

● If you haven't already obtained an *NIE* (see page 72), make this your first job. This number identifies you to the tax authorities even before you start working and is needed when you start filling in forms and doing official paperwork.

● Find out where the relevant tax office (*tributaria*) is and register there for income tax and VAT. This should be the tax office local to where you plan to work, not where you live. Take the original and copies of your *NIE* certificate, your passport and your residence permit if you have one. You will need to fill in a form number 037 and present it to be stamped. The form will confirm which tax regime you come under (see page 130). You must also complete and have stamped form number 845, which registers you for business tax, known as *Impuesto Sobre Actividades Economicas* (*IAE*). Although you don't have to pay this tax unless the profits of your business are over €1 million, you must register for it, as your business or profession must have a tax category and code number (*epigrafe*).

● Go to your local social security office (*seguridad social*), listed in the yellow pages (*paginas amarillas*) and on the Spanish government's social security website (💻 www.seg-social.es/incio), which is only in Spanish but gives addresses and phone numbers of all the social security offices in the country, as well as plenty of other useful information about social security. When you register, you will again need the originals and copies of your *NIE* certificate, your passport and residence permit. In addition, you must bring along a copy of the form 845 that you obtained from the tax office (see above). At the social security office, you will need to complete form TA.0521.

Once you're registered for social security, you will be given a temporary card, which shows your social security number and allows you to register with a doctor. At this point you and your partner and any dependents are entitled to healthcare under the Spanish health system. This includes sickness treatment, maternity care, but not unemployment benefit. **Self-employed workers aren't entitled to unemployment benefit in Spain.**

Non-EU citizens

Non-EU citizens will find it difficult to obtain a visa if they want to work on a self-employed basis or start a business in Spain. You should seek advice from your nearest Spanish embassy or consulate. See also **Permits & Visas** on page 23.

4.

RUNNING A BUSINESS

For many foreigners who are thinking of a new life in Spain, owning their own business is all part of the dream. What better way to escape the daily grind than to be your own boss? According to a survey in 2004, the Costa del Sol had around 10,000 self-employed foreigners – 63 per cent of all self-employed workers in the whole of Andalusia. Of course, anyone who has run his own business, either in his home country or in Spain, will tell you that it is anything but a dream. It's tough in any country; if you plan to start a business in Spain, you will be reminded again and again what it **really** means to be a foreigner when you come up against the full force of Spanish bureaucracy!

One of the first rules of business in any country is that you must know and understand your market inside out. Yet, every year, thousands of foreigners arrive in Spain with the vaguest of business ideas, insufficient money and little or no Spanish. It's a country that seems to induce temporary madness in many people, or maybe it's just the sun and the apparently relaxed lifestyle. **Don't be fooled; if you're going to make your living in Spain, you cannot afford to risk everything on a whim and a prayer. The golden rule is: if you wouldn't do it in your home country, don't do it in Spain!** Whether you want to set up a completely new business or buy an existing one, there are two priorities. The first is detailed research, in terms of the market for your business and more generally in terms of living in Spain, and the second is a long, hard look at how you're going to finance the venture.

RESEARCH

If you have access to the internet, you can begin your general research online, checking out basics such as the legalities of starting a business, where to obtain good advice and the area of Spain you're interested in. There are a number of good websites, but bear in mind that, however good they are, the internet is but a pale impression of the real world. As soon as you've covered the basics in the virtual world, you must get out there and experience the real one (see **Local Research** below).

One of the best websites for all kinds of information about Spain in general and specifically about doing business there is 🖳 www.investinspain.org. Operated by the Spanish Ministry of Economy, it contains a wealth of information in English and Spanish. It isn't just aimed at big business, but also at the small entrepreneur who needs simple, basic information. As well as general information about Spain, it contains links to the sites of all 17 autonomous regions and details of businesses in each region. There's also a step-by-step guide to setting up your business, including information about financial incentives. Of course, a website can **never** be a substitute for professional advice but, if you're aware of each part of the process before you consult a legal adviser, you will be far better informed and able to ask the right questions. It's all part of being one step ahead of the game, which will be a distinct advantage when you come up against that infamous Spanish bureaucracy.

It's worthwhile buying a large map of Spain and seeing how the area you're interested in relates to surrounding areas. Find out about the area's economy in general, which type of products are most in demand and whether any large companies or corporations do business there. Your plans may be affected by local big business, even if it doesn't appear to be directly related.

If you've worked in a similar field in your home country, this should make your research a little easier, certainly in terms of knowing where to start. You will be familiar with business trends and possible problems, but don't make the mistake of many expatriate businessmen, who think that because their ideas went down well in their home country, the same will happen in Spain. If it's a completely new idea, market research into your product or service should be even more intensive. There aren't many profitable gaps left in the market, so look at the lifestyle and spending power of your potential customer base and check any direct or indirect competition carefully.

Many expatriates try to side step the language problem by opting for businesses that offer services only to tourists or other expatriates. The expatriate market is undoubtedly growing, especially in coastal areas and now in more inland areas too. Figures in 2003 from the Spanish government's immigration department show a dramatic rise in the last ten years. The highest concentration of resident expatriates is in the autonomous regions of Catalonia, Madrid, Andalusia and Valencia, but in terms of the whole population, percentages remain relatively low at around 6 per cent.

If you're considering this type of business, make sure you know what custom will be like out of season, when the bulk of your customers may have gone home and the sun won't be shining. Don't ignore the fact that you may earn little or nothing for several months of the year. This type of business is the riskiest of all and requires the most intensive research and the utmost caution. If you're just planning to target tourists or the expatriate community, you may find that this limits your eventual expansion.

For long-term success, it may make more sense to try to appeal to the local Spanish market too. You must be able to give Spaniards the service they require in their own language, and it's important not to underestimate cultural differences. The needs and expectations of the Spanish population are very different from those of the British or Americans. You must canvas opinion on your ideas from as many Spaniards as you can. Even if you don't like what they say, you can be sure they will be honest with you!

Local Research

When you've done as much 'remote' research as possible, it's imperative that you spend some time (as long as possible) in the area where you want to set up your business. If you can, take a temporary job in a similar business, meet people and make contacts, look at the competition and start finding sources of reliable legal and financial advice. **Good legal and financial advice is imperative BEFORE you commit yourself to anything**. If you want to make a smooth transfer from your early research to realistic plans, you must get good advice from those in the know. Everything begins to look very different when you're actually living and working in Spain, rather than just dreaming and surfing the internet. The other essential factor is to gain a realistic idea of the costs involved in setting up your proposed business (see **Chapter 5**).

Chambers of Commerce

An excellent source of advice about business plans is the British Chamber of Commerce in Spain (🖥 www.britishchamberspain.com), which offers considerable support and 'networking' opportunities. Based in Barcelona, the Chamber regularly organises lunches and networking evenings (see page 51) for those living locally, and provides news of similar events in Madrid. A wide variety of information is available in English on its website, especially if you become a member. The Chamber will help you to find interpreters and translators and provide information on the legal and fiscal requirements for your particular business. Employers can register job opportunities for small fee.

The Spanish Chambers of Commerce also offer extensive information and advice to the potential businessman or woman, but you must usually speak fairly fluent Spanish to take advantage of this, although some staff speak English. In theory, their services are available to all budding entrepreneurs, but in practice the service varies from area to area. However, don't dismiss them out of hand for this reason because one of their most impressive and forward-thinking services is the network of 'one-stop' offices (*Ventanilla Unica Empresial/VUE*), which can help you set up your business with the minimum of bureaucracy. There are more than 30 of these offices around the country and they offer advice and information and look at your business plan while you're still at the research stage. Once you decide to go ahead, all the facilities you need to set up your business are provided by *VUE* staff, which saves time, money and an enormous amount of stress for those starting small or medium-size businesses. If your Spanish is minimal and there aren't English-speaking staff, it's well worthwhile employing a translator or Spanish friend to help you take advantage of this service. To find out whether there's a branch in your area, go to 🖳 www.ventanillaempresarial.org/oficinas (in Spanish only).

Town Hall

In areas where there are large numbers of foreigners, you may find that the local town hall (*ayuntamiento*) has a Foreigners' Department, where staff not only speak your language but can also advise you on local business regulations. If you're lucky enough to have a Foreigners' Department at your town hall, make the most of it. Not surprisingly, Foreigners' Departments are dedicated to the needs of foreigners and are an invaluable resource for any new resident, especially those starting a business. Obviously, you must still get professional legal and financial advice, but a Foreigners' Department is an excellent starting point. If they cannot help you, they will be able to direct you to the appropriate department of the town hall, depending on the kind of advice you need, which will help with the required forms, licences and permissions. Even after you've started your business, it's worth paying the Foreigners' Department a regular visit to keep in touch with current events in your area and any changes in laws and regulations that may affect your business.

LEGAL & PROFESSIONAL ADVICE

When you're setting up a business in Spain, there's a considerable amount of paperwork to get through and you're responsible for dealing with it correctly, as well as for obtaining the required licences and paying all necessary taxes on time. **There are no excuses for being a foreigner and not speaking the language. If you don't comply, even through ignorance, you're likely to be faced with large fines.** It's therefore imperative that you use professional help.

This can be a daunting task. Where do you start? How do you find a professional in Spain that can be relied upon? One of the best ways is to do as the Spanish do: judge by recommendation and reputation. This may be easier said than done when you've just arrived in the country and don't even know where to go for a recommendation. However, if you're doing your research thoroughly, you should come into contact with plenty of businesses similar to the one you're planning to start. Ask the owners who they recommend; ask everyone you come into contact with, so that you have several different opinions. Then you will not only know the names of the most highly recommended advisers, but also the names of those to steer clear of.

It may feel too much like stepping into the unknown, especially when your future is at stake, but it makes sense to consult a Spanish professional who has good local contacts and a reputation to protect. If you're in an area where there's a large foreign population, many of the advisers you come into contact with will speak good English (and often other languages as well). They will also be used to doing business with foreigners and so will be familiar with the kind of advice you need. Many people opt for professional firms who operate in their home country and Spain and who work with a local Spanish professional. You may feel safer using this option, but you must still check the firm's credentials with previous clients, as well as those of the local professional it's working with.

There are several types of adviser who can make your life easier in Spain if you plan to start a business, but when you arrive it can be difficult to know which one to consult and when. Probably the first legal adviser you will come into contact with, especially if you're buying property, is a Spanish lawyer (see below). He's likely to make use of a *gestor* (see below), who will guide you through the requisite Spanish red tape. It's also imperative that you find a reliable firm of accountants (see page 90), who can advise you on all the financial aspects of setting up your business as well as your personal taxation. You will need the services of all three types of adviser if you're going to start your own business.

Lawyer

If you're going to get the best start you can, especially in a foreign country, it's vital that you find the best legal advice that's available.

Don't commit yourself to anything – and that means **anything** – until you've found an experienced lawyer. Many foreigners are nervous about consulting a Spanish lawyer (*abogado*). Although it's wise to be cautious, don't forget that lawyers in Spain are qualified professionals just as they are in any other country. They must be registered with the relevant professional body, the Colegio de Abogados, before they can practise.

Nevertheless, you shouldn't engage just any lawyer. Ask other businesses, other expatriates and, most importantly, any Spanish person you know in the community to recommend one. Spaniards value personal recommendation highly and it's the only kind of 'advertising' they take any notice of. A good reputation and useful contacts are everything in Spain and the lawyer you need must possess both.

When you find a lawyer who has been recommended, first check that he's an expert in setting up businesses like yours; second, ask him for an estimate of his charges, in writing; and third, check whether he holds a professional indemnity policy and the sum that it covers. Spanish lawyers aren't obliged to have indemnity, although most do, and it's best to choose a lawyer who does.

If your lawyer is setting up a company for you, he should deal with all the required procedures, beginning with a check that the name you want for your company isn't already listed in the Mercantile Registry. When the paperwork is at the appropriate stage, your lawyer will arrange for you to sign at the office of the *notario* (see page 90) and will then deal with registering your company on your behalf at the tax and social security offices. The cost of these services is usually around €1,500 but varies according to the kind of company you want to set up.

If you're dissatisfied with the service of any Spanish lawyer, you can register a complaint with the Ilustre Colegio de Abogados, the Spanish equivalent of the Law Society, which polices standards among lawyers and sets minimum charges, which are generally lower than in Northern Europe.

Gestor

If you're planning to start a business, the services of an experienced *gestor* are an absolute must, especially if you speak less than perfect Spanish. The *gestor* is a peculiarly Spanish institution; there's no British or US equivalent. Confused foreigners often feel that the profession was created in response to the endless, frustrating Spanish bureaucracy – and that's partly true. The role of the *gestor* originated at a time when illiteracy in Spain was high and, believe it or not, Spanish red tape was even worse than it is now! It isn't a legal requirement to use a *gestor*, but it's unlikely that you will have the time, the language skills or the know-how to deal with the barrage of forms, regulations and officials that you will be faced with. In Spain, it really does matter who you know when you're trying to get things done, and a good *gestor* will have all the right contacts. Make sure that your *gestor* comes highly recommended, tells you in advance what his charges will be and, most importantly, is experienced in the area that you need help and advice with.

Gestores' charges (like almost everything else in Spain) vary enormously and depend not only on the area and the individual *gestor* but also on the amount of work required to obtain, for example, an opening licence. If the process is straightforward, you might pay as little as €300; if not, . . .

A *gestor* is **not** a lawyer or a tax consultant but should be used alongside them. You will probably find that your lawyer has a *gestor* he prefers to use. *Gestores* should be members of the Colegio Oficial de Gestores Administrativos, which regulates the profession.

The first thing your *gestor* must do is check with the Technical Department of your town hall that your business activity is permitted in the area that you want to trade in. Once that has been established, you will need a form to apply for an opening licence (see page 102). It's a good idea to find out as early as possible roughly how long this process will take.

Asesor Fiscal

You're strongly advised to use a specialist financial adviser (*asesor fiscal* – roughly equivalent to a chartered accountant in the UK) if you're planning a new business in Spain. Make sure you use a specialist firm (*asesoria fiscal*) that's been recommended by someone who has used their services. Some companies offer both legal and accounting services, including legally incorporating your company and helping you to manage your accounting and tax obligations.

Notario

The *notario* is a public official (whose role is similar but not identical to that of a notary public in the UK) and doesn't act on behalf of any of the parties involved in a transaction, although he can give them useful advice. He's authorised by the government to draw up and certify legal and official documents. By law, a *notario* **must** be involved in property conveyance, marriage, wills, establishing limited companies and the buying and selling of businesses. In theory, it makes no difference which *notario* you use, as they're all civil servants and provide the same service according to the same laws and charge the same fees. In any case, it's likely that your *gestor* will have a 'favourite' *notario* (i.e. one he works with regularly) and you will simply be taken to him.

BUSINESS PREMISES

Once you know what kind of business you want to run and have decided on the best area, you will need to begin looking for suitable premises, known as *locales*. You will see plenty of premises advertised privately via notices on the buildings themselves or, if you've been in Spain for some time, you may hear of premises by word of mouth, but this route is only for those hardy souls who have been around a while and know the area and the seller well. For most people, it's advisable to use the services of a reputable commercial agent or an estate agent who deals in commercial properties. At this stage in your research, you should know the area fairly well and know which are the main (and most efficient) agents in the area. The next thing to do is to decide whether you want to lease, rent or buy your premises.

Leasing

In Spain, the most common way of securing business premises is on a leasehold basis. You make a one-off payment to buy a lease, which includes fixtures and fittings as well as goodwill if it's an existing business. You then continue to pay the landlord rent for the premises, but you can sell on the lease if you wish.

A lease in Spain has until recently been known as a *traspaso* (literally a transfer, as a lease is transferred from one person to another) but is now called a *cesión*. However, many people (including Spanish landlords) are unaware that the law has changed and that a *traspaso* no longer has any legal validity. You may therefore be offered a *trapaso*. Whether you're offered a *traspaso* or a *cesión*, make sure you obtain legal advice on the terms of your lease and ensure that these are specified in as much detail as possible in the contract.

The rules governing a *cesión* are far more relaxed than those for a *traspaso*, which means that there's more freedom for negotiation between the parties – but also more room for misunderstanding. Your lawyer should check that you aren't simply being offered a rental agreement masquerading as a lease, which will mean that you won't have any rights to sell the lease on to someone else. If you have a legal *cesión*, you're free to sell it on, provided you give your landlord first refusal. He will normally take between 10 and 20 per cent commission on the sale.

When buying a lease, make sure (or ensure that your lawyer checks) that the seller has the right to sell it. This may sound unnecessary, but there are cases of people selling leases they don't own.

In addition to paying an agreed amount for the lease, you must pay a monthly rent to the landlord for your use of the building. The contract should state clearly how much longer the lease has to run. Lease terms are normally between 5 and 20 years, but it's advisable to ensure that your lawyer negotiates the longest possible term. This is because during the term of a lease the landlord can raise your rent only in line with the official rate of inflation (as published by the Spanish government). When your lease runs out, you can usually renew it automatically, but this gives your landlord the opportunity to impose a considerable rent increase, sometimes as much as 20 or 30 per cent.

Renting

There are opportunities to rent business premises, although it isn't as common as leasing. Renting means you don't have the large outlay of buying a lease and have the flexibility to move premises if required. On the other hand, a rental agreement won't give you the same rights as a lease and, if you build up a thriving business in rented premises, there's always the danger that the landlord will decide not to renew your contract or to sell the property. As long as your lawyer negotiates your rental contract properly, however, it isn't easy for a landlord to 'throw you out', as tenants have considerable rights in Spain. If you opt for renting, it's therefore essential that you have a watertight contract by getting professional legal advice and check the terms of the contract carefully, especially the terms under which either party can terminate the agreement. Your business could depend on it.

Your rental contract should contain your details, those of the landlord and a description of the property. You will be expected to pay a deposit equivalent to two months' rent and pay one month's rent in advance. Make sure you get a receipt or proof of payment for your rent. The usual rental period is a year, and this should be stipulated in the contract. A contract can be renewed annually along with your rent, which for the first five years can be increased (or decreased!) only in line with the official rate of inflation.

If your landlord decides to sell the property, as a long-term tenant you have the right of 'first refusal' (*tanteo y retracto*) to purchase it. The landlord should offer it to you in writing, detailing the price and conditions of sale, before offering it for sale elsewhere. If you don't reply or don't wish to buy, he has the right to sell it to whoever he likes. However, if he sells without offering it to you first, you have the right to have the sale invalidated and buy the property yourself at the same price.

Freehold

Freehold premises at reasonable prices are a rare thing in Spain, so if you're offered one at a good price, you should consider it seriously (and take professional legal advice). As the name suggests, freehold offers you more freedom, especially in terms of altering the property for your business needs. It could also give you your own letting or leasing potential and, of course, after the one-off payment to buy the premises, there's no rent to pay. The process of buying a commercial property is exactly the same as buying a residential property, which is described in detail in our sister publication, **Buying a Home in Spain** (see page 323).

BUSINESS ENTITIES

While you're deciding on the kind of business premises you need, you should also consider which kind of company might be the best option for you and your business. There are a number of different types of legal business that you can set up in Spain (at least nine) and you must look carefully at the options with a qualified professional to see what's the most economical and beneficial for your situation. The five options outlined below are those most likely to be relevant to foreign entrepreneurs.

Whichever option you choose, you should decide at an early stage what is to be the registered office of your business. This may be the address of your financial adviser (see page 90), so that all the financial documents are delivered there and dealt with directly by them. This especially recommended if you operate from home, as it will give your business a more 'serious' image.

Sole Trader

If you want to begin small and don't have much capital, you can set up as a sole trader (*empresario individual*). The main advantage of this option is that it's the simplest legal business entity. Your only fiscal obligations are to register for tax, VAT and social security as a self-employed worker and also for tax on your business activities (see **Registration Process** on page 79). A further advantage of being a sole trader is that you aren't obliged to make a specified investment in your company; it can be whatever amount you can afford.

The main disadvantage of setting up your business in this way is that you're personally liable for all the debts of the company and, if anyone decides to sue you or your company, it could be a financial disaster for you and your dependants. If you aren't prepared to take on this kind of risk and have a reasonable amount to invest, it may be worth setting up a limited liability company.

Limited Liability Company

A limited liability company is known as a *Sociedad de Responsabilidad Limitada (SL)*, which is similar to a British limited company or an American limited liability company (LLC). It's the most common form of small and medium-size company. The reasons for its popularity are its simplicity, the relatively small investment it requires and, as the name suggests, the fact that your liability is limited if anything goes wrong or someone sues you. The disadvantage, compared with operating as a sole trader, is that you're liable for corporation tax and VAT as well as your personal tax and social security contributions.

If you start an *SL*, you must invest a minimum capital of €3,005.06 (an exact conversion from the former peseta figure!) and have at least one shareholder (the maximum is 50). You should work with a lawyer and a financial adviser to ensure that your company is legally incorporated and you've gone through all the required procedures before starting business (see **Incorporating Your Company** on page 96).

Sociedad Limitada Nueva Empresa

In April 2003, a modified version of the *SL* was introduced, called a *Sociedad Limitada Nueva Empresa (SLNE)*. The idea behind it was to encourage the incorporation of small and medium-size businesses, and the fact that its fiscal requirements are simpler than those of an *SL* should make it an increasingly popular option. An *SLNE* also differs from an *SL* in terms of the number of shareholders and permissible company names. The maximum number of shareholders allowed with this type of company is five, a move intended to keep *SLNEs* small. The company name must comprise one of the founder's names, a registration number and the letters *SLNE*. The minimum capital required is virtually the same as for an *SL* (€3,012 – all of which must be in cash) but the maximum is €120,202.

Public Limited Company

A *Sociedad Anónima* (*SA*) is the Spanish equivalent of a British public limited company (plc) or an American corporation and is the next most widely used type of business entity in Spain. An *SA* requires a much larger investment than an *SL* so it's usually the choice of big businesses working on major projects that wish to make an investment in Spain. The minimum investment required to form an *SA* is €60,101 and at least 25 per cent of that must be paid into the company bank account before incorporation. The company bylaws must then state what will happen to the remainder, including when and how it will be paid. There can be any number of shareholders in this type of company and they can be of any nationality and don't need to be resident in Spain, although they (or their professional representatives) must sign the necessary documents before a *notario*.

The main advantages of an *SA* are the exemption from personal liability for its shareholders, and the option to float the company, as shares in an *SA* may be quoted on the Spanish Stock Exchange (*Bolsas de Valores*). The disadvantages are the large investment and the complicated accounting required. Annual auditing is also mandatory, and the administration of an *SA* is more strictly regulated than that of an *SL*. If you're starting a small or medium-size business, it's unlikely that an *SA* will be the best option.

Partnership

If you want to make your business arrangement official (and legally avoid paying corporation tax) but don't want to start a business as such, it's possible to establish a partnership (*sociedad civil*). There must be a minimum of two partners and, although there's no minimum investment, they must agree to invest the same amount of money. They must also share the work, the goodwill and the profits equally. There's unlimited liability for partners, which they must share equally. You must still pay 1 per cent of the capital deposited in transfer tax (see page 135) and register for tax on economic activity (see page 132), register for income tax as self-employed workers (see page 130) and register with the social security authorities (see page 138).

Small & Medium-size Businesses

Small and medium-size businesses (*pequeñas y medianas empresas/PYME*) dominate Spain's economy (according to the Ministry of Industry, Tourism and Commerce, 99 per cent of Spanish businesses are *PYMEs*), and the government encourages both their formation and their growth. As a result, many *PYMEs* qualify for grants, incentives and reduced corporate tax rates (see page 133). There are in fact three categories of *PYME*, as follows:

- *Mediana Empresa* – A 'medium-size' business, with between 50 and 250 employees and an annual turnover of up to €50 million;
- *Pequeña Empresa* – A small business, with between 10 and 49 employees and an annual turnover of up to €10 million;
- *Micro Empresa* – A 'micro-enterprise', with fewer than ten employees and an annual turnover of up to €2 million.

Further information about *PYMEs* (in Spanish only) can be found on 🖳 www.ipyme.org.

INCORPORATION

Below is a guide to the steps that should be taken on your behalf to legally incorporate your company. It is **not** a substitute for legal and professional services but may help you to keep your advisers on their toes!

1. The first thing to be done is submit possible names for the company to the Mercantile Registry (Registro Mercantil Central) to check that no other company is registered under the same name. Provided there isn't, you will receive what's called a Negative Name Certificate (*Certificado Negativo de Nombre*). This may not sound like a very interesting piece of paper, but without it you cannot incorporate your company. The Mercantile Registry has recently simplified the checking procedure so that the process takes only a

few days. You can also use the Registry's website (🖳 www.rmc.es – in Spanish only) to consult company names already listed and submit new ones online.

2. The next step is to apply for a provisional company tax identification code (*código de identificación fiscal/CIF*) and register for VAT (*IVA*). **All businesses and self-employed people must register for VAT in Spain.** Your *CIF* will act as your VAT number and allows you to open a bank account in the company's name and deposit the required amount of capital, which you must do before incorporation can take place (see **3** below). You, or your accountant, can apply for a *CIF* at the tax office (*agencia tributaria*) closest to the registered address of your business. You can apply online (🖳 www.aeat.es/agencia/direc) but only if your Spanish is fluent. To apply for your *CIF* number, you must provide the following details: the name of your company (and the Negative Name Certificate from the Mercantile Registry), the registered address of the company, and identification in the form of your passport or residence permit (if you have one). The tax office will then issue you with a certificate called an *Identificación Fiscal* that has your *CIF* number on it.

3. Once you have a *CIF*, you can open a bank account in the company's name and deposit the required amount of capital. The certificate from the tax office states your company name with the addition of the words *en constitución*, which means that your company is in the process of being incorporated. You will receive another certificate (*Certificado del Desembolso Efectuado*) proving that you've paid this amount into your business account. You aren't allowed to withdraw the money you've deposited until the company has been formally incorporated, and incorporation cannot take place unless the *notario* has proof that the money has been deposited, with the above certificate. The certificate is also required to obtain your permanent *CIF* just before you start trading (see **6** below).

4. The company constitution, or deed of incorporation, can then be prepared and signed before a *notario*. This act (and the registering of your business with the Mercantile Registry – see below) is what makes your company legal in Spain, so make sure you know exactly what you and any partners are signing **before** you get to this point. If you aren't clear about the meaning of anything at all, get the relevant documents translated and, if necessary, raise any queries in good time. **The *notario*'s office is the place for signing and official**

rubber-stamping and not for raising questions, so you must be happy with all the paperwork by the time you arrive there. Your lawyer, tax consultant or *gestor* should accompany you to make sure everything goes smoothly. A *notario*'s office is always very and can be a confusing place for foreigners, so you will need someone with you who not only is a fluent Spanish speaker but also really knows the ropes.

Your professional adviser can arrange all the above for you, but you should ensure that one of you brings along the following documentation when you go to sign at the *notario*'s office:

- The Negative Name Certificate from the Mercantile Registry (see **1** above);
- The company's provisional *CIF* (see **2** above);
- The certificate proving that you've deposited the required capital (see **3** above);
- Documents to prove the identity of the founding partners.

The *notario* will also need to see the company bylaws, which should include such details as your corporate name and business purpose, the business address, your capital and the number of shareholders. You will also have to state whether any directors or administrators will be paid and, if so, what the payment arrangements will be. Finally, you must detail your corporate fiscal year, which can be no longer than one calendar year. The fiscal year is from 1st January to 31st December, and it's simpler if your company's fiscal year is the same, as your accounting procedures will be even more complicated if you choose a different period. After the signing, your company bank account can be activated and the authorised signatories registered with the bank.

5. Within 30 days of signing the deed of incorporation, there are two things you must do. The first is to pay 1 per cent of the amount of capital deposited to your local tax office; this is a stamp duty (sometimes referred to as transfer tax). You will need to take along your deed of incorporation and your *CIF* and complete the required form. Second, you must register your company with the Mercantile Registry. For this you will again need your deed of incorporation, along with proof that you've paid the stamp duty and your Negative Name Certificate (see **1** above).

6. The final step in this long-winded process is to obtain your permanent *CIF* from the tax office and register your company for

the 'tax on economic activities' (*Impuesto sobre Actividades Economicas – IAE*) in order to be issued with a business licence. (Confusingly, the licence is also called an *IAE*, although it's often referred to by its former name, a *licencia fiscal*.) For this you will need the certificate showing your provisional *CIF*, your deed of incorporation and a photocopy of your registration with the Mercantile Registry. If your annual turnover is less than €1 million, you may not be liable to pay business tax. However, you must still register for it because your business or profession must have a tax category (see page 79).

If you're running a company as opposed to being a sole trader, you must also register for corporation tax (*Impuesto sobre Sociedades*) after your company has been incorporated and you have all the relevant paperwork. Take it to the tax office and register your company on the Census of Taxpayers by filling in form 037. It's advisable to get an experienced firm of accountants (*asesoria fiscal*) to help you with this and complete and submit your corporation tax returns (see page 133).

Below is a checklist of the various numbers and codes you should have before starting business:

- *NIE* (see page 72);
- *CIF* (see page 97);
- **Social Security Number/***Código Cuenta Cotización* (see page 138);
- **Tax Category/***Epigrafe* (see page 79).

REGISTERING AS AN EMPLOYER

If you intend to employ staff to work in your business, you must register with the appropriate authorities. You should first obtain an application form for a social security insurance policy that will provide accident and sickness cover for your employees. Take a copy of the policy back to the office along with plenty of copies of your *NIE* certificate and your passport, a copy of your deed of incorporation, a copy of your registration for business tax.

On completion of a form TA6 (provided, of course, that all your paperwork is in order), you will be issued with a social security identification number and informed of your obligations as an employer. **If you plan to employ staff, you must register with the social security**

authorities before you start trading. If you want to employ staff at a later stage, you will need to have done this well in advance.

You must also register your business activity with the nearest office of the Ministry of Labour and Social Affairs (Ministerio de Trabajo y Asuntos Sociales) within 30 days of incorporation. You or your *gestor* or financial adviser should obtain a copy of the Ministry's annual guide to labour and social affairs, which is available in English or consult its website (🖥 www.mtas.es – only in Spanish).

PERMISSIONS & LICENCES

Now that you have a legal Spanish company, you can begin to think about trading, although there are still plenty of formalities that must be completed before you can actually do so.

You should visit your town hall as early as possible to find out what's required, as procedures vary from area to area. If the town hall has a Foreigners' Department, that's the best place to start. They can supply you with a list of required procedures for businesses that come under their jurisdiction. However, it's advisable to employ a *gestor* to complete the formalities on your behalf, especially if it's a new business and you're starting from scratch.

It can take months for the relevant officials to examine your proposed business and carry out all the required inspections, and there's no guarantee that it will be approved even after all this has been done.

Installation Plan

You must submit a 'project' (*proyecto*) – more accurately an 'installation plan' – to the town hall, or rather engage a professional architect (*arquitecto*) to do so for you, as the town hall won't accept a plan from anyone else, so it makes sense to use his services from the outset.

When you buy, lease or rent commercial premises, they're normally empty and you must decide how you intend to use them for your business purposes, which may necessitate renovating, rebuilding or extending the premises or simply fitting them out with equipment and furniture. Whatever is the case, your architect must produce a set of plans (even if plans already exist for the premises), showing all the relevant installations, including fire extinguishers, toilets and first aid box (yes, that's a relevant installation!).

You must also make an application for approval of your plan and may need to submit additional paperwork; your architect or *gestor* will advise you of any extra requirements. The cost of an architect's service depends on the size of the premises, as you're charged pro rata, and the type of plan submitted (e.g. a simple redesign or a complete refit). As an example, Teresa Emslie, who needed to fit out a dress shop on the Costa del Sol (see page 204), was charged around €6 per m².

Health & Safety Certificate

Your architect and *gestor* will arrange health and safety and installation inspections. A health and safety certificate (*certificado de salud y de seguridad*) must be obtained before your opening licence (see page 102) is granted.

Building Licence

If your plan requires structural alterations to the premises, you will also need a building licence (*licencia de obras*).

First Occupation Licence

A first occupation licence is required where you're the first business to occupy the premises, even if they aren't new. Your *gestor* should obtain this from the town hall if necessary.

Other Permissions

If you plan to serve food, each of your staff will need a food handler's certificate (*carnet de manipulador de alimentos*), which is issued by the government of the autonomous community in which you live via authorised training companies. Your town hall will give you the contact details for the appropriate company in your area. You must take a short course and a simple test, which is usually quite straightforward. In some areas (mainly coastal areas where there's a high proportion of English-speakers), you can do the test in English. The course costs around €50 per person.

If singing and dancing are included in your plans, you will also need a music licence, which must be applied for at the same time as your opening licence (see below). Policy varies from town hall to town hall, but live music licences are rarely granted and you're more likely to obtain a licence for recorded music. Like so many things in Spain, the cost varies according to local regulations and may even depend on the type of music you wish to play (flamenco guitar presumably being cheaper than heavy metal?).

Opening Licence

When you've completed all these formalities, you may (finally!) apply for an opening licence (*licencia de apertura*). To do so, you must complete the application form and provide some or all of the following (this isn't a definitive list, as requirements vary). If your *gestor* manages to get all this paperwork together and accepted by the local council, hang onto him – he's worth his weight in paella!

- Your *NIE* certificate and residence or work permit;
- The deed of incorporation of your company;
- A copy of your business licence issued by the local tax office;
- A copy of the receipt for the deposit towards the cost of your opening licence;
- Details of your premises – your lease or rental contract or the title deeds;
- Several copies of your installation plan, which must be stamped and approved by the architect responsible for it;
- A security certificate showing that all installations in your premises have been inspected by an engineer;
- A health and safety inspection certificate;
- A building licence, if you plan to make any changes to the premises;
- A first occupation licence (if applicable);
- Other licences as appropriate, e.g. a food handler's certificate and a music licence;
- A receipt showing that property tax has been paid on the premises (see page 136).

The charge for your opening licence may be calculated according to the area of your premises or according to the amount of business tax you must pay; each town hall has a different calculation method (it can even vary with the electricity supply!). The following is an example only – for a new establishment in Mijas:

Area of Premises (m²)	Charge (€)
Up to 100	324
101 – 250	389
251 – 500	428
501 – 1,000	1,100
Over 1,000	1,200

The above charges (in Mijas) are multiplied by various coefficients according to the type of business, e.g. 2 for financial or insurance services and estate agencies, and between 2 and 6 for hospitality businesses.

Obtaining an opening licence can be very difficult without professional help. Requirements vary considerably from one town hall to another and according to the kind of business you want to start. You will almost certainly need the help of a *gestor*, and attempting to manage without one can be a false economy.

Once you finally get that precious opening licence, make sure it's displayed on the premises at all times (no doubt, after all the trouble you've been to to obtain it, you will want to have it framed!) and that you have several copies.

ACCOUNTING

Spanish accounting regulations are contained in the Commercial Code and Corporations Law and they oblige all companies to record every economic transaction appropriate to their activity. The Instituto de Auditores-Censores Jurados de Cuentas de España is the official accountancy body, which is responsible for accounting and auditing standards throughout Spain. However, on 1st January 2005, the entire Spanish accounting system changed, and Spanish-listed companies must now conform to International Accounting Standards (IAS), in order to bring them into line with EU regulations on accounting procedures. You can obtain a copy of the IAS from The International Accounting Standards Board (🖥 www.iasb.org).

Before you can start trading, you must obtain accounting books and take these to the Mercantile Registry office closest to the registered office of your business to have them stamped – and so made legal before you undertake any business activity. You should obtain advice from your financial adviser on the books that are required for your particular business.

In addition to accounting books, the company must have a minutes book (*libro de actas*), which records agreements taken at annual general meetings. If your business is an *SL* (see page 94) you must record the contributions of each shareholder in a *libro de registros de socios* and you also need a personnel registration book (*libro de matricula*), which proves that your staff have been registered with the labour authorities and which must be shown to inspectors when they visit your premises.

Once you start trading, you must file an annual self-assessment tax return. This must be submitted within 25 days of the six-month period that follows the end of your fiscal year. For example, if your fiscal year runs from 1st January to 31st December, you must file for that period within 25 days of 1st June the following year. In addition, you must make quarterly payments in lieu of your annual return during the first 20 days of April, October and December. The amount you must pay is fixed at 18 per cent (or 25 per cent if your turnover exceeds €6,010,121).

When you submit your annual return, the amount you've paid in advance is deducted from the amount you owe. You must also submit corporate tax forms, financial statements and inventories annually to the Mercantile Register. A good financial adviser will fill out the relevant accounting books and submit everything on your behalf.

BUYING AN EXISTING BUSINESS

If you don't want to get involved in starting a business from scratch, buying an existing business may be the answer, especially if you're considering a business such as a shop, a bar or a restaurant. Hopefully, the business will have a good customer base and any licences for the business will already be in place. All you should have to do is register a change of ownership with your local town hall and then build on existing business.

Beware: all may not be as it seems! Try to find out why the owners are selling the business, especially if the price seems reasonable. Thriving businesses aren't sold off at knock-down prices without a good reason. If a business has been badly run and doesn't have a good reputation, you could be buying something that's more of a liability than an asset. Make sure you get at least two **independent** valuations and talk to the current owners at length about their reasons for selling. Is competition too fierce or are there plans afoot to build something close by that will affect your trade? Ask your lawyer to check local planning permission applications for possible rival businesses or anything else that may have a negative effect on your profits.

Another potential disadvantage of buying an existing business is that you must also take on the staff that go with it and you will be subject to all the labour and social security obligations of the previous owner. Make sure that your lawyer checks what kind of contracts are in place for the staff, as you will be the one who has to honour them. Check in particular that there are no outstanding disputes with any staff. The previous employer **and you** are jointly responsible for any claims made before the sale and up to three years afterwards.

Finding the Right Business

Your search for the right kind of business might start on the internet, where you can find out what's available and at what price and form a picture of the market. Your search engine will overwhelm you with sites if you type in something like 'businesses for sale Spain'. You won't find any shortage of agents trying to sell you businesses in Spain, especially in the coastal areas. They may be specialist commercial agents or general estate agents who have businesses for sale.

Private sellers tend to advertise in the classified sections of the English-language newspapers published in Spain (see **Appendix B**); advertisements are usually posted on their websites. Note, however, that you're recommended not to buy privately. *Sur in English* (🖳 www.sur inenglish.com) is the best source of classified advertisements on the Costa del Sol, and details of businesses for sale on the Costa Blanca can be found in *Costa Blanca News* (🖳 www.costablanca-news.com/ property). Details of publications in other areas can be found in **Appendix B**. There may also be specialist publications in your home country that carry details of businesses for sale in Spain. In the UK, *Daltons Weekly* (on sale every Thursday) contains advertisements for businesses for sale, not just in the coastal areas of Spain but also in the big cities such as Madrid and Barcelona.

Once you've arrived in Spain, it isn't necessarily wise to approach an agent or a private seller immediately. Even reputable agents may carry you along on a tide of infectious enthusiasm and persuade you to commit to something before you're ready. Take your time; this is an important decision and you need the chance to familiarise yourself with all aspects of buying and running a business in Spain so that, when you consult an agent, you're in a position to ask the right questions.

Come prepared with a list of agents who seem to be offering the kind of business you're looking for. Put together a shortlist of areas you think will be suitable as well as the type, size and possible cost of the business you wish to buy. Walk around the areas you like at different times of the day and during the evening and see for yourself how other businesses are operating and what the 'traffic flow' is in each area. If you're interested in a seasonal business, try to make at least one of your visits out of season, so that you can see what business might be like when the tourists are long gone – but the bills still have to be paid.

When you feel ready, approach several agents rather than just one, **but don't sign anything until you've taken independent legal advice.** As well as selling businesses, many agents offer a 'hand-holding' service to help you through the setting-up period, providing you with advice and information. The better agents are knowledgeable and can provide valuable support in those confusing early months, but don't forget two very important points about this kind of service. First, however reputable, honest and professional an agent, his principal concern is selling the businesses he has on his books. It's in his interest to move proceedings along and his priorities may not be the same as yours. Second, although it may be easier initially to have all the nuts and bolts of your new life taken care of, the disadvantage is that you don't find out things for yourself and aren't entirely in control of a process that's about to change your life. Take as much general advice as you can from an agent, let him recommend professional advisers and show you where and how things are done, but make sure the decisions are yours and not his. **When you're buying an existing business, it's imperative that you take INDEPENDENT legal advice. It should be independent of the agent and independent of anyone with an interest in selling the business.** When you're trying to find out how things are done in a new country, the best way is to do as much as possible yourself. It's a steep learning curve, especially if your Spanish isn't good, but it will pay dividends in the end.

An agent will need to know what kind of business you're looking for, the areas you're interested in, how much you have to spend and whether you're in a position to spend it immediately. Spanish agents charge the seller, not the buyer, so you shouldn't have to hand over any money until you pay a deposit to secure the business that you eventually choose. According to a leading commercial agent on the Costa del Sol, the most common mistake prospective buyers make is to overstretch themselves financially and sink everything into their business. If the business fails, they lose everything. Don't make the same mistake. When putting together your business plan, set aside plenty of money to live on and a contingency fund for those unforeseen (and always very expensive) problems that have a tendency to arise when you can least afford them!

Before you sign anything, or agree a price for an existing business, arrange for a qualified professional to check its accounts and declared profits. Such figures are often misleading or even meaningless, as the previous owner may have 'cooked the books' in order to pay less tax. However, a professional adviser will be able to tell you if the figures fit the general pattern of similar businesses in the area; he may even have knowledge of the business itself. Make sure that the turnover can be substantiated and, if you can, spend some time working alongside the owner so that you can see for yourself what business is like before you agree to anything.

Purchase Procedure

The procedure for buying a business is essentially the same as for buying any property, but you should tread carefully through it. You must usually pay a 10 per cent deposit to show your commitment to buy, with the balance payable, if all goes to plan, between 30 and 60 days later. The payment of a deposit ensures that the business is taken off the market while all the legal checks are made. You should obtain a receipt and insist that the deposit is paid into a client account until completion of the sale, either by the agent or by a *gestor*, rather than handed over to the seller. This is important, as the legal checks might show that the seller doesn't have the right to sell the business, the leasehold or the property. Once you've paid a deposit, the seller should provide your lawyer with the title deeds (*escritura*) or a copy of the lease and an inventory of what's included in the price. That way your lawyer can check with the Land Registry to make sure that the seller is the legal owner or leaseholder and what the tenancy status is.

Your lawyer should also check that all the licences are in place to operate the business legally (see below) and – most important of all – that there are no debts attached to the business or the property and no outstanding disputes with staff if the business is being sold with employees. In Spain, when you buy or lease a property or a business, you also take on the debts as well as any staff and the attendant social security obligations.

If there are any problems with the contract that are beyond your control (e.g. the seller doesn't have the right to sell, the business isn't licensed as advertised or there are debts or other liabilities that haven't been or cannot be cleared up), your deposit should be returned. You should only lose your deposit if you change your mind without good reason. If your lawyer has made all the relevant checks and is satisfied that all is in order, you can go ahead to completion on the agreed date, at which point the balance must be paid and keys will be handed over to you.

If you're buying a lease, make sure that you can fulfil your responsibilities as leaseholder **before** you sign a contract. During the term of the lease, you must pay all service charges such as water, electricity, telephone and local business taxes.

Licences

One of the main advantages of buying an existing business is that you can generally begin trading more quickly because any licences that are required continue to be valid if it changes hands. You will simply have to register a change of name on the licence. As long as the nature of the business doesn't change, you won't have to wait weeks (or months) while a new application is processed, with no guarantee that it will be granted at all. An agent shouldn't sell you an unlicensed business but unfortunately some do, and unsuspecting purchasers are simply closed down by the police as soon as they open.

If you're buying a business that is trading, it must by law have an opening licence, but make sure you actually see it and get a copy. It should be displayed, or at least available, on the premises. If the current owners cannot provide it, there's a strong possibility that the business is operating illegally.

Your agent should make sure that the business has all the necessary licences (see page 100), and your lawyer or *gestor* should double-check. Don't sign an agreement until you have seen the licences and have copies.

If the business is trading while waiting for a licence, this should be carefully checked with the issuing authority – especially the reason for the delay. In certain circumstances, the business can legally be offered for sale without a licence. If this is the case, your lawyer should check whether there are any potential problems obtaining one and ask for the price to be reduced accordingly.

EMPLOYING STAFF

Think very carefully indeed before you employ staff in Spain. It's no exaggeration to say that you will be stepping into the proverbial minefield. Try not to employ anyone unless you absolutely have to, although you should beware of using unpaid help (e.g. from family and friends), as this is tantamount to illegal labour, although it's common practice, particularly among Spaniards. If you cannot cope with the workload on your own and it's vital to the success of your business to employ someone, make sure you take expert advice from a lawyer who has lots of experience in dealing with labour regulations and can advise you about the law and how it applies to you. If you decide to engage staff, find a professional who can advise you about employment contracts and your social security and tax obligations.

Social Security Payments

As an employer, your main financial obligation is to make social security payments on behalf of your staff. Total contributions in 2004 were 28.3 per cent of an employee's gross pay, of which the employer must pay a large proportion: 23.6 per cent, the employee paying only 4.7 per cent – and enjoying all the benefits! Details of social security payments and benefits can be found in *Living and Working in Spain* (see page 323).

Each new worker must be registered with the social security authorities and within his contract registered with the national employment service (INEM) within ten days. Don't forget about this or be tempted not to do it. If your business is inspected by the labour authorities, you will be heavily fined. To register an employee, you must provide originals and copies of his *NIE* certificate and passport and the relevant completed form (TA.2/S). The INEM should stamp and return two copies of the contract, one of which should be given to the employee and the other retained for your records.

Tax Deductions

You're also required to make monthly deductions from an employee's salary for income tax (usually called withholding tax) provided he earns above the minimum wage, but you aren't liable to make an annual tax declaration on his behalf. You must provide him with a payslip or 'certificate of taxes' (*certificado de retenciones*) showing all the amounts that have been paid by you and your employee, and he makes the declaration himself. Personal tax rates for salaried staff range from 15 to 45 per cent, depending on earnings and allowable deductions, which vary according to circumstances. Details of tax deductions and payments can be found in *Living and Working in Spain* (see page 323).

Employee Rights

Labour laws in Spain have relaxed a little in the last few years, but the rights of employees are still very much uppermost in the eyes of the law. (The main aim of the law is to protect employees from exploitation but, as an employer, you may begin to feel that you're the exploited party when the bills start to come in!) Employees enjoy extensive rights, which include a minimum wage and 14 'monthly' payments instead of 12. These extra payments are to cover the Christmas holidays and the long summer holiday period and are a long-standing tradition. They're also entitled to one month's paid holiday and 14 public holidays (two of which are locally established).

Contracts

The Spanish government is making considerable efforts to encourage employment stability. Permanent or indefinite or 'fixed' contracts (*contrato indefinido/fijo*) are supposed to be the rule and temporary contracts (*contrato temporal*) the exception and, as a result, these are allowed only in certain circumstances (see below). Whichever type of contract you use, you must make sure that it complies with the minimum legal requirements for workers' rights as established in the Statute of Workers and you must obtain advice on this from a specialist in labour law (*asesor laboral*), who will be able to advise you how best to employ someone (legally) in accordance with your needs.

Temporary Contracts

Labour laws in Spain are such a tangled web that many employers often take risks unnecessarily. They take on staff illegally through ignorance and to avoid the time and expense of doing things properly. There are genuine – and legal – circumstances that allow you to employ staff on a temporary basis and they're as follows: for specific training purposes; provision of a specific service or the completion of a specific short-term project; to meet specific production needs or contracts for the temporary replacement of employees, usually due to sickness, maternity leave or retirement. This last reason is the one that employers may use to employ seasonal staff.

This means that you can legally employ staff on a temporary contract, such as a training contract, until you see how they perform in the post, rather than commit yourself to a permanent contract from the outset. You're genuinely training them for the job and, if things don't work out, both parties are free to terminate the agreement at the end of the period. The minimum and maximum duration of temporary contracts depends upon the type of contract and the job that the employee is doing. There are collective agreements to guide you on this. Usually the maximum duration is six months if the employee holds a university degree and two months if he doesn't.

If it's a casual contract to cover an extra heavy workload, you can hire someone for a maximum of six months within a 12-month period. However, you **cannot** keep renewing it indefinitely throughout the year. If you contract someone for a specific project, he may be employed only for the length of that project; if he's replacing a permanent worker, the contract can cover only the period of absence.

When you offer a short-term contract for any of the above reasons, remember that the contract must still be in writing, stating the reason for the temporary employment.

Permanent Contracts

Although you must be very careful about entering into a permanent contract with an employee, it's encouraged by the Spanish government. All manner of financial incentives, in the form of tax benefits and social security reductions, are available if you employ staff on a permanent basis, especially if they're disabled, have been registered as unemployed for more than six months, are aged between 16 and 30 (a group with especially high unemployment in Spain), or are unemployed and over 45 or female.

You should agree, in writing, a trial period, so that you don't commit yourself until you're sure about your employee's suitability for the job, and ensure that the contract states when it comes up for renewal – or it will be virtually impossible to dismiss the person if you need to and you could find yourself faced with an unfair dismissal claim, which will undoubtedly prove very costly.

All contracts must, by law, be written in Spanish, so make sure that your adviser arranges a translation if you aren't fluent in Spanish. Two copies of the signed contract must be sent off to the Employment Service (INEM), who will be stamp and return them, one for the employee and one for your records.

Dismissal

If you want to terminate an employee's contract, you will need to tread with extreme care and, as always, take professional advice from an expert in labour laws. Until recently, Spain's labour laws didn't allow for dismissal unless the employee was guilty of the most heinous crime. Although this has begun to change a little due to pressure from employer's organisations, dismissal is still strictly controlled and, where there's a dispute, courts almost always rule in favour of the employee, leaving the employer with a crippling fine.

There are generally three circumstances in which termination of a contract is allowed, as follows:

- **Economic or Organisational Reasons** – These are what is commonly termed 'restructuring'. As an employer, you can claim that dismissing an employee, or several employees, is the only way to save the business from bankruptcy. This requires the intervention of the labour authorities and, if they decide that dismissal is justified, the contract is terminated and the employee receives 20 days' pay for each year of service up to a maximum of 12 months' salary. If the labour authorities decide against you but you dismiss staff anyway, you must compensate them with 45 days' pay for each year of service, up to a maximum of 42 months' salary.

- **Objective Reasons** – These cover, for example, ineptitude on the part of an employee, an inability to adapt to technological changes after a reasonable period of retraining, and 'continuous and unjustified absences'. To dismiss an employee for any of these reasons, you must give him 30 days' written notice and pay an indemnity of 20 days' salary for each year of service up to a maximum of 12 months' salary.

- **Disciplinary Reasons** – As the name suggests, this covers areas such as insubordination or disobedience, 'serious and wilful non-compliance with duties', verbal or physical abuse of employer or his family, betrayal of an employer's confidence or trust, a continual decrease in the normal accepted standard of work, and habitual drinking or drug-taking which affects performance.

An employee dismissed for either objective or disciplinary reasons must be notified in writing of the reasons for the dismissal. I he doesn't agree, he must file a request for conciliation within 20 days of receiving the dismissal letter. This attempted conciliation at the arbitration office (Servicio de Mediación, Arbitraje y Conciliación) is obligatory before resorting to the labour courts. If arbitration is unsuccessful and the case goes to court, where the dismissal is judged to be fair, the employee receives no compensation. If it's judged to be unfair, you may have a hefty bill to pay: 45 days' pay for each year of service up to a maximum of 42 months' pay. Further details of the law relating to dismissal can be found on the website of the Spanish Institute for Foreign Trade (🖳 www. spainbusiness.com).

5.

MONEY MATTERS

If you're making a living in Spain, in whatever capacity, you will need to familiarise yourself with all kinds of financial matters, so that you remain firmly in control of your new working life. This chapter covers financing your business, banking, taxation, social security contributions, and retirement and pensions.

FINANCING YOUR BUSINESS

When you've reached the appropriate stage in your research, you should put together a business plan and take it along to a professional who's familiar with the economic trends in the area you're interested in and can advise you about the local business environment and any opportunities for obtaining financial support for your venture. There are legal firms that offer a service in your home country and in Spain and specialise in advising on business ideas and financial plans. They can speak your language, they know Spain and its legal system and can help you to present your business plan in a form acceptable to Spanish banks and financial institutions. You will find advertisements for legal advisers who offer this type of service in Spanish lifestyle magazines (see **Appendix B**). These are packed with useful information, articles and relevant advertisements, some of which also appear on their websites. Two of the longer-established magazines are *Living Spain* (🖥 www.livingspain.co.uk), which has a reader's enquiry service), and *Spain* (🖥 www.spainmagazine.info).

The most common mistake people make when they arrive in Spain with plans for a new life is to be unrealistic about what they can achieve and overoptimistic in their financial projections. It's highly unlikely that your business will make substantial amounts of money from day one. At this early stage, make sure your financial projections are pessimistic rather than optimistic. If the bug has bitten you hard, it may be tempting to brush aside those nagging little potential problem areas, hoping they will go away. **If you don't want your dream to turn into a nightmare, don't be tempted to do this!** Make sure that your business plan allows plenty of money to survive on until you can earn some of your own.

Some people suggest having resources to last a year, others as much as two or three years. Many foreigners find that the worst point for them comes at around 18 months to two years after their arrival. The novelty has well and truly worn off, business is slow, money is running out fast, and they don't feel they can stomach any more Spanish bureaucracy.

At this point it's very tempting to give it all up and go home, especially if you have a family with you. It only takes one of them to be homesick or unhappy and your business problems seem to be magnified a thousand times. Make sure you haven't burnt all your bridges and sold all your assets in your home country. If your finances will run to it, keep a small property there so that you can go back and 'regroup' if you need to.

As a foreigner, you will find it doubly hard to make a success of your business – and not just because of the language barrier. Unfortunately, it's all too common to hear of foreigners whose big ideas have turned to dust and who have disappeared overnight, in some cases owing money right, left and centre. However genuine the reasons for this, it doesn't engender trust from customers, suppliers and other businesses. Understandably, Spaniards and other foreigners alike have a healthy suspicion of new arrivals. It's often the reason you're given a wide berth until you've proved you're here to stay. Part of the long hard road to success depends on your ability to prove that you have staying power and commitment within the business community here in Spain. Only you can decide whether it's better financially (and for your sanity!) to cut your losses and go home or to stick it out. Much will depend on how good a start you get with your business and much of that will depend on finances.

Grants & Incentives

An important part of financing your business is to take advantage of any grants or incentives for which you qualify. In theory, there's plenty of financial assistance available in Spain, via the European Union and at national, regional, provincial and local level, especially for small and medium size businesses. However, tracking down the right one for you and actually getting the money in your company bank account is another matter altogether. Try to set the process in motion as early as possible but **don't** factor it in to your financial projections. The application process can take months, even years. Even when a grant is eventually approved, getting it through the system to where you need it – in your business – is a tortuous process.

You will need the advice of someone who's familiar with what's available and knows about regulations and qualifying conditions. The financial adviser who helps you with your business plan is the best place to start finding your way through the maze of financial aid.

Another good source of information about grants and financial incentives for businesses is the website of the Spanish Ministry for

Industry, Tourism and Trade (▣ www.investinspain.org). This contains detailed information about the criteria for grants from central government and those awarded by autonomous communities, municipalities and city councils. Some of the Spanish Chambers of Commerce also have information, as do the one-stop business creation offices (*Ventanilla Unica Empresarial/VUE* – see page 86), although their information is not always available in English. The Madrid Chamber of Commerce has information available in English on its website, which is a useful reference point (▣ www.cameramadrid.es/ingles). Finally, the Dirección General de Política de la PYME (▣ www.ipyme.org – in Spanish only), the association of small and medium-size businesses in Spain is an important organisation in the Spanish business world and can give entrepreneurs a considerable amount of support. If you aren't a fluent Spanish speaker, find someone who is to help you make contact with them.

Bear in mind that any grant or incentive offered by the state or by an autonomous community is governed by the regulations which the EU has established for all its members. Aid and incentives are permitted only in areas which meet EU criteria, of which details can be found on the Invest In Spain website (▣ www.investinspain.org).

European Union Grants

European Union (EU) grants can be particularly difficult to track down, but a number of websites can facilitate your search, including the following:

▣ www.grant-guide.com – An EU-funded website called 'GUIDE', which aims to simplify the hunt for information about grants (both state and private) available throughout Europe. Information is available in all official EU languages. There's a searchable database of literally thousands of grants, loans, cash awards and venture capital schemes.

▣ www.grant-guide.com – Grant-Guide is a consortium of three grants consultancy firms, in the Netherlands, Spain and the UK. The Spanish grant search information is linked with the leading grants consultancy firm in Spain, Econet. Some services aren't free.

▣ www.econet.es – Run by Spain's leading grants consultancy firm, Econet and providing information in English;

▣ www.europa.eu.int – The European Union's own website, which you can access in English (click on 'Enterprise' and then 'Grants and Loans');

⌨ www.ipyme.org – The website of the Dirección General de Política de la PYME (see above). Go to 'SIE Bases de Datos' and then 'Ayudas de la Union Europea' (in Spanish only).

Grants at National Level

Many of the information sources of information about grants and subsidies at a national level are only in Spanish. However, Econet's website (⌨ www.econet.es) can be accessed in English. Econet acts as an intermediary between applicants and awarding bodies, helping with advice and qualifying information and is one of the key organisations to contact in order to obtain the grant you need. The association of small and medium-size businesses (see above) will also help with grants and incentives at a national level, some of which are aimed specifically at small and medium-size businesses (*pequeñas y medianas empresas/PYME* – see page 96). Details of loans available to *PYME*s are detailed below.

Grants at Autonomous Community Level

Each of the 17 autonomous communities in Spain has an investment promotion agency. The website of the Spanish Ministry for Industry, Tourism and Trade (⌨ www.investinspain.org) provides links to all the relevant websites (click on 'Regional Agencies'). A few of them are available in English, but most are only in Spanish and. Bear in mind that any grant or incentive offered either by the state or any autonomous community is governed by the regulations which the EU has established for all its members. Aid and incentives are only permitted in areas which meet their criteria. This information is also detailed on the Invest In Spain website.

Other Grants & Incentives

Financial incentives are offered at various levels (autonomous community, municipal and city council) to companies which create and foster employment among 'disadvantaged' groups. If you employ people who have been unemployed for more than six months or you employ women, especially older women, in an industry where women are traditionally underrepresented, you will qualify for rebates of between 20 and 100 per cent on your employer's social security contributions. If you create jobs among the local community, you may also benefit from significant subsidies, especially during the first year after your company is incorporated. Your local Chamber of Commerce will give you details incentives that apply to your situation, and further information can be found on the Invest in Spain website (🖥 www.invest inspain.org).

Loans

Many of the people who contributed to this book had difficulty securing bank loans to start up their businesses. Although the Spanish banking system has improved dramatically in the last 15 years, when it comes to lending, banks aren't generally great risk-takers. They're particularly cautious about lending to foreigners, even those who are resident in Spain and have some collateral, such as a house. Even fairly senior banking staff don't have the autonomy to approve loans in the same way as they do, for example, in France. They often require a guarantor for the loan or ask for evidence that the business has been making some money, which isn't usually realistic when you're at the start-up stage! In theory, under EU regulations, both residents and non-residents should be equally eligible for a loan in any currency, but in practice you may find that you come up against closed doors.

If you need a bank loan, you must prepare a thorough and realistic business plan, which should include how you plan to repay the loan if it's granted. Professional advisers who have offices in the UK and Spain, such as John Howell and Co., solicitors and international lawyers, The Old Glass Works, 22 Endell Street, Covent Garden, London WC2 9AD (☎ 020-7420 0400, 🖥 www.europelaw.com), will work through your business plan with you and help you to present it in a form acceptable to a Spanish bank.

If you secure a loan, you will be expected to put in at least an equal amount of investment and the repayment period is usually between five and seven years. Rates vary considerably with the bank, the amount and the loan period, so it's advisable to shop around with the help of your professional adviser.

Small and medium-size businesses (*PYME*) are entitled to preferential access to credit facilities offered by Spain's state owned financial agency (Instituto de Crédito Oficial/ICO), which is part of the Ministry of the Economy and Finance. For example, they can obtain a loan of up to 70 per cent of the net investment and, provided you have no other loan or grant, you can apply for the Micro-Credit Facility, which provides up to 95 per cent of the net investment (up to a maximum of €25,000). The ICO's website (🖥 www.ico.es) is available in English and provides details of the loans available; click on the section entitled 'Financing Facilities', then on 'Domestic Investment'.

BANKING

Banking in Spain has changed out of all recognition in the last few decades, during which period the number of banks and branches has increased considerably, although some have also gone bust. Many banks went broke in the '70s and '80s, but Spanish banking has since emerged from the dark ages and is now much more efficient. Banking has become highly automated in recent years, although many Spanish banks remain frustratingly slow and inefficient compared with banks in many other EU countries. Where human involvement is concerned, Spanish banks remain Neanderthal, although with regard to electronic banking they compare favourably with other European countries and their ATMs (cash dispensers) are among the world's most advanced (how many other countries' ATMs 'talk' to you in a number of languages?). Most banks also offer home banking services via telephone and/or the internet, which is an invaluable service if you're busy setting up and running a business.

There are also around 50 foreign banks operating in Spain, although there are fewer (with an overall smaller market share) than in most other European countries. However, competition from foreign banks is set to increase as EU regulations allow any bank trading legitimately in one EU country to trade in any other EU country. Most major foreign banks are present in Madrid and Barcelona, but branches are rare in other cities. Among foreigners in Spain, the British are best served by their national banks, both in the major cities and resort areas. The most prominent British banks in Spain are, in order of the number of branches, Natwest, represented by Solbank (some 65), Barclays (28 branches) and Lloyds TSB (around 10). These banks are full members of the Spanish clearing and payment system and can provide cheque accounts, cash and credit cards, and direct debit/standing order services. The Royal Bank of Scotland also operates at some BSCH branches. Note, however, that foreign banks in Spain operate in exactly the same way as Spanish banks, so you shouldn't expect, for example, a branch of Barclays in Spain to behave like a branch in the UK or any other country. Surprisingly, considering the size and spending power of foreign residents and tourists in Spain, most Spanish banks make few concessions to foreign clients, e.g. by providing general information and statements in foreign languages and having staff who speak foreign languages.

Opening Hours

Normal bank opening hours in Spain are usually from between 8.15 and 9am until around 1.30pm, Mondays to Fridays, and from 8.30 to 9.30am until 1pm on Saturdays in winter (banks are closed on Saturdays from around 1st April to 30th September). Savings banks open all day on Thursdays (until 7pm) but are closed on Saturdays. Some branches in major cities remain open continually from the morning until 4 or 4.30pm from autumn to spring, although they may close earlier on Fridays. Some banks are experimenting with longer hours at certain branches and opening from, for example, 8.15am until 8.30pm (or they may open from around 8.15am to 2pm and again from around 4.30 until 7.45pm). Banks in shopping centres may also open all day until late in the evening (some are open the same hours as hypermarkets, e.g. from 10am until 10pm). At major international airports and railway stations in major cities, there are banks with extended opening hours, although they often have long queues. Banks are closed on public holidays, including local holidays (when banks in neighbouring towns often close on different days), and they may also close early during local *fiestas*. Note that many bureaux de change have long opening hours and some are even open 24 hours during the summer in some resort areas.

Opening an Account

Ask your friends, neighbours or colleagues for their recommendations and just go along to the bank of your choice and introduce yourself. You must be at least 18 and provide proof of identity (e.g. a passport), your address in Spain and your passport number or *NIE* certificate (see page 72).

Non-Residents

Until you become resident in Spain, you're entitled to open a non-resident euro account (*cuenta de euros de no residente*) or a foreign currency account only. An important point for non-resident, non-EU citizens to note is that the transfer of funds for the purchase of a property (or any other major transaction) in Spain must be verified by a certificate from your bank (*certificado de cambio de divisas*). This allows you to re-export the funds if necessary at a later date. This is unnecessary for EU nationals. If you're a non-resident you can do most of your banking via a foreign account using debit and credit cards, but if you own a home in Spain, you will need a Spanish bank account to pay your utility and tax bills (which are best paid by direct debit). You can have your correspondence (e.g. cheque books, statements, payslips, etc.) sent to an address abroad if necessary.

Residents

You're considered to be a resident of Spain if you have your main centre of interest there, i.e. you live and work there almost permanently. To open a resident's account you must usually have a residence permit (*residencia*) or evidence that you have a job in Spain. It isn't advisable to close your bank accounts in your home country, unless you're sure you won't need them in the future. Even when you're resident in Spain, it's cheaper to keep money in local currency in an account in a country you visit regularly than to pay commission charges to change money. Many foreigners living in Spain maintain at least two current (cheque) accounts, a foreign account for international transactions and a local account with a Spanish bank for day-to-day business. If you want to open a company account, you must deposit a minimum sum depending on the type of company you're setting up (see **Business Entities** on page 93).

TAXATION

Before starting a business in Spain or starting work there, it's important to find out what your tax liabilities are likely to be. Before you make any other decisions, and certainly before you move to Spain, it's advisable to consult a tax adviser who's familiar with taxation laws both in your home country and in Spain. That way you can prepare well in advance for the move and hopefully reduce your tax liability in both countries. You should also inform the tax office in your home country of intended your move abroad, as you may be entitled to a tax refund, although this will depend on a number of factors.

In the UK, the Inland Revenue has a Centre for Non-Residents (☎ 0151-472 6067, 🖥 www.inlandrevenue.gov.uk/cnr), which can provide the necessary information. They will need evidence that you're moving abroad and should give you a form P85 to complete. It's a good idea to do this with the help of your tax adviser, as the form will be used to decide where you will be resident in Spain for tax purposes. The Inland Revenue can also advise you about your tax situation in general and any double-taxation agreement that your country has with Spain. Double-taxation agreements have been set up so that you don't have to pay tax in two countries at once, so it's important to check this.

Two good sources of information on tax issues, both personal and corporate, are the website for the Spanish Ministry for Industry, Tourism and Trade (🖳 www.investinspain.org – available in English) and the website of the Spanish Commercial Offices in the US (🖳 www.spain business.com), which is also available in English. Both these sites are useful when you're initially looking at the tax implications of your venture and subsequently.

Back in the '60s and the '70s, taxes were very low in Spain and tax evasion almost a way of life. Although there have been increases over recent years, Spanish income tax rates are still among the lowest in Europe and there are a myriad of tax concessions and allowances both for companies and individuals, depending on your circumstances. The tax authorities have also begun to realise that inefficient and complicated tax collection is costing them money! Consequently, there have been some major tax reforms in the last few years, which are designed to make things easier for the taxpayer as well as to cut down on fraud: along with it being easier for you to declare your income correctly, you're more likely to incur heavy penalties if you don't. Large fines are incurred for serious breaches of tax law and tax evasion. Although there are still many 'fiscal nomads' (those who manage to avoid being resident in any country for tax purposes) in Spain, they're beginning to find it more difficult to avoid paying Spanish taxes. **If you think you can escape the taxman by moving to Spain, forget it!**

Nevertheless, Spain is no different from any other country in the sense that there are ways of taking advantage of the system legally. Once you begin to move ahead with your plans, and even after you've started a business, you will also need to check that you're up to date with the ever-changing tax requirements. For these reasons, you should engage a reputable financial adviser or accountant (see page 90). Your lawyer may be able to recommend an accountant or you can ask people you trust for their recommendations; this is always a good bet in Spain.

Many foreigners hand over all their tax affairs to their adviser or accountant, and this makes sense, especially if your Spanish isn't fluent. He can deal with your own and your employees' income tax and social security contributions, your VAT returns and your end of year tax returns. However, as with so many areas of your new life in Spain, it's vitally important that you're always aware of what other people are doing on your behalf and in your name (or company name). Specialist legal and financial procedures must always be left to qualified professionals, but try and be as informed as you can and make sure you have a rough idea of what your accounting obligations are right from the word go.

Despite recent reforms, the Spanish taxation system is still complicated. It's important to understand that the country as a whole operates on three levels: national, regional and local or municipal – particularly when it comes to taxation. National taxes are levied by the Spanish central government tax agency, the Agencia Estatal de Administración Tributaria, whose website (💻 www.aeat.es) has some useful information, but most of it only in Spanish. Its headquarters are in Madrid, but its assessment and tax collection centres are in provincial capital cities. Regional taxes levied by autonomous community governments and local taxes by municipal authorities.

If you're lucky enough to live in Alicante province, you can obtain lots of help and advice (in English, French or German) on all kinds of local and regional tax issues, including payment of the local council tax (*IBI*), the tax on economic activities (*IAE*) and the vehicle registration tax (*IVTM*), from an organisation called SUMA, which is part of the Alicante Provincial Council. SUMA calls itself the 'autonomous organisation for tax management in Alicante' and aims to make tax paying a simpler business! Even if you don't live in Alicante, you can find a lot of useful general information on the SUMA website (💻 www.suma.es – in English, Spanish and Valenciano), but check that it applies in your area. SUMA also runs a telephone enquiry service (☎ 965 148 561), which is available from 9am to noon on Mondays, Wednesdays and Fridays in English, French and German.

Personal Income Tax

Spanish income tax is known as *Impuesto Sobre la Renta de Las Personas Fisicas/IRPF*). It's a national tax, but part of it goes to your autonomous community government. It applies only to residents; non-residents are taxed in a different way. Your liability for income tax in Spain depends on whether you're resident there for tax purposes. Under Spanish law that means for more than 183 days per year (whether or not you have a residence permit) or if your economic interests, such as your business and investments, are in Spain. If this applies to you, you will have to pay tax on both earned and non-earned worldwide income. In addition to any salary or income from business interests, you will be taxed on your pension, any capital gains, property and investment income and any employee benefits that you enjoy if you've been relocated by your company.

Allowances

To work out your taxable income, you can deduct various allowances from your gross salary depending on your circumstances. These include the following (all figures are for the 2004 tax year):

- **Personal Minimum Allowance** – €3,400 for a single person and €6,800 for a joint tax return (more if you're over 65 or disabled);

- **Salary or Pension** – You can deduct €3,500 if your annual income from a salary or pension is lower than €8,200. If your income is between €8,200 and €13,000, you can deduct €3,500 minus 22.91 per cent of the difference between €8,200 and your income. If your income is over €13,000, you can deduct €2,400. If you're over 65, all the above allowances are doubled.

- **Social Security Payments** – All social security payments are tax deductible.

- **Relocation** – If you were previously unemployed and moved to a different area to take up a job, you may deduct €2,400 from your gross salary.

- **Dependent Children & Elderly People**– You can deduct €1,400 for a first child, €1,500 for a second child, €2,200 for a third child and €2,300 for a fourth and each additional child. In addition, you can deduct €1,200 for each child under three. If you're caring for elderly people, you can deduct €800 for each person between 65 and 75 and €1,000 for each person over 75.

- **Child Support Payments** – If you're a divorced parent and have to pay child support payments as a result of a court decision, you may deduct these from your income.

- **Disability** – There are a number of deductions that you (or your dependants or parents) can make if you have a disability. The amount depends on the level of disability and is €2,000 if your level is between 33 and 65 per cent, plus deductions of €2,800 from income and €2,000 for care if you have mobility problems. If your disability is above 65 per cent, you may deduct €5,000, plus deductions of €6,200 from income and €2,000 for care if you have mobility problems.

- **Professional & Trade Union Fees;**

- **Spanish Company Pension** – If you're paying into one of these schemes, you may deduct contributions up to a limit of €8,000 if you're under 52. If you're between over 52, you can deduct €8,000 plus €1,250 for each year over 52 up to a maximum of €24,500.

- **Annuity** – Depending on your age, you can deduct a percentage of any annuity (either life or fixed period annuity). For example, if you begin receiving an annuity at 39 or less, you're taxed at 45 per cent but, if you start at 65, you're taxed at only 20 per cent.

- **Legal Expenses** – Expenses of up to €300 incurred as a result of action connected with your work may be deducted.

- **Dividends** – You may deduct 60 per cent of any dividends paid to you.

- **VAT (IVA)** – 75 per cent of any VAT paid as a result of a property sale can be deducted.

- **Principal Residence Costs** – You may deduct 15 per cent of the cost of purchase or renovation of your principal residence up to a maximum of €9,015 (renovation doesn't include additions such as a garage or swimming pool, or normal repairs and maintenance). You can also deduct mortgage payments up to €9,015 and 15 per cent of an amount invested in a mortgage savings account up to €9,015.

- **Charitable Donations** – You may deduct 20 per cent of the value of donations of cultural items to charities and 10 per cent for cash donations, up to a maximum of 30 per cent of your taxable income.

- **Spanish Life Premiums** – You can deduct 10 per cent of the cost of Spanish life premiums or premiums for an invalidity policy.

- **Income Taxes Paid in Another Country** – If you've already paid income tax in another country, you may deduct this.

Although this is a fairly comprehensive list, it should be used as a guide only. A good firm of accountants will ensure that you make all the deductions you're entitled to, thereby ensuring that you pay the minimum tax necessary – and still stay within the law!

Income Tax Rates

Your net (or taxable) income after the deduction of allowances is taxable at between 15 and 45 per cent above a tax-free limit, as shown in the table below:

Earnings after Allowances (€)	Tax Rate (%)	National/Autonomous Community Split
Up to 4,000	15	9.06 /5.94
4,001 – 13,800	24	15.84/8.16
13,801 – 25,800	28	18.68/9.32
25,801 – 45,000	37	24.71/12.29
Over 45,000	45	29.16/15.84

If your Spanish is fluent (and you're au fait with the tax system), you can calculate your tax using a CD-ROM, which can be bought cheaply from the tax office or via the tax office's telephone or internet services (⌨ www.agenciatributaria.es).

Tax Declaration

If you have any kind of income in Spain – whether you're a salaried employee or self-employed, own a business, are retired or are unemployed, and whether you're a resident or non-resident of Spain – you must submit a tax declaration. There are a few exceptions to this rule. For example, you don't need to declare if you're a salaried employee earning less than €22,000 and with no other source of income and your employer has deducted withholding tax throughout the year, or if you're non-salaried with earnings below €8,000. However, you should still keep detailed records of all earnings and check with the tax office or a financial adviser that you don't need to declare.

If your earnings are above these levels, you must make a declaration – and the responsibility lies with you and your advisers. No one will send you a form; you must obtain one from the tax office or from a tobacconist's (*estanco*), where they're sold for a few cents.

There are three types of form; an abbreviated declaration (*declaración abreviada*), Form 103, which is used if you need to declare earnings from pensions or investments that have already been subject to withholding tax; a simple declaration (*declaración simplificada*), Form 101, which must be used if you have income from letting, certain business and agricultural income or capital gains from the sale of a permanent home where the total gain is to be reinvested in another property in Spain; an 'ordinary' declaration (*declaración ordinaria*), Form 100, which is for all sources of income other than the above and covers all business and professional activities and capital gains. Unfortunately, for most people trying to make a living in Spain, this form – 13 pages long and the most complicated of the three – is the one that's required!

However, help is at hand, either from your tax adviser or from the tax office in the form of an innovative computer programme called the Personal Income Tax Return Help Progamme (*Programa de Ayuda a la Declaración del Impuesto sobre la Renta de las Personas Fisicas/PADRE*), which is the result of a major effort on the part of the tax authorities to help you declare your tax correctly. (They claim that it's "a simple, secure and trustworthy system, because it was written by the Tax Agency itself"!)

To use the *PADRE* system, you can go to the tax office, where staff will help you to enter your information into the computer programme, which runs on the Windows operating system. Because the tax office is keen to promote the system, if you use it for your declaration, you will be first to receive any refunds that are owing to you. However, don't just turn up at the tax office. You must phone ☎ 901 223 344 and make an appointment to see a specific member of staff. In areas where there are large numbers of foreign residents, there may be a member of staff who speaks English, but don't depend on it. When you go to the tax office for your appointment, you should take along your bank statements showing interest received and your average balance; any papers relating to stocks, shares, bonds and any property that you own in Spain or abroad; any declarations and receipts for taxes paid in another country; and, of course, those vital documents, your passport, residence permit and *NIE* certificate You can find a fuller explanation of the *PADRE* system in English on 💻 www.aeat.es/agencia/ memorias/02/ingles – scroll down to the section called 'Citizen Assistance Services'.

If you can't face the tax office, you may find that your bank has the *PADRE* programme and can enter your information via their computer, in which case a member of their staff should help you to make your declaration. However, if your tax position is complicated or if you prefer expert and independent help, it's best to consult a tax adviser. Many of them have access to the *PADRE* programme and charge around €35 for a simple tax return and around €60 for a more complicated one.

The Spanish tax year runs from 1st January to 31st December, and employees must submit their declarations between 1st May and 20th June of the following year, although if you think you're entitled to a refund, this deadline is extended to 30th June. You pay your income tax in arrears, so for income earned in 2005, you would declare between those dates in 2006. The self-employed must make quarterly declarations (see below).

Late payment, even by a day, will incur a surcharge, usually of 20 per cent, although you can officially request a payment deferral. If you have an adviser taking care of your tax affairs for you, check that he pays on time and gets receipts for payments. If he doesn't do this, it will be **you** that's liable for the penalty.

You should keep copies of your tax returns for at least five years, which is the maximum period that returns are liable to be audited by the tax authorities. After five years, any unpaid tax cannot be collected.

Employees

If you're a salaried worker, your personal income tax situation is relatively simple. There's a 'pay-as-you-earn' system and your employer deducts the relevant tax contribution (called withholding tax) throughout the tax year, so that you should have nothing more to pay. Recent improvements in the system mean that this amount is calculated so that it matches as closely as possible your tax liability and allowances. Normally, even if you work for an employer, although income tax is deducted from your salary, you're responsible for filing your tax returns, not your employer. However, if you earn less than €22,000 per year and your salary is your only source of income, you won't need to declare. The national tax agency calculates what you owe or what's due to you and sends you a form (105) to check, sign and return; any refunds due to you are made before the end of April.

Self-employed

If you're self-employed, you have different accounting and tax obligations from those of an employee. There are two types of self-employed tax 'regime'. Go to the tax office nearest to where you plan to work and complete and hand in Form 037. This form is stamped by the tax office and will confirm how you pay your taxes.

If you're a sole trader operating without a specific business entity (such as an SL or SA – see page 93), you may have to begin paying taxes under the *modulos* system (this is decided for you by the tax office, and you have no say in the matter!). Under this system, the tax office assesses what your business income is likely to be and you pay tax on this amount each quarter, irrespective of your actual earnings, even if they amount to zero. The advantage of this system is that you don't need to keep accounts or prepare VAT invoices and you simply submit an ordinary return at the end of the financial year.

Otherwise, you will make payments according to the standard system, known as direct estimation (*estimación directa*), but this means you must make quarterly tax and VAT declarations and either operate a double-entry book-keeping system yourself or engage an accountant to do so on your behalf. At least with the direct estimation system, if you earn less you pay less. You can change from the *modulos* system to the direct estimation system after a year if you think it would be better for you.

Either way, you must pay the balance of the income tax you think you owe at the same time as you make your declaration (see **Tax Declaration** on page 128). You can either pay the whole amount when you submit your form or 60 per cent with the declaration and the remainder by the following 5th November. You can take your returns to the tax office where you're resident for tax purposes and pay there or file your return and pay direct from your account at any of the designated banks in the area. If you pay at the tax office, payment must be made in cash (watch out for muggers!). If no payment is due, you must still file a return.

Most self-employed people end up paying too much tax, as their quarterly payments are set at 20 per cent of earnings, and are due a rebate. If you think this will be the case, you can apply for a rebate at the same time as you submit your tax return. If you haven't paid enough, you will be sent a bill for the difference!

Wealth Tax

Known as *Impuesto Extraordinario sobre El Patrimonio* but usually referred to simply as *patrimonio*, this is a regional tax, which must be paid in addition to income tax (and at the same time) and is levied on residents and non-residents alike, although it affects non-residents differently.

Residents

If you're resident in Spain, your liability is based on the value of all your worldwide assets, including property, vehicles, business assets, cash deposited in bank accounts, jewellery, stocks and shares and anything else which might contribute to your wealth. You must produce your year-end bank statements, showing any interest received and an average balance.

Husbands and wives must each make a separate declaration and are each entitled to the first €108,102 (total €216,204) of their assets tax free. If their assets include their principal residence, both the husband and wife are entitled to a further deduction of €150,253. So, for a couple, declaring separately, deductions can amount to €516,710. You can make further deductions if you have a mortgage or loan on your property. Tax rates in 2004 were as follows:

Asset Value Above Allowance (€)	Tax Rate (%)	Cumulative Tax (€)
Up to 167,129	0.2	334
167,130 – 334,253	0.3	836
334,254 – 668,499	0.5	2,506
668,499 – 1,337,000	0.9	8,523
1,337,001 – 2,673,999	1.3	25,904
2,674,000 – 5,347,998	1.7	71,362
5,347,999 – 10,695,996	2.1	183,670
Over 10,695,996	2.5	

Non-Residents

Non-residents only have to declare their property and any assets in Spain but aren't entitled to an allowance against wealth tax. The above tax rates apply.

Business Taxation

If you have your own company, are a sole trader or are self-employed, you will have to pay not only your own personal income tax (see above) but also possibly a tax on your economic activities, and all Spanish companies – but not the self-employed and sole traders – must pay corporation tax. These taxes are described below.

Tax on Economic Activities

Spain levies a 'tax on economic activities' (*Impuesto sobre Actividades Económicas/IAE*), which must be paid by businesses, self-employed workers and professionals with an annual turnover of more than €1 million. It used to be a local tax but now comes under the jurisdiction of the national tax authorities. The *IAE* is levied annually, irrespective of the type or size of your business. Because of the turnover limit, introduced in 2003 to encourage the set-up of small businesses, most businesses don't have to pay this tax; however, whatever your turnover, **you must register for *IAE*, as your business or profession must have a tax category and a code number (*epigrafe*), which are assigned when you do so (see page 79)**. *IAE* is likely to be replaced by another tax in the not too distant future, not least because local councils have lost a considerable amount of revenue since the introduction of the turnover limit.

Corporation Tax

Corporation (or company) tax applies to companies only (not sole traders or the self-employed, unless they've formed a company). It's known as *Impuesto sobre Sociedades* and is levied on any company which is resident in Spain for tax purposes, which means that it was incorporated under Spanish law (see page 96), or that its registered office is in Spain or that its management headquarters are in Spain. The government is keen to encourage foreign companies to operate in Spain and so company taxation laws have recently undergone a series of changes designed to make their set-up simpler. There are also considerable tax incentives for small and medium-size companies (see below).

If your company is incorporated in Spain, it will be taxed on all its worldwide profits, earned and unearned, including income from investments and asset transfers, at a rate of 35 per cent. However, if you qualify as a small or medium-size company (see page 96), you will pay a reduced rate of 30 per cent and if you happen to set up a business in the Canary Islands, you will benefit from their special company taxation system and may only have to pay between 1 and 5 per cent corporation tax, depending on whether you comply with the required conditions (see page 133).

It's advisable to get an experienced firm of accountants (*asesoria fiscal*) to complete and submit your corporate tax returns. Corporation tax must be paid within 25 days of the company's Annual General Meeting, which must be held within six months of the end of the fiscal year (31st December).

Small & Medium-size Businesses: The government is keen to encourage the setting-up of small and medium-size businesses (see page 96), which are therefore entitled to a reduced rate of 30 per cent corporation tax for the first €90,151.82 of taxable income, but thereafter must pay the standard rate of 35 per cent.

Companies that have net sales of less than €3 million in the preceding tax period also qualify for certain tax advantages. Full details of these can be found on the Invest In Spain website (🖳 www.investinspain.org – in English) under 'Corporate Income Tax'.

Capital Gains Tax

Capital gains tax (*Impuesto sobre Incremento de Patrimonio de la Venta de un Bien Inmueble*) is payable on the profit from the sale of certain assets in Spain – and not only property. You must also pay capital gains tax (CGT) when you make a profit from the sale of antiques, art and jewellery, stocks and shares and property and businesses.

When you're buying property or a business, be very careful that the purchase price declared on the sale contract (*escritura*) isn't too low. Although, under-declaration is illegal, it has been common practice in Spain for the seller to have a very low value placed on the *escritura*, so that he pays as little CGT as possible when he resells it. However, this is beginning to change, as the authorities try to crack down on the practice and collect the tax owing to them. Don't get caught in the middle. If you, as a buyer, accept a low declared value, you will find that you're the loser. When you come to sell, and you appear to have made a larger capital gain than you have, you will be liable for more tax. Note, however, that you may not find anyone willing to sell you premises or a business if you refuse to compromise whatsoever on the declared value. Take advice from your lawyer (some of whom express surprise that this practice is so alien to foreigners!) in order to achieve a satisfactory compromise.

There are a few situations in which you aren't liable for capital gains tax. If you're a resident of Spain and are 65 or over, you will be exempt from CGT. Residents below the age of 65 are also exempt from CGT provided that the property they're selling is their principal residence, they've lived there for three years and they plan to buy another home in Spain within three years.

A capital gain should be declared within three months of the sale and rates are 15 per cent for residents and 35 per cent for non-residents. If you buy from a non-resident (whether you yourself are resident or non-resident), you're obliged by law to withhold 5 per cent of the total purchase price and pay it directly to the Spanish tax authorities within 30 days of the sale. You must make the declaration on Form 211. This payment means that it's more difficult for the seller to avoid paying CGT on the sale. As a buyer, provided you pay the 5 per cent during the 30 day period, you cannot be held liable for any additional CGT that the seller might owe. Once you've paid the 5 per cent to the tax office, you must give the seller a copy of Form 211 and he then applies to the tax office (on Form 212) for the return of the difference between the 5 per cent and his CGT liability. If he doesn't do this in the required time, the tax office will keep his money. **If you're buying from a non-resident, failure to subtract and hand over the required 5 per cent means that you're liable to pay any CGT from the sale and could also face a hefty fine.**

Property Transfer Tax

If you're legally incorporating a business or buying a property, you will also be liable for a regional tax, known as *Impuesto de Transmisiones Patrimoniales y Actos Jurídicos Documentadas*, on the following types of transfer:

● **Corporate Transfers** – You must pay one per cent of the bank deposit made to incorporate your company (see page 96) within 30 working days of incorporation.

● **Mergers & Revaluations** – You must pay transfer tax at the same rate on any business merger or share capital increase or decrease.

● **Property & Land Transfers** – Resale properties incur transfer tax at a rate, which is usually 6 per cent of the purchase price declared in the contract, although it varies from one autonomous community to another. Remember that all parties may want to declare a value much lower than the real value, to reduce this tax (see above) but, if its declared value is considerably lower than expected, tax inspectors may be alerted and you may be subject to heavy penalties. Ask your lawyer for advice and ask him to check with the tax office the average market value for the property you intend to buy. If you're buying a new property, you won't have to pay transfer tax, but you will have to pay 7 per cent of the purchase price in the form of VAT, as it's seen as a business transaction between you and the developer.

Stamp Duty

Stamp duty must be paid when you sign any documents in front of a *notaio* (these are known as *actos jurididicos documentales*), which you must do if you're incorporating your company or buying property and public deeds or registry office documents are involved. The rate varies according to the kind of transaction and the autonomous community but is usually between 0.5 and 1 per cent.

Plus Valia

You must also pay a tax on the increased land value since the last sale. This depends on what you buy and how long it is since the last sale. The official value of the land is always lower than the market value and you can find out how much this tax might be by going to your local tax office, where there are records for each property and staff can tell you what the assessed value of the land is.

Property Taxes

Spanish property tax (*Impuesto sobre Bienes Inmeubles Urbana/Rustica* or simply *IBI*) is a local tax, similar to council tax or rates in the UK. It's payable by resident and non-resident owners and is used for local services such as street and beach cleaning, education, cultural and sports amenities and local council administration. *IBI* is payable on commercial as well as residential property but, if you rent your business premises, the landlord should pay it for you – make sure this is specified in your rental contract. **Check when you're buying property or business premises that there aren't any outstanding taxes to pay.** If there are any unpaid taxes, you, as the new owner, become liable for them. Note, however, that it's now obligatory for the seller to produce his last *IBI* receipt, proving that his taxes are up to date.

When you buy a property, you must register your ownership with the local town hall within two months of signing the contract and you can be fined if you don't do this. Local authorities have become tough on those who don't register because, until fairly recently, they were losing a tremendous amount of potential revenue from undeclared and untaxed properties.

Your *IBI* is based on what's called the *valor catastral*, which is similar to a rateable value and is usually around 70 per cent of the market value, but this varies considerably with the local authority. The value is calculated according to the size and general assessment of the property (whether it's considered 'luxury', 'normal' or 'simple') and how close it is to services, amenities and roads. Rates are generally higher in coastal and resort areas than inland, as services are usually better. The tax rate is usually 0.5 per cent of your *valor catastral* for urban properties and 0.3 per cent for agricultural properties, but make sure you check this, as rates are set locally and can vary considerably according to the local government's expenses (and debts!).

Pay a visit to your local town hall and find out what you should have to pay and when. Some send out bills, but many don't, and it's your responsibility to make sure this tax is paid by the due date. It's prudent to set up a direct debit to authorise your bank to pay the tax when it's due so that you aren't caught out. If it isn't paid on time, surcharges will be applied: usually between 10 and 20 per cent plus interest and collection costs, depending on how late the payment is. Some town halls have a system of discounts to encourage residents to pay their bills early.

If you live in an area with a large foreign population, your town hall may have a Foreigners' Department which can advise you, in your own language, about the best method of payment. Payment dates vary with the local council, but you usually have two months in which to pay a bill. If you haven't set up a direct debit, you must usually take a cash payment to the tax collection office, although you can sometimes pay by bank draft or credit card. Check the acceptable payment methods before you go.

Rubbish Collection & Mains Drainage Tax

'Rubbish and drains' (*basura y alcantarillado*) is an annual tax payable by both resident and non-resident property and business owners. It's usually separate from *IBI* and it varies according to the size of the property or business, the location and the amount of rubbish that you produce. Expect to pay between around €150 and €200 per year.

Value Added Tax

If you're self-employed or own a business, you must register for value added tax (*Impuesto sobre el Valor Añadido/IVA*), irrespective of your turnover. Value added tax (VAT) applies in all of mainland Spain and the Balearic Islands, but not in Ceuta and Melilla, nor in the Canary Islands, where a lower sales tax applies (see page 44). The standard rate of VAT is 16 per cent, although there are reduced rates for some items. Certain things are exempt from VAT, such as the rental of private property, exports, insurance and financial services. The transfer of a business is exempt from VAT, provided the buyer is going to continue the existing business. VAT is applicable to goods purchased outside Spain and, if you're supplying goods or services, you must add VAT to all your invoices.

You must register for VAT with the tax authorities at the same time as you apply for your tax identification number (*CIF* – see page 97). This number must appear on all invoices for services or goods that you provide, of which you should keep copies for inspection, along with records of any VAT that you've paid on purchases. You're obliged to keep detailed accounts and file a quarterly VAT return – unless your business has an annual turnover of more than €6 million, in which case you should file a monthly return.

As in other countries, you may be offered goods and services net of VAT, provided you pay in cash. Not only is it illegal to do so but, if you're VAT registered, there's no advantage, as you can reclaim the VAT.

Road Tax

A road tax (*Impuesto de Circulación*) is payable for all Spanish-registered cars. It's payable annually, usually at your town hall, and the cost depends on the make and size of your vehicle; expect to pay around €85 for an average car. When you buy a new car, you will have to make the first tax payment at the time of purchase; take the receipt for the car to the town hall and register it for road tax.

SOCIAL SECURITY

If you work or own a business in Spain, you must, by law, pay into the social security system. Although payments are high, benefits are excellent and the system is comprehensive, covering all healthcare, including sickness and maternity; unemployment insurance; old age pensions (the retirement age in Spain is 65 for both men and women); industrial injury compensation; invalidity and death benefits. Your social security payments differ according to whether you're an employee, an employer or self-employed. The system is outlined below; further details can be found on the Social Security website (⌨ www.seg-social.es), which contains comprehensive information but is only in Spanish. There are details of social security regulations and payments for all circumstances. For those starting a company, there's a section called *Empresarios*; the self-employed section is headed *Autónomos*. The site also provides contact details for all social security offices throughout the country.

Employees

Employees have the best deal in terms of social security, as a large percentage of their contributions are paid by their employer, the remainder being deducted automatically from their salary. Your contributions are based on official minimum and maximum limits set by the government for each type of work, known as the *nómina*. There are specific social security programmes for certain types of worker, such as seamen, civil servants, agricultural workers, military personnel and coal-miners. Most other workers come under the general social security programme, which requires contributions of 28.3 per cent of gross pay: 4.7 per cent deducted from employees' pay and the remaining 23.6 per cent paid by employers. Your employer will register you for social security before you start work.

Employers

If you have your own business and will be employing others, you must register your company with the social security authorities **before** you start trading (see **Registering with Social Security** on page 138). Once this is done, you will be issued with a social security identification number and the tax office will explain what's required of you as an employer. Employers' social security contributions on behalf of their staff are high (see above) and, of course, they must also make their own contributions.

Self-employed

The self-employed come under a different social security scheme from employees, known as the *régimen especial de autónomos* ('special' meaning 'expensive'!). You must pay far more in contributions, as you don't have an employer to pay a large proportion of them for you. In 2004, the monthly minimum contribution was €225.11. **This is the minimum amount you must pay every month, irrespective of your earnings, even if they amount to nil.** The maximum contribution is around €2,575. The more you pay, the larger the pension you receive when you retire; you can also pay an additional amount for temporary incapacity/sickness benefit.

To receive a Spanish pension, you must have contributed to social security for at least 15 years, of which at least two must have been in the 15 years preceding your retirement. The amount of pension you receive is calculated according to your contributions during the last eight years (known as your 'earnings base'), so it's to your advantage to make higher contributions during these eight years. Note that, if you have two different self-employed activities, you must pay social security contributions twice!

You will receive much the same benefits as a salaried employee, except that you won't receive unemployment benefit if you're out of work. When you register for social security at your local office, you will be supplied with payment slips so that you can pay your contributions directly into the bank. A list of offices can be found on the Social Security website (🖥 www.seg-social.es).

RETIREMENT & PENSIONS

Making a living in a new country is tough going, whether you're trying to get a new business started or generate enough business to pay the endless stream of bills. So probably the last thing on your mind is your retirement and putting aside money for a pension. Of course, you should be thinking about providing for your retirement from day one, especially if you intend to retire with a pension you can live on. You will also need to check whether you can claim a pension from your home country as well as from Spain.

Home Country Pensions

All European Union countries and the US have social security agreements with Spain, which mean that as long as you have made pension contributions in your home country and have reached its official retirement age, you can claim your state pension in Spain. British citizens should contact the Inland Revenue's Pensions Service via its International Pension Centre (☎ 0191-218 7777 – open 8am to 8pm UK time) or its website (🖥www. thepensionservice.gov.uk), which has a dedicated section for non-residents who want to claim their UK pension from another country. US citizens can get information from any US embassy or consulate or via the US Social Security website (🖥 www.socialsecurity.gov).

If you're being paid a pension by your home country, you should be aware that it may be subject to income tax in that country. However, if you're also receiving a Spanish pension (see below) and are taxed in Spain, you should be able to avoid this under a double-taxation agreement; check with the tax office in your home country for information. In the UK, the Inland Revenue's Centre For Non-Residents offers advice during office hours on ☎ 0151-210 2222.

Spanish Pensions

Spain, like many other European countries, has an impending pensions crisis. Life expectancy in Spain is 78 years, higher than the OECD average, and experts believe that the combination of an increasing long-lived population and Spain's very low birth rate means that by around 2020 there won't be enough taxpayers to fund the pensions of those over 65. In the meantime, as long as you've been paying social security contributions for a minimum of 15 years (at least two of which must have been in the last 15), you can claim a Spanish state pension from the retirement age of 65, which is the same for both men and women.

If you've made 15 years of contributions, you're entitled to 50 per cent of your 'earnings base' as a pension. Your earnings base is usually calculated as the average of your income that was subject to pension contributions over the preceding eight years. For each additional year of contributions, your pension increases by between 2 and 3 per cent up to 35 years' contributions, which will entitle you to 100 per cent of your earnings base. The annual minimum pension in 2003 was €6,603.52 for someone over 65 with a dependent spouse and €5,607.56 for someone with no dependents. You will receive 14 pension payments per year, just as you received 14 salary payments.

Until recently, you had to give up work completely before you could claim your pension, but in the last few years a more flexible method has been introduced which allows you to combine your pension with part-time employment, although your pension is reduced pro rata if you continue to work. You can also opt for early retirement and a reduced pension: your pension is reduced by 8 per cent for each year below 65 (if you've made 30 years of contributions).

If you reach retirement age and haven't paid into the social security system, you can claim a non-contributory retirement pension, provided you're over 65 and have been legally resident in Spain for at least ten years since the age of 16 and you don't have a disposable income over

€3,689 per year. In 2003, the non-contributory pension amounted to just over €260 per month.

More information about pensions and general information about living and working in Spain is available in English on the website of the Labour and Social Affairs Department of the Spanish Embassy in the UK (⌨ www.mtas.es/consejerias/reinounido/working).

6.

COMMUNICATIONS

Whichever way you plan to make a living in Spain, communications will be vital, especially if you want to start your own business. This chapter looks at telephone and internet services and the infamous Spanish postal service!

Although Spanish technology isn't highly rated, its communications services have improved considerably in the last decade. Anyone running a business will need access to fixed and mobile telephones, and the majority of businesses will operate more efficiently by using the internet. Note that broadband (*banda ancha*) connection isn't available in all areas of Spain (see page 155). Information technology and internet-related businesses are discussed in **Chapter 11**, where expatriate entrepreneurs explain how the internet has revolutionised their businesses, giving them far more flexibility and new opportunities.

TELEPHONE SERVICES

Telefónica, the former state-owned monopoly, is still the main telephone service provider in Spain, despite increased competition and 'market liberalisation' during the last few years, having over 80 per cent of the market share. Other companies have tried to compete, but without much success, and Telefónica is still the only company that offers a complete service, including the installation of telephone lines, the others providing only call services.

Nevertheless, some other companies may offer call charge packages that suit your business needs and it's worth investigating the alternatives. There's a variety of tariffs, so make sure you check each one carefully.

Private Telecommunications Providers

The main providers for private telephone communications in Spain are:

- Âlo (US Communications) – Offers specialist business communications services (telephone and internet). The website (🖥 www.alo.es) is available in English and there's an English-language customer service line (☎ 800 900 400).

- Auna (owned largely by Endesa and Telecom Italia) – Also offers business communications packages both for telephone and internet. The website (🖥 www.auna.es) isn't available in English. Auna has a business customer service line (☎ 902500 090).

● **Jazztel (Nortel)** – Provides telephone and internet services via its own high capacity fibre optic network. The website (🖳 www.jazztel.es) is available in English.

● **SpanTel (Spantel Comms Inc)** – Also offers customised business packages. The website (🖳 www.spantel.es) is available in English.

● **Tele2 (Netcom)** – Offers specialised business services. The website (🖳 www.tele2.es) is only in Spanish.

● **Uni2** – Offers specialised business services. The website (🖳 www. uni2.es) is only in Spanish.

There are also regional providers, such as Madritel in Madrid (🖳 www. madritel.es) and Euskaltel in the Basque Country (🖳 www.euskaltel.es).

Installation & Line Rental

Telefónica is the only provider allowed to install and operate your telephone line. **Before you commit yourself to a property, whether residential or commercial, check that you can be easily connected to the telephone system and, if necessary, the internet, within a reasonable period of time.** Don't take anything for granted, especially if you're planning on working from home or running a business in a remote area of Spain. Even properties slightly inland from the coast may be difficult to connect to telephone and, particularly, broadband lines. Many people find themselves trying to run a new business with a couple of mobile telephones which always seem to lose their signal at the wrong time!

To have a telephone installed or reconnected, you can visit your local Telefónica office (Oficina de Atención al Usuario or Oficina Comercial), telephone them (☎ 1004, where you can ask for an English-speaking operator) or can fill out an application form online (🖳 www.telefonica.es). If you choose to go to an office, you should take along your passport or residence permit (*residencia*), proof of your address such as a recent electricity bill, and a copy of your property deed (*escritura*) or rental contract. If you're renting and don't have a residence permit, you must pay a deposit of €200. In response to demand, Telefónica have also recently launched a 'Telefónica in English' service for foreigners (☎ 952 449 020, 🖳 www.telefonica in english.com).

In January 2005, installation of a standard telephone handset cost €110.59, a second line costing €58.30. Monthly rental per line is €16.52. If you're taking over a property from the previous occupants, you should arrange for the telephone account to be transferred to your name from the day you take possession. **Before buying or renting a property, check that all previous bills have been paid; otherwise you may find yourself liable for them.**

Bills

Bills are sent at varying intervals depending on the company, although the usual period is monthly, and you have 20 days to pay. VAT at 16 per cent is levied on all charges, and itemised bills (*factura detallada*) are provided. Bills can be paid in cash at most banks, via a bank account or in cash at a Telefónica office. You can have your telephone bill paid by direct debit from a bank account, which is always advisable, as it ensures that you aren't disconnected for non-payment. If your bill isn't paid within 20 days, your line may be cut without further warning, although a new system has been introduced whereby lines with unpaid bills are reduced for ten days to incoming calls only before the service is stopped altogether. If your line is cut, there's a reconnection fee, which depends on the amount owing and the elapsed period, after which it should be reconnected within two working days. All companies offer the possibility of checking your bills and telephone usage online.

Call Charges

To save money you should shop around and choose the company with the lowest rates for the type of calls you intend to make; it's even possible to use different providers for different types of call, although this can make life complicated. Note that rates for calls may not be consistently low in the same company and that some companies have aggressive marketing campaigns with cheap offers which often expire soon after a client has signed up. It's worth noting that Telefónica hardly ever offers the cheapest rate! For information on services and tariffs, visit the websites of Telefónica and the main private call providers (see page 146).

Domestic Calls

Domestic tariffs are divided into local (or metropolitan) calls (*metropolitana*), calls within your province (*provincial*) and calls outside your province (*nacional/interprovincial*).

Local Calls: Telefónica has now lost its monopoly on local calls, and there are a number of providers offering services. Competition is intense and call charges are expected to continue to fall. Tariffs are very difficult to compare because of special offers and conditions. Most providers charge an initial connection fee of €0.07 and typical rates are €0.01 (Tele2) or €0.02 (Auna and Telefónica) per minute during 'normal' times and €0.005 (Tele2) or €0.01 (Auna and Telefónica) per minute at other times. Some charge a fixed monthly fee and then offer reductions on call charges. Normal hours (*hora normal*) are from 8am to 6pm, Monday to Friday, and reduced (*reducida*) hours at all other times.

Provincial & Interprovincial Calls: Most companies offer these services and prices vary considerably, as do the normal and reduced rate periods. Auna, Tele2 and Telefónica charge a €0.08 'connection fee' for each call; most other providers don't charge. Some companies, such as Auna and Telefónica, have two rate bands on weekdays, e.g. 8am to 8pm on weekdays (normal) and other times (reduced). Others, such as Tele2, have a flat rate at all times. Matters are further complicated by special deals offered by practically all companies. Examples of provincial call charges are €0.02 per minute flat rate (Tele2) and €0.04 per minute normal tariff (Auna and Telefónica). Examples of interprovincial call charges are €0.03 a minute flat rate (Tele2) and €0.07 per minute normal tariff (Telefónica).

International Calls

It's possible to make direct International Direct Dialling (IDD) calls from Spain to most countries. A full list of IDD country codes is shown in the information pages (*páginas informativas*) of your local white pages, along with codes for main cities and tariffs. To make an international call you must first dial 00 to obtain an international line. Then dial the country code (e.g. 44 for Britain), the area code without the first zero (e.g. 20 for London) and the subscriber's number. For example, to call the central London number 020-7123 4567 from Spain you would dial 00 44 20 7123 4567. To make a call to a country without IDD you must dial 9198 for European countries plus Algeria, Lebanon, Syria and Tunisia, or 9191 for all other countries.

There's normally a high surcharge for operator-connected international calls, but Spain subscribes to a Home Direct service (*servicio directo país*) that enables you to call a number giving you direct and free access to an operator in the country you're calling, e.g. for the

UK dial ☎ 0800-890034 (BT) or 0800-559 3145 (C&W). The operator will connect you to the number required and will also accept credit card payment for a call and reverse charge (collect) calls. Countries with a Home Direct service include Argentina, Australia, Austria, Belgium, Bolivia, Brazil, Canada, Chile, China, Cyprus, Czech Republic, Denmark, Finland, France, Germany, Greece, Guatemala, Hong Kong, Hungary, Iceland, India, Indonesia, Ireland, Israel, Italy, Japan, South Korea, Malaysia, Malta, Mexico, Morocco, Norway, the Netherlands, New Zealand, Portugal, Russia, South Africa, Sweden, Switzerland, the United Kingdom, Uruguay and the US. Information about Home Direct services is provided in the 'international communications' (*comunicaciones internacionales*) section of telephone directories, on the Telefónica website (🖥 www.telefonica.es) under *España Directo* or by calling 11825.

To obtain an operator from one of the four major US telephone companies, call ☎ 1-800-247 7246 (AT&T), ☎ 0-800-937 7262 (MCI), ☎ 1-800-676 4003 (Sprint) or ☎ 1-800-746 5020 (Worldcom). You can either use a domestic US telephone card or make collect (reverse charge) calls.

Competition for international call customers is fierce, and rates are constantly falling. Auna, Tele2 and Telefónica levy a €0.12 fee for 'connecting' each call, a service provided free by most others. Most companies have peak and reduced rates (e.g. Auna, TeleConnect and Telefónica have a peak rate from Mondays to Fridays between 8am and 8pm with reduced rate at all other times), while others, such as Tele2, have a flat rate at all times to anywhere in the world. Examples of low call charges are €0.08 per minute flat rate (Tele2), €0.06 per minute reduced rate for calls to Western Europe (TeleConnect), €0.10 per minute peak rate (TeleConnect) and €0.24 per minute reduced rate to the US (Uni2). Calls to Gibraltar are charged at the domestic rate for interprovincial calls (see above).

Many foreign (i.e. non-Spanish) companies offer low international call charges, e.g. Direct Telecom, which works in partnership with British Telecom. You can sign up for the service via its website (🖥 www.direct-telecom.es), which is in English, or by telephone (☎ 922 787 111). Examples of Direct Telecom's charges are €0.05 cents per minute to a UK landline or €0.26 cents per minute to a UK mobile. National calls range from €0.029 to €0.035 cents per minute and calls to Spanish mobiles are €0.23 cents per minute. These rates apply at any time of day, throughout the year.

Note that if you're using a service other than Telefónica, you may need to dial the company's prefix, e.g. 1050 for Auna and 1073 for Tele2, before making a call, although most companies offer a pre-set dialling service whereby the company's prefix is automatically set on your telephone line and precedes all numbers you dial.

Callback Companies: An increasing number of expatriates (and Spaniards) make use of a callback service, such as those provided by Telegroup Global Access (☎ 966 922 285, 💻 www.affinitytele.com) in Spain. Subscribers 'call' a local freephone number or possibly simply dial a code before numbers. In some cases you call a number abroad (e.g. in Britain or the US) and are called back and given a new line on which to make calls.

Using the Telephone

The tones used in Spain are similar to those in other European countries, e.g. the dialling tone (*señal para marcar*) is a low continuous burr (similar to those in the UK and the US), a ringing tone is a repeated long tone, and the engaged (busy) signal is a series of rapid pips. If you get a recorded message after dialling, it may be telling you that all lines are engaged and to try again later. The message may also be telling you that the number you've dialled doesn't exist (*el número marcado no existe*). To make a reverse charge call (*cobro revertido*), dial 1009 for numbers within Spain, 1008 for the EU, Algeria, Libya, Morocco, Tunisia and Turkey, and 1005 for all other countries.

The usual Spanish response when answering the telephone is *diga* or *dígame*, meaning literally 'speak (to me)'. The caller may preface what he has to say with *oiga* (listen). 'I'm trying to connect you' is *le pongo/paso* and 'go ahead' may be simply *adelante*. Other useful vocabulary includes 'to answer the telephone' (*coger*), 'to hang up' (*colgar*), 'to dial' (*marcar*), 'connect me' (*póngame con*) and 'wrong number' (*número equivocado*).

Telephone numbers are usually dictated two digits at a time. If someone asks you to spell (*deletrear*) something on the telephone, such as your name, you should use the telephone alphabet, given below (with the pronunciation of each letter in brackets). Obviously to use it you need to be able to pronounce the alphabet in Spanish and the words listed below. For example if your name's Smith you say, '*Essay para Sábado, emay para Madrid, ee para Inés, tay para Tarragona y achay para Historia*'.

A (ah)	Antonio	N (enay)	Navarra
B (bay)	Barcelona	Ñ (enyay)	Ñoño
C (thay)	Carmen	O (oh)	Oviedo
CH (chay)	Chocolate	P (pay)	Paris
D (day)	Dolores	Q (ku)	Querido
E (ay)	Enrique	R (eray)	Ramón_
F (efay)	Francia	S (essay)	Sábado
G (zhay)	Gerona	T (tay)	Tarragona
H (achay)	Historia	U (oo)	Ulises
I (ee)	Inés	V (oo-bay)	Valencia
J (hota)	José	W (oo-bay-doblay)	Washington
K (kah)	Kilo	X (ekiss)	Xiquina
L (elay)	Lorenzo	Y (ee greeyay ga)	Yegua
LL (elyay)	Llobregat	Z (thayta)	Zaragoza

Telephone Directories

Telephone directories (*guías telefónicas*) are published by province, each province having its own telephone book and code number. Some provinces have more than one volume, e.g. the Madrid white pages (*páginas blancas*) and yellow pages (*páginas amarillas*) each have two volumes. The directories for the province where you live or have your business are provided free of charge. If you want other directories, they're available from provincial Telefónica offices for around €3 each. New directories aren't published every year (and they aren't all updated at the same time) so information contained in them is often out of date.

The white pages directory contains a number of information pages (*páginas informativas*), including emergency and useful local numbers; Telefónica service numbers; national and international codes; instructions on how to use the telephone (in English, French, German and Italian) and possibly tourist information. The second section in the white pages is the alphabetical list of subscribers. White pages information can also be accessed via the internet (⌨ www.paginas-blancas.es).

The yellow pages directory contains useful local numbers at the front, a list of towns covered by the directory and local information. Yellow pages information is also available by phone (☎ 906 365 024) and via the internet (🖳 www.paginas-amarillas.es). Blue pages (*páginas azules*) are also published in Spain and contain an alphabetical index of streets and subscribers by street number.

Euro Pages is a European business directory containing details of some 150,000 suppliers (☎ 900 131 131, 🖳www.europages.es). In some areas there are English-language directories, e.g. the English Speaker's Telephone Directory (ESTD) for the Costa del Sol and Gibraltar (☎ 956 776 958, 🖳 www.esp.gi/publications).

When you have a telephone installed, your name and number is automatically included in the next edition of your local white pages directory unless you choose to have an unlisted number (*no registrado*), for which there's no charge. Subscribers are listed in the white pages under their town or village (*ciudad*) and not alphabetically for the whole of a province. When looking for a subscriber's number, you must therefore know the town, not just the province, where they live. You will receive little or no help from directory enquiries unless you know the town where a subscriber is located. There are no town codes in Spain, where each province has a code (*prefijo* or *códigos territoriales*). All numbers have nine digits and include the area code, which must be dialled whether you're making a local call or calling Spain from abroad. Area codes are shown on a map in telephone directories.

Directory Enquiries

National and international directory enquiry services are offered by Telefónica and other telephone companies. Dial ☎ 11818 for Telefónica's domestic directory enquiries, and ☎ 11825 for international enquiries. International operators may speak English or other foreign languages, but don't expect national operators to speak anything but Spanish or the local regional language. There's a charge of €0.35 for Telefónica domestic directory enquiries (free from telephone boxes) and €2.70 for international enquiries. Trying to obtain international numbers from directory enquiries is time-consuming and costly, and it's usually easier to call someone abroad and ask them to find the number for you. Telefónica's telephone offices contain a full set of Spanish telephone directories. Note that national directory enquiries now offers a connection service (costing €0.30), whereby you're directly connected to the number you've asked for.

Mobile Telephones

Mobile telephones (*móviles*) were relatively slow to take off in Spain but recently prices have fallen dramatically as a result of the price war that has been raging between the three service providers in the last few years, and sales have rocketed. All the major population areas are covered by both analogue and digital networks, although sparsely populated areas aren't served or reception is difficult. Spain has both analogue (Moviline) and digital (Amena, MoviStar/ Télefonica and Vodafone) networks, although the analogue Moviline network is due to shut down in 2007. The combined networks cover around 90 per cent of the country and 98 per cent of the population. All mobile numbers in Spain start with the number 6.

The three main mobile telephone providers offer both pre-paid ('pay as you talk') and contract arrangements. Competition is fierce and so prices and packages are constantly changing. Below is a current guide to rates, although there are numerous different payment plans to choose from, depending on where and when you make most of your calls. Those offered by the three digital networks can be found on their websites (🖳 www.amena.com, 🖳 www.movistar.com and 🖳 www.vodafone.es). A company called The Phone House has compiled the rates of all the operators and posted them on its website for easy comparison, although the site is only in Spanish (🖳 www. phonehouse.es/commerce/servlet/eses-companyinfo-Networks).

Mobile Telephone Tariffs		
Company	Pre-paid Rate	Contract Rate
Amena	21 cents per minute	18 cents per minute (€18 monthly minimum)
MoviStar	30 cents per minute	15 – 30 cents per minute (€30 monthly minimum)
Vodafone	19 cents per minute (only to fixed line and Vodafone mobile phones)	19 cents per minute (€20 monthly minimum)

If you have a pre-paid phone, you can top it up (*recargar*) in many shops and supermarkets or via ATM cash machines at many banks (simply key in the telephone number and the amount and it's debited directly from your account).

If you arrive from the UK or another European country, you can usually bring your mobile telephone and use it in Spain, as Spain operates on the GSM network. However, calls are routed through your home country and are therefore expensive, so it's advisable to buy a Spanish mobile telephone as soon as you can, or have a Spanish SIM card fitted to your existing telephone. This system works well if you're travelling frequently between Spain and your home country, as you can simply change the SIM card before you go.

INTERNET

If you're starting a business in Spain (or anywhere else), you cannot afford not to have internet access. Almost equally important is a broadband connection. The commercial internet only really began to take off in Spain in the mid-'90s, mainly due to the high cost of local calls for the dial-up service and the relatively small number of computer owners. Now it's catching up fast and broadband technology is taking Spain by storm in much the same way as mobile telephones. However, broadband isn't available in all areas of Spain, where many small villages and rural areas are unlikely ever to have access, as it's impossible (or uneconomical) to lay the necessary cables. You should therefore make sure that your chosen area for doing business is (or will soon be) wired for broadband. You can do this via the Telefónica in English website (🖳 www. telefonicainenglish.com – go to the ADSL section, where there's a link to a map of Spain showing which areas are covered.

Note also that Telefónica's installation service is generally not the fastest but you cannot get round it by going to another provider, as they themselves must go through Telefónica. In some areas ADSL installation is taking months and in others a matter of a week or two.

Competition for clients is fierce among the various companies offering internet services, although their initial charges and monthly rates are similar. In October 2004, Telefónica announced that it would cut its broadband internet prices, which would lead to a price war between them and other providers and bring down prices for consumers. Most providers charge for installation and then a monthly fee of around €40, although competition means that better deals are becoming available all the time. British Telecom, under the trading name BT España, offers a specialist business communications service, including a Virtual Business Centre offering online services to business customers 24 hours a day. Its website (🖥 www.bt.es) is available in five languages, including English and Spanish.

In early 2005, Telefónica were offering three levels of ADSL to business users. The line connection charge was €38.10 for all levels, with an additional cost for a 'router' of €72.61, and monthly charges varied from €74.58 to €150.57, depending on the speed of connection. Other providers of ADSL services include

Ya.com (🖥 www.acceso.ya.com) and Wanadoo.es (🖥 www.wanadoo.es), both of which offer 512 speed ADSL for around €35 per month, and Gonuts4free, which operates in both the UK and Spain and offers ADSL connection for €49 per month (speed 512–1000) and a BT or Telefónica connection (speed 512) for €39 per month, as well as English telephone support (☎ 807 517 045).

Satellite Internet Services

If your business doesn't have access to cabled broadband connection, you may want to consider a satellite connection. Speed of transmission is the same as cable-connected ADSL, but installation costs are much higher (around €1,300) with monthly charges starting from around €60, and you need to install a satellite dish. The other disadvantage of satellite internet connection is that European satellite broadband capacity is shared. If you have a lot of material to transfer, this can be a problem. Some companies offer a monthly 'priority traffic' allocation, but above this you will have to share the service with other users and, at peak times, you may experience a reduction in connection speed. Satellite internet providers covering Spain include Avonline (🖥 www.avonlinebroadband.co.uk), Business Comm (🖥 www.bcsatellite.net), Global Telephone and Telecommunication (🖥 www.globaltt.com).

POSTAL SERVICES

The Spanish postal (*correo*) service has a reputation for being one of the slowest and most unreliable in Europe, so it isn't a good idea to start a business that relies on the postal service! If you know that sending important post is going to form a large part of your business, it's advisable to set up an account with an international courier service as soon as you can (see page 157).

It's advisable to send international post by airmail (*por correo aéreo*). Even then, delivery times in Europe vary considerably according to the

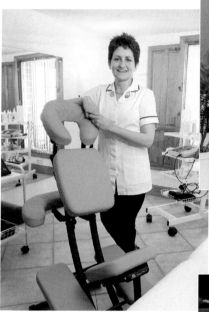

▲ *Foreigners' Department, Mijas Town Hall*
© *Brian Hall ARPS*

▲ *Estelle Mitchell, Physiotherapist*
© *Bodyworks Health Clinic*

▼ *Fruit & Veg Stall* © *Brian Hall ARPS*

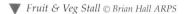

▲ *Willies Sausage Company* © *Graeme Chesters*

▼ *Giles Birch and Jonathan Buzzard,*
Ski Center, Sierra Navada
© *Ski Center*

▲ Gardener © Brian Hall ARPS

▲ English Pub © Graeme Chesters

▲ Market Stall © Brian Hall ARPS

▲ Estate Agent © Graeme Chesters

◄ Flowerseller © Survival Books

Painter © Brian Hall ARPS

Susan Sorrell & Sophie Watts,
The Language House
© Brian Hall ARPS

Telephone Shop © Graeme Chesters

Pavement Artist © Survival Books

Gerry McKenna, Irish Butcher
© Brian Hall ARPS

◄ Café © Survival Books

▲ Food Shop © Graeme Chesters

▲ Water Sports Centre © Graeme Chesters

▼ Ikonia Boutique, fashion show
  © Brian Hall ARPS

▲ James Jewell, yoga teacher
  © Brian Hall ARPS

country of destination and where letters are posted (possibly even the post box used), and letters may arrive sooner when posted at a main post office – but don't count on it! Although letters posted in Spain often arrive at European destinations in two to four days, it's advisable to allow around seven days. Airmail letters between Spain and North America usually take five to ten days, although you should allow up to two weeks. **You can never rely on any European post being delivered in less than ten days, as instances of letters taking many weeks to arrive at a European destination are common.**

Even sending letters by express (*exprés/urgente*) post isn't the answer, as there's no guarantee that they will arrive earlier than those sent by ordinary post. The only way to ensure express delivery within Spain or from Spain to another country is to use a courier (see below) or to communicate by fax or email.

The Spanish post office has a website (💻 www.correos.es – in Spanish only) which details all its services (some of which are available online) and its prices (*tarifas*), as well as a special service for businesses (*Empresariales*) which includes direct marketing, bulk postal services and a guide about how your company can make the best of the Spanish post office.

The charges for letters (up to 20g) are €0.28 within Spain, €0.53 to Europe and €0.78 to the rest of the world. Parcel post to Europe costs €17.50 (up 20kg). The charge for North America is €12.00. There's also a priority parcel service (*EMS postal exprés*), which is slightly more expensive.

Courier Services

You may want to consider an international or national courier service (*mensajería* or *transportes*) as an alternative to the postal service. There's a good selection available in Spain and all companies offer similar services, from local same-day delivery to national and international delivery. All the main companies also offer online tracking of your parcel. There are no standard prices, but all companies have a customer service line offering price information or you can enter the specifications of your parcel online for an instant quote. The three main international courier companies are as follows:

- **TNT** – Offers a range of services from Special Express service, which is the fastest method possible, to Economy Express for less urgent parcels. Visit TNT's website (💻 www.tnt.com) for more details.

- **United Parcel Service (UPS)** – Offers services similar to those of TNT, including overnight delivery to 70 per cent of all business addresses in the European Union, with a choice of delivery by 10.30am or by noon. You can organise collection, delivery and the tracking of your parcel via the website (🖥 www.ups.com), which has a page in English dedicated to Spain.

- **DHL** – Offers same day delivery to eight main Spanish cities, provided the package can be collected before 11am. DHL's customer service department number is ☎ 902 122 424 and its website for Spain (🖥 www.dhl.es) is available in English.

Shipping Services

DHL offers one of the most comprehensive rail, air and road shipping services, both to and from Spain. Its Euroconnect road freight service covers business areas in Europe for shipments over 31.5kg and offers a choice of full- and part-load shipment services to all European countries. There's a downloadable customs information sheet and a Trade Automation Service, which offers comprehensive trade and customs information. The British International Freight Association (BIFA, 🖥 www.bifa.org) can help with information about members in the UK which ship between Spain and the UK.

FLIGHTS

Most major international airlines provide scheduled services to Madrid and many also fly to Barcelona and other major cities. The Spanish state-owned national airline, Iberia, is Spain's major international carrier. There's a wide range of flights from airports in the UK to many airports in Spain, although some regions are less well served than others. The Costa Blanca, Costa del Sol and the Canaries are the best served, with year-round flights offered by several airlines. Flights to the Balearics (especially Minorca) are greatly reduced in winter and you may need to travel via the mainland, which will increase the cost.

Note also that the instability of the airline business means that airlines can (and do) merge or go bankrupt, which often results in a cut-back of services or the disappearance of a route. Budget airlines also frequently change their routes and prices.

Scheduled Flights

Iberia provides good connections to Central and South America and throughout Europe, but few connections to North America (New York and Miami only). However, Iberia is a member of the One World alliance along with British Airways, American Airlines, Cathay Pacific and Qantas, among others. This allows them to offer flights to most destinations in the world via other airlines in the alliance at competitive rates. Most transatlantic flights from North America are routed via Madrid. If you're unable to get a direct flight to Spain from North America, it's usually best to fly via London, from where there are inexpensive daily flights to airports throughout Spain. British Airways and its subsidiary GB Airways, for example, operate daily flights to the main Spanish airports from several destinations in the UK. Fares on scheduled flights to Spain have fallen in recent years due to increased competition, although they're still high compared with charter fares. Increased competition from airlines such as Air Europa (Spanish owned) on many routes has forced Iberia to reduce its fares, particularly on domestic routes.

Budget Airlines

The introduction of 'no-frills' flights has been revolutionary and has provided some welcome competition, forcing British Airways and Iberia to reduce their prices. There are several advantages to using budget airlines, including speed and ease of internet and/or telephone booking, ticket-less flights and no seat allocation. Fares are generally lower, although they've risen in recent months and in many cases are no cheaper than scheduled flights (particularly if you're able to take advantage of special offers from British Airways and Iberia, where the price includes a newspaper, drinks and meal). Budget airline advertised prices usually don't include airport taxes, which can be high (e.g. €17.50 from Luton) and you will probably be charged for using a credit card, e.g. €5 to €7. Food and drinks on budget airlines are also expensive.

Budget airlines often advertise very cheap fares, although these are usually limited to a few seats and involve travelling at unsociable times or at short notice, which may not suit your business schedule. Remember that if you're flying backwards and forwards to an area of Spain that's popular with tourists, flights in high season or on popular routes are generally as expensive as those offered by scheduled airlines, and may be booked up weeks in advance.

Airports & Flight Information

This section contains a survey of Spain's major international flights, plus a few in neighbouring countries convenient for Spain, and lists the UK airports serving them. Comprehensive information for all Spanish airports can be found via the internet (💻 www.aena.es – click on 'English' and then use the 'Choose Airport' menu).

Madrid

Madrid's Barajas airport is Spain's busiest, handling some 34 million passengers per year, and the main Spanish airport for intercontinental flights as well being the hub of domestic flights. The airport (15km/9.3mi to the east of the city) has been extensively modernised and a new terminal is currently under construction that will double the passenger capacity. The city centre is easily accessible by public transport, including the metro. Madrid airport is served by regular flights from Birmingham, Dublin, Edinburgh, Glasgow, Liverpool, London-Gatwick, London-Heathrow, London-Luton and Manchester airports. Airport information is available on ☎ 902 353 570.

Barcelona

The region's main airport is Barcelona's El Prat de Llobregat, located 14km (9mi) from the city centre. It was extensively modernised for the 1992 Olympic Games and is one of the best in Spain. The airport is very busy and offers a wide range of chartered and scheduled flights to both domestic and international destinations. Note that weekend flights to Barcelona from the UK are in high demand and can be expensive. Public transport from the airport to the city is quick and efficient, although getting to the Costa Brava and Costa Dorada from El Prat can be slow due to traffic congestion. Barcelona airport is served by regular flights from the UK and Ireland from Birmingham, Bristol, Dublin, Edinburgh, Glasgow, Leeds/Bradford, Liverpool, London-Gatwick, London-Heathrow, London-Luton, London-Stansted, Manchester and Nottingham-East Midlands. Airport information is available on ☎ 932 983 838.

Valencia & Costa Blanca

The Costa Blanca is served by three airports: El Altet (Alicante), Manisses (Valencia) and San Javier (Murcia).

Alicante: The main airport and international gateway to the Costa Blanca is El Altet (11km/7mi from Alicante city centre), which is one of Spain's busiest airports. It provides a wide range of flights (mostly charter) to over 20 countries, although most are from the UK and Germany, plus a range of domestic flights. Communications to both the north and south of the Costa Blanca are good, and taxis and hire cars are plentiful. Alicante airport is served by regular flights from Belfast, Birmingham, Bristol, Cardiff, Dublin, Edinburgh, Exeter, Glasgow, Leeds/Bradford, Liverpool, London-Gatwick, London-Heathrow, London-Luton, London-Stansted, Manchester, Newcastle, Nottingham-East Midlands and Teeside. Airport information is available on ☎ 966 919 400.

Valencia: Manisses airport, some 8km (5mi) from Valencia city centre, handles many regular domestic flights plus scheduled flights to some European cities. Manisses airport is is also a good alternative to El Altet (Alicante) for the northern part of the Costa Blanca, although traffic congestion around Valencia tends to increase journey times. Valencia airport is served by regular flights from Dublin (Aer Lingus), London-Gatwick (GB Airways), London-Heathrow and Manchester (both Iberia). Airport information is available on ☎ 961 598 500.

Murcia: Murcia's San Javier airport serves the southern part of the Costa Blanca and the Costa Cálida, and is also useful for reaching the northern region of Almería. San Javier is a small airport, although air traffic has increased considerably in recent years, and offers a growing number of charter and budget flights to airports in the UK and Germany, as well as Dublin. Murcia airport is served by regular flights from from Birmingham, Leeds/Bradford, London-Gatwick, London-Luton, London-Stansted, Manchester and Nottingham-East Midlands. Airport information is available on ☎ 968 172 000.

Malaga & Costa del Sol

Malaga: The region's main airport is Malaga's Pablo Picasso (8km/5mi to the west of Malaga city), the third-busiest in Spain handling some 10 million passengers a year. It's well served by domestic and international flights, particularly from the UK, Germany and Ireland, with between 50 and 100 flights daily. Scheduled flights operate from most major European destinations throughout the year and charter flights are also widely available, although flights from some destinations (such as Exeter and Southampton in the UK) are suspended during the winter months. The airport was modernised in the '90s and is spacious and generally efficient. A new control tower was completed in 2001 and a second terminal is under construction with a second runway planned. Bus and train services link the airport with Malaga and the rest of the Costa del Sol, and taxis and car hire companies are plentiful.

Malaga airport is served by regular flights from Birmingham, Bristol, Cardiff, Dublin, Edinburgh, Glasgow, Leeds/Bradford, London-Gatwick, London-Heathrow, London-Luton, London-Stansted, Liverpool, Manchester and Nottingham-East Midlands. Flight information is available on ☎ 952 048 804.

Gibraltar: Gibraltar airport also serves the Costa del Sol, although there are few flights and they're almost exclusively to and from the UK. Queues to leave Gibraltar are often long and customs checks lengthy. There's no public transport to Gibraltar from the Costa del Sol except taxis. **You may require a visa to enter Spain from Gibraltar.** Gibraltar airport is served by regular flights from the UK from London-Gatwick (GB Airways), London-Luton (Monarch) and Manchester (Monarch). Flight information is available on ☎ +350 73026 from abroad or ☎ 956 773 026 from Spain.

Balearics

The three main islands have airports, which are among the busiest in Europe during the summer months.

Majorca: San Juan airport in Majorca (situated 11km/7mi east of Palma) is Spain's second-busiest, handling around 20 million passengers a year. Flights (mostly charter) are available from most major European cities, particularly in the UK and Germany. Flights from mainland Spain are also frequent, the least expensive being from Barcelona and Valencia.

Palma airport is served by regular flights from Belfast, Birmingham, Bristol, Cardiff, Dublin, Edinburgh, Glasgow, Leeds/Bradford, Liverpool, London-Gatwick, London-Heathrow, London-Luton, London-Stansted, Manchester, Newcastle, Nottingham-East Midlands and Teeside airports. Airport information is available on ☎ 971 789 681.

Minorca: Minorca has a small international airport situated just south of the capital, Mahon. There are charter flights from several European capitals, although they're concentrated during the high season, and in winter there are no direct flights from some destinations. Domestic flights to mainland Spain are also available, although fares are high. Mahon airport is served by regular flights from Glasgow (Excel Airways), London-Gatwick (Excel Airways and GB Airways) and London-Luton (Excel Airways and Monarch). Airport information is available on ☎ 971 157 000.

Ibiza: Ibiza airport handles mainly charter flights from the UK and Germany, which are greatly reduced in the winter. Flights to mainland Spain are mostly via Barcelona and Valencia, and are expensive. Ibiza airport is served by regular flights from London-Gatwick (Excel Airways, EasyJet and GB Airways), London-Stansted (EasyJet), Manchester (Excel Airways and Bmi Baby) and Nottingham-East Midlands (BMi Baby). Airport information is available on ☎ 971 809 000.

Canary Islands

All the inhabited islands have airports, but the smaller islands of El Hierro, La Gomera and La Palma are served by tiny airports with virtually no international flights and only a limited number of flights from Gran Canaria or Tenerife. Several budget airlines now fly to the Canaries and numerous charter flights are available.

Tenerife: Tenerife has two airports, Reina Sofía in the south near the Costa del Silencio and Los Rodeos in the north near the capital – recently refurbished and with a new terminal. Los Rodeos handles mainly domestic and inter-island flights, while Reina Sofía handles most international traffic with an abundance of charter flights, mostly from the UK and Germany. A second runway is planned. Public transport to the capital and resort areas is generally good, and taxis and hire cars are plentiful.

Reina Sofía airport is served by regular flights from Birmingham (MyTravelLite), Glasgow (Excel Airways and FlyGlobeSpan), London-Gatwick (Excel Airways and GB Airways), London-Luton (Monarch), London-Stansted (Excel Airways), Manchester (Excel Airways, MyTravelLite and Monarch) and Newcastle (Excel Airways). Airport information is available on ☎ 922 759 200 (Reina Sofía) and ☎ 922 635 999 (Los Rodeos).

Gran Canaria: Gando airport on the east coast of the island is one of the busiest in Spain. It's served by frequent charter and scheduled flights from mainland Spain and Europe, particularly the UK and Germany. Flights are inexpensive and available all year round. There are also flights to the other Canary Islands. The airport is well connected with both the north and south of the island, and public transport to the capital and southern resorts is good. Taxis and hire cars are plentiful.

Gando airport is served by regular flights from Birmingham (MyTravelLite), London-Gatwick (Excel Airways and GB Airways) and Manchester (Excel Airways). Airport information is available on ☎ 928 579 130.

Fuerteventura: Fuerteventura has an international airport to the south of the capital. There are frequent flights from Barcelona, Madrid and many European cities during the summer, although flights are considerably reduced during the rest of the year. The airport is served by flights run by Excel Airways from Glasgow, London-Gatwick and Manchester. Airport information is available on ☎ 928 860 500.

Lanzarote: Lanzarote's Guacimeta airport is situated just outside the capital, Arrecife, and has frequent services to the other islands, mainland Spain and Europe, particularly the UK and Germany. Public transport links the airport with the capital and the main resorts. Lanzarote has flights from Birmingham (MyTravelLite), Glasgow, London-Stansted, Manchester and Newcastle (all Excel Airways). Airport information is available on ☎ 928 846 001.

7.

BARS, RESTAURANTS & HOTELS

You certainly won't be alone if you've ever sat and dreamt about running a bar, a restaurant or a small hotel in Spain. That kind of business seems to hold an almost dreamlike fascination, especially for those who have spent time in the country on holiday. What better way to make a living than sitting in the sun, chatting to customers over a beer?

If you think this is the kind of business you would like to run in Spain, you must forget those dreams and swallow a large dose of reality. The hospitality trade, especially bars in tourist areas, is one of riskiest in Spain. In coastal areas, bars and restaurants open and close with depressing regularity. This is good news for the owners of the premises and the agents involved, who receive a percentage of the sale every time a bar changes hands, but it's often a personal and financial disaster for expatriates who have sunk their life savings into a dream.

The chances are that your dreams are based on holiday experiences during the summer months, when the bars and restaurants are bursting at the seams with customers, and the owners have smiles on their faces. Try sitting in those same bars during the winter months, when strong winds and rain have left the beaches and promenades empty and bar owners are desperate to lure what few holidaymakers there are away from the competition.

Of course, many foreigners make a success of running a bar or a small hotel in Spain, but they don't do so on a whim and a prayer. This chapter looks at why those people have been successful and explores some of the pitfalls that lie in wait for the unwary and the ill prepared.

EXPERIENCE

Peter and Pam Carey made a success of their Costa del Sol bar partly because of their experience in the industry in the UK. This gave them a more realistic view of potential problem areas, which many would-be bar owners overlook because they get in the way of their dream. Peter and Pam were publicans before they came to Spain and it was their son, Richard, who suggested that they open a bar in Fuengirola. They had owned a second home in Spain for some time and were familiar with both the area and their likely customer base. However, Peter and Pam were still cautious: "From experience, we knew that running a bar is incredibly hard work." said Peter. "It was only when Richard suggested that he and his partner, Willow, share the workload with us that we thought it could work. There are no licensing hours in Spain and bars tend to close when the last person has gone home. Pam and I knew we couldn't handle that on our own, but Richard suggested that we did the day shift and he and Willow would run it at night and into the early hours. That way we could stay open for longer and appeal to a wider range of customers.

"It was the perfect arrangement: during the day we had plenty of custom from the older expatriate community, who came to the English theatre nearby, and Richard and Willow took over in the evening when the bar was popular with a younger, more Spanish, crowd. Both Richard and Willow speak fluent Spanish so that wasn't a problem and we had, literally, the best of both worlds."

They opened their bar in October 1993. It's officially called The Brewers Bar but has become known locally as the Jugglers Bar (no apostrophes), because Richard, an excellent juggler, began to sell juggling equipment, which locals try their hands at in the courtyard outside. Their local knowledge meant that they understood how important it was to get established with the locals out of season. By April of the following year, when the tourists started to arrive, the place was buzzing, which attracted the visitors too.

FAMILY

Peter and Pam's bar was an immense success and Peter feels that much of this was due to the fact that all the family members involved were happy with the arrangement: "Don't underestimate how that kind of thing can make or break any business, especially one in the hospitality industry," he says. Running a bar, restaurant or hotel can put enormous strain on family relationships. If you've never worked with your partner for 16 to 18 hours per day, it's likely to come as something of a shock. Combine this with exhaustion and possible financial worries and you have all the ingredients for disaster in a relationship. Try to avoid this by being prepared for the worst. Think about what you will do if one of you gets ill, homesick or just needs a few days' break.

If you have children to care for, especially young children, think seriously about whether it's the right thing for your family. Most people who have tried it would agree that it's almost impossible to look after a family and work the kind of hours that are needed to run a bar or restaurant. If you're thinking along these lines, make sure your financial planning allows for the cost of employing an extra member of staff to help out.

RESEARCH

Steve Timewell, owner of Fiesta Property Services, a commercial agency selling businesses on the Costa del Sol, says that during their busy periods they can receive up to 100 enquires per week from those who think they want to buy a bar in Spain. "The first thing we do," says Steve, "is get them to fill out a lengthy buyer's questionnaire. This gives us not only information about the kind of bar they're looking for, but also an insight into the kind of people they are. This can mean the difference between success and failure. We can tell immediately from the questionnaire whether or not they've done their research properly and we try to be as realistic as possible with prospective buyers. They have to realise that it's incredibly hard work running a bar. The long hours, the financial commitment and, in some cases, working with your partner full-time, can all take their toll if you aren't used to them. Many of the people who contact us have never even worked in a bar before and have little or no idea what they would be getting into." **If you have no experience of working in a bar or restaurant and wouldn't consider buying such a business in your home country, don't do it in Spain!**

If you're serious about this kind of business and think you're strong enough to overcome the potential hurdles, make sure your market research is as thorough as possible. If you don't have any experience in the hospitality trade, get yourself a temporary job working in a bar or restaurant in the area of Spain that you're interested in. There's nothing like a few long hard shifts behind the bar or waiting at tables to help you decide whether it's for you. Remember that when you're a bar owner, you must be the first person there in the morning and the last to leave, probably in the early hours of the following morning. If your work experience doesn't put you off, you will have gained some valuable experience in the industry, made some useful contacts and begun to see what's involved first hand. Get to know the busy spots in your preferred area and make sure you're realistic about the kind of competition you will be facing.

The Costas and the Spanish Islands are popular locations for would-be bar owners but the big cities, especially Madrid and Barcelona, are also seeing increasing numbers of expatriate owners, and trade there is less seasonal and doesn't depend so much on the weather. Many foreigners opt for popular tourist spots on the Costas, believing that the combination of tourism and a large expatriate community is a guarantee of success. Sadly, it isn't, simply because the competition is intense. In that sense, these are probably the most difficult areas in which to open a bar. In most of the popular coastal areas, the port and seafront areas are jam-packed full of 'English' pubs, cafes and restaurants and there just isn't enough trade to go round. You may have three or four months in the summer when trade is relatively brisk, but that leaves another eight or nine when custom is thin on the ground but the bills and the rent still have to be paid.

Steve and Pat Mallen, who own Bar sin Problemas – known locally as Sin's – on the Costa Blanca, bought their bar 15 years ago as a going concern from a couple who had run it for only a year. Steve and Pat had both had bar experience in London and locally in Spain before they took it over and thought they knew what they were letting themselves in for. Pat says that, despite their experience, they didn't do enough research about the level of out-of-season custom: "The area is really quiet for eight months of the year and there are a lot of retired people living here who don't go to bars on a regular basis. Competition is tough and in the last couple of years at least half a dozen English bars have opened in the local town. Luckily, we've got a well established customer base, in terms of both regular holiday-makers and local people, so we've weathered the storm, but some of the newer bar owners haven't."

FINANCES

Overstretching your finances is one of the biggest problems for expatriates who come to Spain intending to buy a bar or restaurant. Many have burnt their bridges and sold their homes to raise the money to start a new life. Steve Timewell of Fiesta Property Services warns: "If you've raised, say, £100,000 from the sale of your house, don't look at bars or restaurants at that price. Work out how much you will need to live on for a while and think hard about extra costs, then deduct that amount and a bit more and that will give you a more realistic figure." Don't forget that, once you've bought your bar, there will be stock to buy (although sometimes this is included in the price), lawyer's fees, licences to pay for, staff wages if you decide to employ others and your own tax and social security payments – without forgetting rent and utility bills.

Most important of all, allow sufficient funds to live on for around a year. If you have children, research the available schools carefully, as English or international schools in Spain are generally fee-paying, which is an expense you may not have had at home.

THE CITIES

If you think you might want to open a bar or restaurant in one of the big cities, such as Madrid or Barcelona, you will obviously have to cater for a very different market from the Costa crowd and ensure that your Spanish is far more proficient. You may get away with basic Spanish on the Costas, but you won't in Madrid or Barcelona. Indeed in Barcelona, you would be well advised to speak Catalan as well (see page 31). Matthew Loughney, owner of Kitty O'Shea's Irish bar in Madrid, says that, although theirs is an authentic Irish bar, they never forget that they're in Spain. Their staff can speak both Spanish and English and offer Spanish food alongside traditional Irish and British dishes. In the cities, your customer base is generally a far younger one and Irish bars in particular are highly popular. If you're thinking of jumping on the bandwagon, however, bear in mind that when Matthew first came to Spain just over five years ago, there were only a dozen or so Irish bars in Madrid; now there are more than 70 and competition is intense.

Matthew prides himself on offering a 'comfort zone' to new arrivals in Madrid. Their best customers are the British, who are looking for familiarity, advice about life in Madrid and someone to share a drink with in their own language. In areas of Spain where little English is spoken on a daily basis, an Irish or British bar can be a welcome haven, and Matthew works hard to make sure that Kitty O'Shea's is just that. His advice to would-be bar owners in either Madrid or Barcelona is to try to find premises that aren't too far off the beaten track; no one will ever find you and there are too many other bars along the way. The obvious locations are the popular tourist areas, but it's also important to be within easy reach of the financial and business districts. "Go and see the bar at different times of the day and the year. It isn't the same kind of seasonal problem as on the coast, but of course custom varies from time to time. One of the most important things to be aware of in a city, where everything is far more contained, is potential noise pollution. You only need one neighbour who's disturbed by your music and the comings and goings of your customers and you will be closed down before you've had a chance to get going."

PREMISES

General information on finding commercial premises in Spain is provided on page 91. If you're planning to buy a bar, hotel or restaurant, you should note the following in particular:

- Walk around the areas you like. See which bars and restaurants are the most popular, preferably in winter as well as summer, and find out why. How do they attract customers and keep them? Sit outside a few, watching the customers come and go. What type of people are they, what do they buy and which are the busiest times?

- Bars and restaurants, especially in coastal areas, are usually sold as going concerns, so when you take one over, you buy the lease from the current leaseholder and pay an agreed amount for 'goodwill' (see below). Thereafter you will pay the owner (who may be different from the leaseholder – see **Leasing** on page 91) a monthly rent.

- Bars and restaurants have particular legal obligations, as they're offering food and drink to the public. First, **your menus must be available in Spanish as well as in English or another language; it's illegal not to do this**. Second, everyone working on the premises must have a food handler's certificate (*carnet de manipulador de alimentos*). This isn't difficult to obtain (see page 101) but you must attend a short course and take a simple test. In some areas, courses have translators available and you can do the test in English, but don't rely on it.

- If you want music in your bar or restaurant, full-scale live music or simply background recorded music, you will need a separate licence for that (see page 101). The cost varies according to the kind of music you want and which region of Spain you're in. If the business doesn't already have a music licence, your lawyer should check whether it's likely that one will be granted for your premises.

The 'goodwill' payment obviously varies according to a number of factors, including the position of the bar, the fixtures and fittings and whether or not there's a well established client base. **Make sure you find out whether the business you're buying has a reputation worth paying for.** Once you know the area, you can ask locally, and your professional advisers should be able to help. Have the business's accounts checked by a qualified accountant before you agree on a price and, if possible spend some time working alongside the owner, so that you can see for yourself what trade is like on a daily basis.

Other important things that your lawyer should check include the following:

- That there are no outstanding debts on either the business or the property or any social security obligations that you don't know about;

- That all the necessary licences are in place and transferred to your name once the sale is completed. Reputable agencies only have legal businesses on their books, but always get your lawyer to check. The opening licence (*licencia de apertura* – see page 102) should be clearly displayed by the current owner; if it isn't visible, ask to see it.

Emmerson Wade and his wife Yvonne decided to find their own premises after a frustrating time working with agents who couldn't come up with what they wanted. They'd decided to open a small hotel in Spain, after 29 years of running their own restaurants and bars in the UK. Their guesthouse, called Ciudad Quesada in Rojales on the Costa Blanca, is also their home and, after trading for only two years, 90 per cent of their business is returning customers. They did extensive of research, spending several months on the Costa del Sol before arriving on the Costa Blanca. They found plenty of small and medium-size bars and big hotels, but nothing in between. "That's why we decided on an English-style guesthouse, which offers a personal service and really good quality food, including," says Emmerson, "the best English breakfast served anywhere!"

STAFF

Like many owners of bars, restaurants and small hotels, Emmerson and his wife are the only two employees, working hard together to make a success of their venture. Employing staff in Spain is something you should only do once you've taken advice from a specialist in labour laws (see page 87). If your bar or restaurant is a relatively small operation, it's usually possible to keep costs down by doing all the work yourselves, especially when you first start trading. It's perfectly legal to do so provided that one of you is registered as self-employed and pays tax and social security contributions on all earnings (see **Chapter 4**). That way, your dependants will be covered for treatment under the Spanish health service.

If you need to hire staff, things become a little more complicated. Bar staff are often hired on a casual, one-off, cash payment basis. Although plenty of bars and restaurants do this, it's illegal and, if you're caught, you may have to pay a heavy fine. **In popular tourist areas, inspectors make regular visits to check the contracts of the people who are working on the premises.** Details of contracts and of your responsibilities as an employer can be found in **Chapter 4**. You can legally employ someone for a short period, although it must be properly registered with the labour authorities as a temporary, training contract. Matthew Loughney of Kitty O'Shea's in Madrid always employs his staff initially on a six-month training contract, to see if they're suitable for the job and fit in well. That way, he's employing them legally but isn't obliged to keep them on after six months if they haven't made the grade. If things work out, he offers them an indefinite contract.

CUSTOMERS

Matthew Loughney spoke of the 'comfort zone' his Irish bar offers customers, giving them a sense of security and familiarity in the midst of a foreign country and culture. This is an important element for a successful bar, restaurant or hotel in an area with a large tourist or expatriate population, but Matthew's bar also offers something to the Spanish population, which is a must in a big city. Many expatriates in coastal areas don't even consider what the Spanish may want from a bar or a restaurant and consequently lose out on a substantial amount of trade. The wise ones, like Peter and Pam Carey on the Costa del Sol, don't underestimate the possibilities of that market and manage to cater to both.

Matthew Loughney advertises in publications such as the *Time Out* guide to Madrid and local free magazines and newspapers, but ultimately he believes that word of mouth is the best advertising – and it's free. Emmerson and Yvonne Wade chose the internet for advertising when they first opened: "In the early days, it was a great way to grow the business, and now our guesthouse is listed on five or six websites as well as our own. Mind you, once our guests get here, we really look after them. We make sure we take time to talk to them and give them all kinds of information about the area. We really do care that they're comfortable and have a good holiday. Only two years down the line, 90 per cent of our guests are returning business or have been recommended by others, so we must be doing something right."

Emmerson and his wife, like many successful owners in the hospitality industry, understand the importance of a good atmosphere and derive genuine pleasure from serving their guests. If you're going to work hands-on in the business, as all those who have made a success of it agree, you must be there because you want to be, not just for financial reasons. Pat Mallen from Sin's bar near Alicante sums it up: "It's so much more than all the practical things behind the bar; to run a successful operation in the hospitality industry, you need to be a cross between a therapist, a priest and, in the worst cases, a referee!"

8.

PROPERTY

If you're thinking about working or setting up a business in any property-related field in Spain, the first thing you should do is familiarise yourself with property market trends in Spain, which can directly or indirectly affect your business. **The most important thing to bear in mind is that, particularly in coastal areas, the property market is all but saturated with foreigners trying to make a living**. You will therefore need to be especially enterprising, hard-working and, possibly, lucky to make a success of a property-related business.

This chapter looks at working in an estate agency and whether it's possible to make a success of starting your own estate agency business. Many agents combine sales with lettings and property management, so these areas are also explored. There's information about relocation services (an ever-growing market, especially in Spanish cities and coastal areas), construction and building services and property maintenance, which includes gardening, swimming pools, cleaning and house- and pet-sitting.

RESEARCH

As you begin to research the property market in Spain, you will soon discover that almost every day there's a new report predicting either that the property market is either about to crash or that it's healthier than ever. Don't believe anything you read until you've looked at the source to see whether the authors have an interest in promoting upward or downward trends. Obviously, it's in the interest of most agents to talk the market up, and consequently it's difficult to obtain an unbiased view from them. One of the few independent companies, which produces excellent, objective, property market reports, is Spanish Property Insight (🖳 www.spanishpropertyinsight.com), which works with the high profile Spanish property magazine, *Inmueble*. Its website is operated by Mark Stucklin, a graduate of Spain's leading business school in Barcelona, who has had extensive experience of the property market in Spain. It will give you a clear insight into the market generally, as well as area-specific market information. CB Richard Ellis, agents and property consultants, who have offices all over Spain (🖳 www.cbre.es) also provide good market information, especially for the Spanish cities, as does Knight Frank (🖳 www.knightfrankglobal.com).

Wherever you obtain your information, remember that it's only a guide to the market and no one knows for sure what the future holds. You must also do your own research, and you can only do that once you're in Spain and in regular contact with agents and other professionals in and around your chosen area. You need to be living in the area or at least visiting it regularly for at least six months, preferably longer. Try to find a temporary job in a related area so that you can make plenty of useful contacts in the industry.

ESTATE AGENCY

Even if your goal is to set up your own agency, it's advisable to start by working in an existing, established agency for a couple of years so that you can learn the ropes and get a feel for the market. As a foreigner yourself, you're more likely to get a job and to be able to do business in an agency that deals with foreign buyers, even if you speak fluent Spanish. This means living and working in the kind of areas where foreigners buy in significant numbers, principally the main coastal areas and the islands.

Working in an Agency

Selling property is far more complicated than many people imagine, and you should be under no illusions about how difficult it is to do well. If you work in an agency in one of the coastal areas or the islands, with large numbers of English-speaking agents, you will find that competition for sales is tough and the stakes are high. It will help your chances enormously if you've had experience in estate agency in your home country. At the very least, you should have experience of sales and marketing in a service industry.

Mark Stucklin suggests you choose your employer carefully: "You're likely to be put into sales to start with, especially if you have little or no experience. Your basic salary will be very low, often not enough to live on, so your incentive to sell and make your commission is high. It's pretty standard practice, but it can foster some aggressive sales techniques and unpleasant internal cultures and there's less incentive to spend time looking after the client's long-term needs."

As an employee, you should make sure you're given a proper contract and understand both the contract and its implications, especially in terms of how much and when you will be paid. In any country and any industry, there are good and bad employers, but the estate agency business is so competitive in some areas of Spain that it has more than its share of dubious practitioners. Recently, there have been a few well publicised cases of estate agents not paying commission due to employees until several months after the sale has been completed – sometimes not at all. Other employers take advantage of the fact that their employees cannot speak Spanish and don't know where to go for advice if they're unsure or unhappy about their treatment. Remember that as an employee in Spain, you have the same rights as a Spanish person and a foreign employer has the same responsibilities as a Spanish employer – **as long as you have a valid contract** (see page 75).

If you experience any problems with your employer, seek advice from a lawyer or a *gestor*. There are plenty of English-speaking lawyers and *gestors* in coastal areas who can help you for a moderate fee.

Setting Up an Agency

If you're planning to set up your own estate agency in Spain, especially in the coastal areas, exercise extreme caution. If you've spent some time working in the sector in Spain, you will understand the culture, the market and the competition you will face if you intend to set up on your own. In most areas, the market is virtually saturated, and the intense competition means that you must be determined and even ruthless to have any chance of creating a viable business. Mark Stucklin explains how things have changed since the boom years of the '70s and '80s: "At that time, the market was driven by enormous numbers of foreign clients, and Spanish agents couldn't speak their language and found it difficult to cater to their property needs. There was a huge gap in the market for agents who made the client feel secure, simply by speaking their language. Now the market's rationalising; it isn't enough just to speak English. You must be bilingual, so that you can make the most of Spanish as well as English-speaking contacts, and most importantly know how to market successfully in an extremely crowded marketplace."

Marion Atkins, who has been in business in Spain for 18 years and owns Key Property Services, a chain of five estate agencies on the Costa Blanca, agrees: "If you've worked as an estate agent in your home country, that's a good start, especially if you're a member of a professional body, such as the National Association of Estate Agents (NAEA) in the UK. However, it's a completely different market out here, perhaps not quite as gentlemanly as it is in the UK! You must have some experience of sales and marketing, in any kind of business, that's imperative. That aside, you must do your homework, have plenty of money behind you and take every opportunity to make useful contacts of any nationality in any professional area. If you've come over here and left your support network at home, you will need people you can go to for help if you experience problems. Get a good lawyer, accountant and *gestor*. If you've got good professionals working for you, you can concentrate on your business. Most importantly, work professionally. It sounds obvious, but simple things like opening up on time **every morning** are really important, as well as keeping promises to clients and sticking to a code of conduct. I'm a member of the NAEA, which has a Spanish chapter. Members must keep to a strict code of practice, and it's a qualification that English clients recognise."

Regulation

Until 2000, only highly trained and well qualified professional estate agents, known as *Agente de la Propiedad Inmobiliara (API)*, were permitted to sell property in Spain. However, *API*s had their position in the industry challenged in the '90s by another group of professionals with a qualification known as *Gestor Intermediario de Promociones y Edificaciones (GIPE)*. In June 2000, after years of disagreement and legal battles between the two groups, the law was changed and selling property became a completely deregulated industry in Spain, where there are no regulations or minimum qualifications required to work as an estate agent.

Not surprisingly, the property industry has since become something of a free for all. Although the title of *API* still exists (a few foreign agents are *API*s) and *API*s have a regulatory body, which is the most widely recognised in Spain, the qualification is no longer a requirement nor one that non-Spanish clients recognise or understand. Various organisations are pressing for the establishment of standards – the NAEA (🖳 www.naea.co.uk) is one of the organisations campaigning for regulation, as is the Spanish Association of Real Estate Companies (Asociación Empresarial de Gestion Inmobiliaria (AEGI, 🖳 www.aegi.es) – but currently anybody can set himself up as an estate agent, and thousands of foreign hopefuls, thinking they can cash in on a buoyant market, do just that.

Mark Stucklin says: "The industry lacks the stamp of professionalism because of deregulation. Commission rates for sales are high in Spain, around 5 to 15 per cent, so financially it's a very tempting road to go down, especially when you realise that you only need to achieve one or two big sales per year to make enough to live on. One impressive website and a mobile telephone later and another hopeful 'estate agent' has joined the thousands who are vying for business. Now that the market is stabilising, I expect many agents to go out of business because of the intense competition and the fact that they aren't properly run, professional organisations." You have been warned!

Rental & Letting

Many estate agents also deal in rentals and lettings, so if you're (still) planning on setting up an estate agency, this is a related service that you could include. With more than 50 million tourists visiting Spain each year and more northern Europeans than ever emigrating to warmer climes, the potential for lettings is significant. However, a letting service isn't just an add-on extra but a specialised area, so you should try to gain experience in lettings as well as sales before you go it alone. If you already have an estate agency and want to move into lettings, make sure you employ someone knowledgeable about the rental market to deal with that side of the business initially.

RENTAL & LETTING AGENCY

If you just want to run a rentals and lettings agency, rather than include it as an estate agency service (see above), it's often best to start small, even on a private basis, until you've had time to familiarise yourself with what's available. It's the kind of thing that you can only do successfully if you're really well informed about both the area and the properties that are available to rent. As with sales, it's imperative to work for at least a short period in an established lettings company, so that you can do some market research while earning a salary.

Making the right contacts is everything, especially if you're going to start small and handle a few private lettings. Owners will have to know and trust you before they will allow you to rent out and look after their property on their behalf. Many will prefer to pay the charges of the large companies to enjoy a more comprehensive service and to ensure redress in the event of mismanagement (e.g. a property is left unlocked and is burgled); as a small agent, it may be difficult for you to obtain insurance to cover such eventualities. Making contacts and establishing relationships takes time, so don't expect to walk straight into this option and make a living immediately.

Most holiday homes are empty for several months of the year, so owners can generate a substantial income if they're prepared to let their properties. If you're living in Spain throughout the year, you're in a good position, not just to let property on behalf of owners, but also to become involved in property management and maintenance (see page 191). As well as an income, the owner has peace of mind if he knows there's someone reliable regularly checking the property, keeping him informed and arranging minor repairs in his absence.

There are various levels of service that you can offer. Many owners prefer an all-inclusive package, which means that you advertise the property, administer bookings and payments, deal with tenants and make sure that the property is maintained in good condition. However, if you're responsible for letting a number of properties on a short-term rental basis, this can involve you in a considerable amount of work, especially during the busy summer season and you may prefer simply to offer a 'caretaking' service.

Location

Whether you do letting on a large or a small scale, the location of the property is everything. If you're planning to tap into the holiday letting market, which is the most lucrative, make sure any property you take on is in a good position. The properties that usually bring in the most money in terms of rent are those in the main tourist areas, such as the *costas* and the islands. If you're in a coastal area, think about the needs of the type of holidaymaker who will come for sun, sea and sand. They will usually want access to a swimming pool – and you can charge more if the property has one – and will want to be close to a major airport and to amenities such as a beach, shops and restaurants, bars and nightlife. If you have access to inland properties, such as a house in the countryside or the mountains away from the coast, remember that this kind of property will attract a different kind of customer, who may cause you fewer headaches, but probably won't bring in as much income.

Charges

Charges vary considerably depending on the package you offer, so ask around other agencies to get an idea of prices in your area. Some charge an annual management fee (e.g. €500) and then a percentage of all rentals, which includes cleaning and linen. This is usually around 15 to 20 per cent but can be as much as 30 per cent. The management fee would include, among other things, regular checks on the property, arranging pool-cleaning, paying bills and carrying out any urgent repairs, although these last are usually billed separately. Laundry and cleaning are normally extra and charged at around €15 per hour.

Advertising

One of most effective ways of advertising, especially for holiday lets, is to put the property on a holiday rentals website, as an increasing number of people are booking their holidays entirely via the internet. There are a number of excellent websites covering all areas of Spain, which will charge you a fee to advertise with them and then alert you to any enquiries about the property. There are also specialist holiday rental magazines, such as *Dalton's Weekly* in the UK, which has combined with the property directory *Private Villas* to form the Dalton's Holidays website (🖳 www.daltonsholidays.com), where advertisements can be placed. Don't forget also the English-language newspapers and magazines in Spain (see **Appendix B**). If your properties are in a good location and of a high quality and your support service is good, you may find that tenants keep returning and you need to rely less on advertising.

Contracts

Whilst holiday lets offer a good income, you need to achieve a high turnover of tenants, whereas longer lets can be a simpler option if the owners don't want to use the property for long periods. Maintenance of a property is cheaper, as tenants are expected to do the basics themselves as well as pay their utility bills. However, if you're going to deal with longer rentals, there are a number of issues to consider – not least Spanish law, which favours tenants' rights over those of the landlord. Holiday lets aren't affected by this law and don't allow tenants rights to automatically extend their contract. However, tenants renting for more than a year can automatically extend their contracts for up to five years. The rent can only be increased annually by the rate of inflation and it can be virtually impossible to evict tenants should you need to.

Make sure you obtain good professional advice about long-term contracts. There are two types of contract for long-term letting: a 'seasonal' contract (*arriendo de temporada*), which is for less than a year, and a 'housing' contract (*arriendo de viviendas*) for more than a year. Surprisingly, you can buy a standard, pre-printed contract at a tobacconist's, but don't let this lull you into a false sense of security and make sure it's checked by a lawyer before anything is signed by anyone.

RELOCATION SERVICES

Most people associate relocation services with corporate moves abroad. Big companies hire relocation consultants to handle anything and everything to ensure that their employees enjoy a smooth ride settling into life in a new country. In Spain's two main cities, Madrid and Barcelona, the relocation market is huge, but most of the big relocation agents tend to deal solely with corporate clients rather than individuals. However, Spain is seeing the growth of another side to the relocation market.

Dominic Tidey of the Association of Relocation Professionals (ARP, 🖳 www.arp-relocation.com) in the UK, which promotes high standards and best practice in the industry, says that Spain is one of the few countries that also has a thriving private relocation market: "It exists happily alongside a mature corporate market. The private acquisition market has grown up in response to demand from second-homeowners and those moving permanently to coastal areas and the Spanish islands. It tends to be run by expatriates who have made the move to Spain themselves and can give advice based on their experience. It's a major growth area in Spain."

Dominic emphasises that, if you want to work in the relocation business, whether it's in one of the cities or a coastal area, the vital thing is that you have extensive local knowledge: "You must have a substantial contacts file on all topics that might be useful to those coming to live and work in the area. The other recommendation is, naturally enough, that you have good language skills. All of the staff in the big corporate relocation agencies in Madrid and Barcelona speak two or three languages, and are usually native Spanish speakers. If you're working in a coastal area, you will still need languages to have the edge over any competition. Obviously English and Spanish are the main languages, but German is also a big plus, as there are still plenty of German buyers in some coastal areas. The other thing to remember is that the private relocation side of the business is usually property led – the client needs a home first and other services later – so it's useful to have experience in the property market."

Qualifications & Professional Standards

Qualifications and high professional standards are vital for the benefit of both clients and your business, as the relocation business is becoming more and more competitive. The ARA offers training and education for relocation providers as does the European Academy of Relocation Professionals (EARP, 💻 www.earp.eu.com), which is the profession's training body and provides both country-specific and general training in all aspects of relocation services. The aim of the ARA and the EARP is to ensure that the industry has a recognised qualification specific to the European industry. Dominic Tidey says that corporate users particularly look for this seal of quality in relocation agents, as they know that members are required to abide by a certain code of conduct. However, membership of the ARA is open only to UK-registered agents.

Setting Up a Relocation Business

If you're thinking of setting up your own business in this area, you must have many skills – negotiating skills, people skills, language skills – as well as extensive local knowledge and contacts. It isn't wise to try to go it alone until you've learnt the ropes working as an employee for one of the large relocation agents. Make sure you've built up an extensive network of 'local correspondents' – people who live in a particular area and can supply you with information on a one-off freelance basis should you need it. Dominic Tidey of the ARA says: "You cannot be everywhere and know everything. The big corporate suppliers in Madrid and Barcelona use self-employed staff on an occasional basis when they need them."

Jane Craggs, whose company Valencia Relocation SL has been operating for five years, says that she wouldn't consider working with anyone who hadn't been living in the area for a number of years: "They need to be well integrated into the community and fluent in Spanish and English," but there's more to it than that. "Anyone who works in this business must know how the system works in Spain, be aware of what's going on and have a really good cross-cultural understanding. That applies at whatever level you work in the business."

Jane's company deals with both corporate and private clients and she says that during the last few years she has seen a significant change in the private relocation market: "Valencia is largely a working city and, until fairly recently, foreign residents were hardly noticeable because they integrated so well into the community. Now there are more and more people coming out to start a new life and their needs are completely different from those of the corporate clients we deal with. It's a new area for us and it's a difficult and complex one. Many of them arrive with little or no Spanish and in Valencia there's virtually no English spoken at street level – it's quite different from the coastal areas, which have large expatriate communities. Private clients are often on a tighter budget and trying to find work rather than having a guaranteed job with a multi-national company.

"This kind of client has a whole host of problems we don't normally see with corporate clients and they require different relocation skills. Many of them have seen the difficulties that others have encountered in moving abroad and they're prepared to employ professionals to speed up and ease the transition into their new life. You need to tell them in couple of days what might take them six months to discover if they were going it alone."

Jane, who is a member of the European Relocation Association (EURA, 🖥 www.eura-relocation.com) and the European Academy of Relocation Professionals (see above), sums up the qualities required of a relocation consultant: "Professionalism and experience are everything. This isn't the kind of business that can be established overnight; it needs long-term commitment and will only pay dividends if time and professionalism are invested in it. Relocation, as a service industry, requires high levels of personal understanding – never more so than now with the new breed of younger expatriates making the move to all areas of Spain."

CONSTRUCTION & BUILDING SERVICES

If you're going to work or do business professionally in construction and building services, you will need a solid background in the building trade and the qualifications to prove it. Bring any qualifications you have with you and make sure they're translated into Spanish. Many people come to Spain, especially to areas with large numbers of expatriates, with few qualifications and charge inflated prices on the basis that they're native English speakers.

Lars Tristan, a Danish citizen, started his own construction company on the Costa Blanca in 1991 and named it after himself: Tristan. He gets extremely frustrated with the 'cowboys': "Everyone's a plumber here and that devalues the hard work of companies like ours, who try and do things legally and professionally. Spanish bureaucracy doesn't make it easy, especially for foreigners, which is why so many people are working illegally. The legal processes are frustrating to begin with, but it pays to have all your papers in order, pay your taxes and do everything properly. I have no problem with healthy competition, but competition from cowboys means it isn't a level playing field. We have to charge VAT and pay it to the government. Those who are working illegally obviously don't do that, which immediately makes our quotes more expensive. However, at least I can sleep at night, because I know I'm doing a good job and I'm doing it legally. My company guarantees all its work and so far I've had no complaints."

Tadeusz Sieracki (known as Tadeo) came to the Costa Blanca from London 16 years ago with experience of working in the family's building and construction company in the UK. "My father had his own construction business and I worked for him once I was old enough. When I arrived in Spain, most English people living here were retired and needed someone who could speak English to do minor repairs and painting and decorating for them. Because I knew the building trade, I began operating in a small way as a self-employed person and I've built up a good client base over the years."

Tadeo says it's important to stick with what you know when you first come to Spain: "It's hard enough starting afresh in a different country, so you need something to hang on to – your trade or your experience in a particular area. I've seen so many people come over and try to work in areas that they have no experience of whatsoever. They're just setting themselves up for failure from the start. My advice is that if you wouldn't do it in your home country, don't try to do it here! If you have the relevant experience and you want to work or set up a business in property maintenance or the building trade, find out as much as you can about the different methods of working in Spain before you arrive. The Spanish ways of working, their tools and their materials are quite different from, for example, those in the UK. That's not to say they're any better or worse, just different, and it takes a while to get used to them. For example, plastering in Spain is done completely differently; it's fascinating watching the experts doing it and you will need to learn the Spanish method of doing things."

Language

Lars works with all nationalities but, when he first started his business, most of his customers were expatriate Scandanavians who felt more comfortable with a builder who spoke their language. Importantly, though, Lars also speaks English and Spanish fluently. He says it would be impossible to operate a business like his without fluent Spanish. Jeremy Kaye, who has been in the building and construction business near Denia on the Costa Blanca for seven years, agrees: "I'm lucky, I'm English, but I went to school in Spain, so I speak fluent Spanish and I know I couldn't run my business as successfully and efficiently if I couldn't communicate with Spanish suppliers, contractors and tradesmen. Our customers are almost entirely English-speaking expatriates and they trust us because we're an established company and can speak their language, but we couldn't do our job properly if we didn't understand the Spanish market as well as the English one."

Qualifications

Jeremy began by setting up as a sole trader and then formed his company, Argent Silver SL, at the end of 2003. He had specialised qualifications as a master bricklayer and says that he tends to only employ Spanish technical tradesmen, such as electricians and gas fitters. "In Spain, you must have a licence to work in any of those trades and it's difficult to get a licence as a foreigner. It's possible, but you must be a resident and be willing to sit the necessary exams in Spanish at a technical college. In this area, you can do that in Alicante or Valencia. Your language skills will have to be pretty advanced and you will need to know the specialised vocabulary used in the profession. However, I've heard that this may change in the future and you may be able to take the exams in English.

"It's difficult to work here legally in either electrics or plumbing because they're strictly controlled. For instance, the electricity system works completely differently here from, say, in the UK, so it's extremely dangerous if a foreigner who isn't familiar with the system tries to do electrical work. General building work isn't a problem and if you have qualifications in that area in your home country that are generally acceptable here."

Jeremy adds a final piece of advice: "You must be adaptable. The methods of building are quite different here, but any builder worth his salt, who is experienced and keen to learn, will soon pick them up."

PROPERTY MAINTENANCE

Property maintenance covers a host of smaller building and maintenance needs and there's a significant market for these services, especially amongst expatriate retirees who can no longer do these jobs for themselves. Tadeusz Sieracki (see above) started working in property maintenance. Like Jeremy Kaye at Argent Silver (see above), Tadeo says adaptability and open-mindedness are important, but not at the expense of professionalism: "There may be a lot of expatriates living here and a lot of English spoken, but this isn't the UK or any other country; it's Spain. It sounds obvious, but I see so many people trying to apply the same rules here as they do at home. It's perfectly natural; they're looking for some kind of anchor, but you can't expect the same kind of attitudes or to be able to charge the same kind of prices as you did in your home country. When you're new to a business, you have to prove yourself first. Drop your prices a little, but not the quality of your work, and the customers will keep coming back. "Remember that, even if you were starting from scratch in your own country and in your own language, it would take around three years to build up a good network of contacts and establish this kind of business, so it isn't going to happen overnight in Spain. You must have sufficient funds behind you to survive for at least a couple of years without earning any significant amount of money."

Like so many other expatriates, Tadeo says that to make the most of your opportunities and succeed in business, you must learn Spanish: "When I first came out here, almost no one spoke English so I was forced to learn Spanish, which was difficult at the time, but once I'd cracked it, it paid dividends. Don't rely too much on books or tapes, but get out there and meet and talk to as many Spanish people as you can. Don't worry about your mistakes; the Spanish won't mind. Just get on with it."

Gardening

There are many expatriates, especially retired people, who need someone to care for their gardens and prefer to use a native English-speaker. However, there's also a substantial market for Spanish clients in some areas, but you must research this well and, of course, be able to speak Spanish. It's important to understand that the concept of employing a gardener is quite different in Spain. Many other nationalities, especially the English, like to dabble in gardening themselves but have someone to help with heavy work. The Spanish tend to leave it entirely to professionals. Either you live in an apartment and just have a few pots on your terrace or you have a garden which is tended, almost exclusively, by a gardener. It's difficult to find out information about plants that are sold in garden centres, as most of their customers are gardeners, who are knowledgeable about such things as planting conditions.

If you want to work in Spain as a gardener and make a success of it, your first job (as with any venture) is to do as much market research as possible. Your second is to find out as much information as you can about plants, gardens, soil and weather conditions, which can be unlike those in northern European countries. David Carr, an English gardener who has been working as a garden designer and landscaper on the outskirts of Barcelona for six years, says that you must not only know what you're doing but also have a love for the job: "Whatever you do, **don't** come for the weather. The heat's a big factor here, of course, but not necessarily a positive one if you're working outdoors. As a gardener you will be spending a fair amount of time slaving in oppressive temperatures, especially during the summer, in a rather underpaid profession."

David has traded on the fact that he's English, and his website has an 'English country garden' feel to it. He says his clients love it: "Gardening and especially garden design is not as big here as it is in the UK, so it's quite a different concept, especially for my Spanish clients. During the last ten years or so, the outskirts of Barcelona have seen the development of numerous satellite towns and much of my business comes from those areas; around 80 per cent of my clients are Spanish people who want something a little different for their gardens. The other 20 per cent of my clients are English expatriates who tend to want garden maintenance, as they would in the UK."

Setting Up

David's background is a creative one, backed up by practical garden design experience in the UK. He has a degree in Fine Art and worked for the Parks Department as well as with private clients in London before coming to Barcelona in 1995. "I started by advertising in a glossy publication in San Cugat, a dormitory town outside Barcelona, and I registered myself as self-employed. I didn't want the responsibility of forming a company until I could see how things were going. I'm still debating whether I want to go down that road or not. At present, I tend to work on my own and employ casual labour or sub-contract the work under my supervision to a Spanish colleague who has his own company when I need to. I enjoy the flexibility that allows me.

"As it happened, I became established through one big client who employed me to do extensive garden design and construction work. It was a great start, but I needed to employ others and it involved me in so many administrative headaches that I've pulled back now. I find that I enjoy my work far more if I do less and can really concentrate on the gardens and the design, rather than worrying about paperwork and staff."

Bureaucracy

Even after six years, David finds the bureaucracy stifling: "Tax is the biggest problem. When you're self-employed you must have a quarterly assessment and that seems to come round pretty quickly. The Social Security payments are also very high, especially if you don't work for a while. You have to pay more than €220 per month even if you aren't earning anything at all. As for VAT, in my kind of business almost no one wants to pay it, but I'm legally obliged to charge it and, of course, hand it over to the government. It's pretty difficult to be competitive when you're operating in a relatively small way. You're also financially vulnerable because there are some customers who won't pay their bills. It's virtually impossible to do anything about it because Spain has no organised channel for small claims. It's something that seems to happen quite frequently – and not just to foreigners: I have Spanish friends who have had similar, and far worse, experiences."

Getting Established

It has taken David a long time to feel established: "I've been in Barcelona for around ten years now and feel as if I'm finally getting there, albeit in a relatively small way. I don't advertise any more and just use the website and word of mouth recommendations. In terms of the work I do, I prefer quality to quantity. It hasn't been easy; in a business sense, things don't work quite the same way here as in the UK. That's partly to do with different attitudes and the Spanish work culture, but you know you've jumped an important hurdle when you stop tearing your hair out and start laughing a bit more about things. I'd say, all in all, it's been worth all the hard work."

Swimming Pools

Swimming pools are big business in Spain. According to a market research report by the US Trade Department in 2003, the Spanish swimming pool market is the second-biggest in Europe after that of France. The annual rate of growth of new swimming pool construction has been 10 per cent during the last ten years and the biggest growth area is in pools for private homes. This means that there's potential not only for swimming pool installation but also for associated products, such as pool covers, cleaning and heating systems and chemicals, and for pool maintenance services. This might appear to be the perfect job – out in the sun all day working on beautiful properties – but it requires a lot of knowledge and skill and is far more complex than it looks.

There's potential in all the popular destinations for expatriates in Spain, including Catalonia, Valencia, Murcia, the Balearics and the Canaries and Andalusia. Although the use of pools is largely confined to the summer, they need cleaning and maintenance during the winter months and installation can be carried out at almost any time of year. If you're planning to sell associated products, such as chemicals and equipment, business tends to be limited to the spring and summer months.

Note, however, that swimming pool maintenance is a difficult area to find work in as a foreigner. Established companies prefer to hire only experienced staff with experience of working in Spain (and usually Spanish nationals), so you may need to work for nothing initially in order to become 'approved'. It's also a highly competitive sector, especially in areas with a large number of second homes. It isn't something you can do as a sideline, e.g. if you're a gardener, but is a highly specialised job and, if you don't know what you're doing, it can be dangerous.

If swimming pool installation or maintenance appeals to you, a good place to begin your research is the biannual International Swimming Pool Exhibition in Barcelona, where you can obtain a wealth information about this growing sector. The organisers have a website (⌨ www.salon piscina.com), which is available in English.

Cleaning

Cleaning services are much in demand, especially in coastal areas and cities. There's also enormous demand from those letting holiday homes, who need their properties cleaned between lettings. Cleaning is hard work, but it can be profitable. If you want to earn money temporarily or plan to start your own agency, employing a team of cleaners, your services will be much in demand.

However, you must remember that your customers need to be able to trust you in their homes, and you must have excellent references that can be checked, which can be difficult to achieve if you're new to a country. Bring some character references with you, both related and unrelated to any cleaning experience you might have had in your home country. Obviously, references from former employers are particularly relevant. People tend to ask friends and other business people in the community if they need a cleaner and always prefer to employ someone who is recommended. Try working through an agency to start with, in order to build up confidence in yourself and the quality of your work, before going it alone.

The going rate for cleaning varies from area to area, but in the cities and coastal areas, an experienced, highly regarded cleaner can charge between €8 and €10 per hour. As in many other countries, the vast majority of domestic cleaners work on the black market, but remember that if you do this, you have no rights or employment protection whatsoever; you probably won't get paid for holidays and won't be insured for any damage you might cause unintentionally while doing your job.

If your plans include starting an agency offering cleaning services, you must research the market in your area thoroughly and have plenty of experience so that you understand the practicalities of the job. Check your local English-language press in Spain (see **Appendix B**) to get an idea of what kind of demand there is and what the going rates are in your area.

House-sitting & Pet-sitting

These services are popular only in areas where there are plenty of expatriates. Although house- and pet-sitting are common in many other European countries, there's little demand for them in Spain. As with cleaning, you must build up a good reputation before anyone will trust you sufficiently to leave you in charge of their house or their pet. You should bring as many references as you can from your home country, and potential customers must be able to check them. You can advertise in local English-language newspapers and leave notices in vets' surgeries about a pet-sitting service.

9.

RETAILING

Shopping habits in Spain are changing fast and, although you can still find plenty of small local traders, shopping centres and chain stores are edging their way into the lives of many Spanish shoppers. This is partly due to the growing number of working women, who demand longer opening hours and need to be able to find everything under one roof, so that they're able to do a 'one-stop' shop on the way home. However, for the time being, small retailers and supermarkets seem to exist quite happily together, and many housewives still visit independent traders daily for their fresh produce but also enjoy a family visit to a shopping centre for all kinds of goods.

Retailing can offer a wealth of opportunities for expatriates, and an obvious avenue is to look at what your fellow countrymen might miss from home. English or international book shops have been springing up in cities and coastal areas of Spain over the last few years, sometimes also offering greetings cards and stationery. Small supermarkets, specialising in the type of product that expatriates are familiar with, are also popular. If you're thinking along these lines, you must research your market carefully; many foreign products are far more readily available in Spanish supermarkets than they were a few years ago, especially in areas popular with tourists and foreign residents.

You may prefer to look at the feasibility of a product which appeals to Spanish customers and the expatriate market. The key, as with any business anywhere in the world, is to find a gap in the market, offering a product that isn't readily available in a certain location. A report in *The Scotsman* newspaper in summer 2004 told of the unexpected success enjoyed by MacKay's Ltd, the Dundee preserves manufacturer, which is re-exporting Spanish oranges to Spain in the form of jams and marmalades for the expatriate market in coastal areas.

You must also decide whether you want to buy a business that's up and running, or whether you would prefer to start with a blank canvas. In coastal areas it's fairly easy to find ready-made retailing businesses on the books of commercial agents or advertised in English-language newspapers. Both *Sur in English* on the Costa del Sol and the *Costa Blanca News* on the Costa Blanca carry advertisements for going concerns. If this is what you're looking for, tread carefully (see page 104). This chapter looks at three retailing operations started by expatriates in Spain: an English book shop in Barcelona, a small supermarket selling English goods in a village near Alicante on the Costa Blanca, and an Irish butcher on the Costa del Sol.

RESEARCH

Whether you want to buy an existing business or start your own, your first move must be to do as much market research as possible, and this should include the level of potential competition for your business, both from other small traders and from any nearby large chain stores or supermarkets – and you should check at the town hall whether there are plans to build new shops in the area. If it's an area that you're unfamiliar with in commercial terms, start by spending as much time as you can in and around your intended location watching the flow of people. Look particularly carefully at those people who are likely to be your target market and make sure there will be plenty of potential customers passing your way every day. Talk to as many people as you can and ask as many questions as you dare – both of expatriate and of Spanish consumers – to find out the needs and buying habits of the locals and, if relevant, tourists, in order to get a feel for the potential demand for your product or services.

Book Shop

Frank Sirett, who opened an English book shop called Elephant in Barcelona in 2001, had been aware of the gap in the market for some time. "I've lived in Barcelona for 15 years," he says, "and for many of those years I was desperate for English books at reasonable prices." His love of reading meant that he regularly trawled the second-hand English book shops in the area and that's how he began his market research. He often offered his services to the book shops and so made some good contacts, was able to see how they did things and learnt from a few of their mistakes. When the opportunity to open his own book shop came up, his eagerness to start trading didn't deter him from carefully researching his market to work out who his likely customers might be and the areas of Barcelona they tended to frequent. This information was crucial when he began to put together his business plan. Frank went to Barcelona Activa for some initial information. Barcelona Activa is an organisation run by the local council (Ajuntament de Barcelona) which will give you an assessment of your business plan and advise you on the practicalities of setting up. There's a high success rate among businesses that approach them. Further information can be found on the Barcelona Activa website (🖳 www.barcelonanetactiva.es), which is in English, Castilian Spanish and Catalan.

Butcher's

Gerry McKenna, who has been operating G.T. McKenna, an Irish family butcher's in Calahonda on the Costa del Sol for almost three years, says he did around 18 months' detailed market research and his own feasibility studies before he made the decision to open his shop. He knew how important it was to be on the spot to do so: "I was travelling backwards and forwards from Ireland every couple of weeks," he says. "I must literally have walked the length of the Costa del Sol, from Malaga to Sotogrande. It was the only way I could really see what was already available and I spent a long time talking to expatriates and tourists in local supermarkets to find out what they missed most from home. The answer that came up every time was, believe it or not, really good sausages! They also wanted to be able to buy cuts of meat they were familiar with." Gerry's professional background as a supermarket executive in Northern Ireland, specialising in fresh meat and food control, meant that he knew his products and had plenty of experience in the industry, but he realised this didn't automatically mean he knew the market in Spain. "I contacted the British and Irish Embassies and the Tourist Boards here in Spain and they gave me average numbers of tourists that visit the area and expatriate residents here. When I saw those figures, I knew the potential market was enormous."

It's that kind of research that makes the difference between success and failure, Gerry's family butcher's is now thriving, and people travel miles to buy his home-made sausages and familiar cuts of meat from the UK and Ireland.

There are plenty of other factors to consider during your research, which are often forgotten by over-eager potential entrepreneurs. Seasonal variations in trade can cause you big problems, especially in coastal areas. Is your product a seasonal one, or is the area you're looking at only busy in the summer period, when the tourists are there? Something like a gift and souvenir shop could be very popular during the summer but custom will be far thinner on the ground during the winter. It makes far more sense to go for a product that's likely to be in demand all year round and to find premises in an area that's regularly frequented by expatriate and Spanish residents alike.

Supermarket

Julie Day and her daughter Georgina are old hands compared with Frank Sirett and Gerry McKenna. The two women opened a small supermarket called Codayma in Orba, a small village near Alicante, eight years ago, but they had lived in the area for ten years prior to that, doing market research almost without realising it. Julie already knew many expatriates and Spanish people. She had worked in bars and restaurants as well as for a company which was selling British products by mail order. "I come from a family of small traders and had served in both my grandparents' and parents' shops as a child," explains Julie. "I enjoy serving the public and decided on a supermarket because at the time the area badly needed somewhere you could buy British foods." They sell all manner of things: food, greetings cards, household products, newspapers and much more. They're also a focus for the expatriate community: "We tend to be an information centre too; everyone comes in for advice, a smile and a chat as well as for their shopping."

FINDING PREMISES

Julie was lucky enough to find a small, rather run down shop in the main street of Orba, which had previously sold ceramic pots. "It was in a good position, but we had very little capital and I thought it was going to be too much of a commitment. Then I was left a small amount of money in a friend's will and that went towards buying the fixtures and fittings from the previous owner. It was in a bit of a state but we painted it inside and out and tried to make it look as good as possible on limited funds." Julie rents her premises; she has made attempts to buy them from the landlady, but she doesn't want to sell. Julie and Georgina are good tenants and she can increase the rent by the cost of living each year. Spanish owners aren't keen to sell outright, as they see the income from property letting as a welcome supplement to their pension and as a way of providing an income for generations to come.

Frank Sirett used up a lot of shoe leather looking for premises before he found something suitable. "It was a two- to three-year process and very frustrating," he recalls. "We did approach estate agents but it was a waste of time and in the end we just walked round and looked for suitable premises that had 'to rent' (*se alquila*) signs up and then made appointments to view them. Sometimes it's easier do it yourself." He made a conscious decision to open in the Poble Sec area of Barcelona, as it was reasonably priced, close to the metro and within walking distance of the centre of the city. He could have spent more on premises with more passing trade, but he didn't feel the extra cost warranted it. "We're unique and serve a limited sector, so we just work harder on our advertising. It stops us from taking things for granted." Frank rents his premises and has no plans or resources at present to buy them. He made sure he used a lawyer to check the rental contract.

Gerry McKenna's needs for his butcher's shop were far more specialised, as he needed space at the back of the shop for refrigeration and for preparing products such as sausages. He eventually took his current premises on a rental basis, and he strongly advises that you read all the small print and make sure you understand every word of your rental agreement. He also suggests you get someone independent of the transaction to translate it for you. "I nearly got caught out with the first premises I found." said Gerry. "Everything seemed fine, but the last line of the agreement stated that either party could terminate the contract with only seven days' notice." Luckily he noticed this point and refused to sign. Had he not been so astute, he would have immediately signed away all of his usual tenant's rights, which are fairly extensive in Spain (see page 92). If his landlord had exercised his right to terminate the contract, it could have meant the end of Gerry's thriving business. Whichever kind of agreement you have – whether it's a sale contract, a lease or a rental agreement – make sure you use a lawyer that comes highly recommended and that **you yourself** read every last word and understand what it means before you sign anything.

SHOPFITTERS & SUPPLIERS

You can probably get to this stage without speaking much, if any, Spanish (provided you have your contract translated), especially in areas with a large number of expatriates, where most lawyers speak English. However, once you're past this point and are ready to fit out your premises, things begin to get more complicated in terms of language. It's fairly difficult to find expatriate shopfitters in Spain, although the UK National Association of Shopfitters has a list of members who operate internationally on its website (🖳 www.shopfitters.org). This will obviously be a more expensive option than using a Spanish company, which may therefore be preferable if your Spanish is more fluent. As with any service in Spain, it's best to seek recommendations, but a good way to begin is by looking in the local yellow pages (*paginas amarillas*) under *Instalaciones Comerciales y Equipamiento*.

Teresa Emslie, who opened a women's fashion shop called Ikonia, in the Port of Duquesa on the Costa del Sol in 2004, couldn't speak much Spanish when she came to Spain, so she had to be resourceful when it came to finding suppliers and shopfitters for her shop. She found out where the nearest industrial estates (*polígonos industriales*) were. These are generally well sign-posted and contain all manner of retail suppliers. Teresa decided that this was the best way for her to familiarise herself with companies that might be useful to her. So she simply drove round and knocked on doors: "At first, I approached them with trepidation and found a few English speakers, but not many, so we used a mixture of animated sign language and calculators to do business. I'm a lot better now and my vocabulary has improved immensely, but I would say it's essential to have as much Spanish as possible, even in expatriate areas. In my case, I also had to approach suppliers in Madrid because they had some of the best stock, and I found that almost no one spoke English there."

Gerry McKenna, the Irish butcher, and Julie at Codayma both found the language problem easier because they were able to call on the skills of their children. Although Julie is reasonably fluent, her daughter studied at a local Spanish school and speaks fluent Castilian Spanish and *valenciano*, the local dialect. "We have lots of Spanish customers and Spanish suppliers," says Julie, "so it's vital." Gerry McKenna's daughter is also a fluent Spanish speaker and made all the necessary telephone calls and accompanied him when he had dealings with suppliers, contractors and the authorities. He also used contacts he had built up during his market research to find suppliers of the specialist equipment and shopfitting material he needed. "Much of the machinery I'd used in Ireland was made in Spain, so with the help of my daughter, I tracked down the local representative of the equipment companies and we approached them here in Spain."

LICENCES & PERMISSIONS

It's important to be clear about your needs and to find out what the regulations are **before** you commit yourself to any particular premises. If they don't meet the requirements, it could be a complicated and expensive business to bring them up to scratch, which may also mean a long delay before you can obtain your opening licence (*licencia de apertura*) and may even result in a refusal. Seek advice from a lawyer or a *gestor* about the requirements for your particular business and remember that they may vary from one local authority to another. You can visit the town hall yourself and ask for a list of things you must provide before they will consider giving you a licence (see page 100), but, as you will need an architect to submit an installation plan, it's advisable to find one who can deal with the relevant departments at the town hall and liaise with your *gestor*.

Frank Sirett decided to install a small bar in his book shop, which meant a separate licence. Before he could open, an approved architect needed to present his case to the local town hall. Fortunately, the architect understood both Frank's needs for his shop and the requirements of the authorities. Julie Day found a good *gestor*, who took care of everything and who remains her friend to this day. She needed a licence for selling tobacco and a food handler's licence, both of which must be renewed periodically; the shop is visited regularly by Health and Safety inspectors.

As he was going to be selling food for human consumption, Gerry McKenna knew that he had to be especially careful. There are strict European Union laws on food safety, but the standards that are required in order to pass the relevant inspections depend on how those laws are interpreted by the Spanish authorities. Gerry had to approach local representatives of The European Food Safety Authority (EFSA), which governs all levels of the food industry across Europe. In Spain the agency concerned is the Agencia Española de Seguridad Alimentaria, which is part of the Ministry of Health; there is some information in English on its website (⊟ www.aesa.msc.es).

Your application and inspections will be dealt with by the local provincial office of the autonomous community government. In Gerry's case, his premises had to be inspected by representatives of the health department of the government of Andalusia to ensure that they were fit for the purpose of preparing meat for human consumption. "I made sure I knew what the requirements were as early as possible, so that I could bear them in mind when I was looking for a good site. I also found out which building contractors specialised in this kind of outlet because they also know what's required to comply with the regulations," explains Gerry.

INSURANCE

Insurance is a vital consideration if you don't want to lose everything you've worked for. You will need building insurance against obvious risks such as fire and water damage. If you rent the property from a landlord, he should already have this, but you should check the details of the policy before you sign your rental contract. Then there are the contents of shop, the fixtures and fittings and your stock, which will need insuring against damage and theft, including when stock is in transit. You must also ensure that you have sufficient public liability insurance, which means that should any customer injure himself in your shop and claim against you, your insurance company will pay (unless you've been negligent). If you employ others, you will also need employer's liability insurance and to pay social security contributions on behalf of your staff so that they're covered for accidents, illness, etc. (see page 138).

Ask around for a reliable broker or insurance agent, as there are plenty of companies offering insurance to businesses, some in specific business sectors and others offering services in English and other languages to the expatriate market.

MARKETING

It's natural, after all that hard work in setting up, to want news of your business to reach as many people as possible, but you must be ruthlessly selective and spend plenty of time researching the most cost-effective way of reaching the most potential customers. Indeed, you should have combined this with your market research.

As soon as you open your shop, you will find yourself bombarded by people trying to persuade you to part with your money, when what you're trying to do is make some of your own. The most persistent will be those trying to sell advertising space in publications. Many publications are free to readers and consequently only make their money through advertising. Remember that their priorities won't be the same as yours. Look carefully at **all** the publications you can, talk to other businesses that advertise in them and ask about their success rate. You can spend a large proportion of your advertising budget on a glossy magazine advertisement only to find that you get little or no custom from it.

In the early days, it may not be necessary to spend a lot of money advertising in magazines or newspapers. You could start by distributing flyers to areas where you think your customers may see them, or ask if you can display them in other relevant areas. Flyers can be printed relatively cheaply and initially they will help you to see what kind of feedback you get. Many people interviewed for this book agreed that word of mouth was the most effective, and obviously the cheapest, method of 'advertising' in Spain. The Spanish in particular almost always prefer to have a recommendation and will rarely contact a business 'cold' from an advertisement.

Once you're a little more established, your marketing needs will become clearer and you will be able to be more discerning about how you spend your money. Julie Day, Frank Sirett and Gerry McKenna all agree that, however successful you are, the best way to keep the customers that you have is to be constantly one step ahead. "Advertising can become boring for you and your customers," says Frank. "The customers stop noticing it and, once you get to that stage, it has done more harm than good. Keep them guessing about what might be different next week; give them plenty of variety."

In this sense, running a retailing business in Spain is no different from running one anywhere else: you can never afford to rest on your laurels. Gerry McKenna is always looking for new ideas to increase his business: "I'm constantly chatting to customers to find out what else they'd like to see on the shelves and I've begun selling other English or Irish products that my customers are familiar with. They might come in to buy their Sunday roast and realise they can also get sauces to go with the meats, Irish milk and even fresh cream to pour over their desserts. Fresh cream is hard to come by in this part of Spain, so it has been very popular. Whatever you do, you cannot afford to sit back and think you've made it. The minute you start doing that, the customers go elsewhere and it's almost impossible to get them back."

10.

TEACHING

For many expatriates, teaching in Spain means only one thing: teaching English as a foreign language. Although this is a popular option, and an area where there's considerable demand and opportunity, there are other teaching avenues available and this chapter looks at some of them. Teaching an art or craft is one. Another is joining the staff of an international school, teaching in English or Spanish.

Information about teaching English as a foreign language for EU and non-EU citizens and how to obtain the relevant qualifications and find a job in a language school is followed by the experiences of two women who have taken things a step further and opened their own language school. There are details of how to go about giving private lessons on a freelance basis, which is an increasingly popular option with expatriates.

TEACHING ENGLISH

Teaching English as a foreign language is a route that many English-speakers choose, at least initially, to make a living in Spain. Whether you're a young graduate wanting experience of another country and culture, someone planning to live and work in Spain long term, or a professional taking a career break who wants to try something different, teaching English can be a relatively easy way to earn a living. At the very least, it's a useful stopgap until you become more established and a great way to make contacts with both English-speakers and Spanish people when you're new to the country. What's more, teaching English is one job where you really don't need any Spanish. In fact, one language school owner said that it was a definite advantage if you couldn't lapse into Spanish and help your pupils out.

Teaching English to children is a major growth area as a result of the government's initiative to introduce English as early as possible into the Spanish curriculum. From September 2004, the teaching of English in public primary schools became compulsory from the age of six and the Spanish government has worked in partnership with the British Council for many years to encourage the teaching of English through an integrated curriculum in some Spanish infant schools. In the past, students were mainly adults who needed to learn for business or social reasons and, although that's still a significant market, teaching children, or English for Young Learners (EYL), is becoming almost as important if not more so. If you think that might be an area for you, make sure you're properly trained and qualified in this specialist area. The website of the British Council (💻 www.britishcouncil.org/english/eyl/spain) has details of teaching English to young learners in Spanish schools as well as privately and in specialist language schools.

Non-EU Citizens

EU citizens who are native English-speakers have a big advantage when it comes to teaching English in Spain because, unlike non-EU citizens, they can live and work in Spain without a visa. Unfortunately, EU regulations make it almost impossible for an employer to legally take on a non-EU citizen. Many language schools therefore hire non-EU citizens with just a tourist visa and there are plenty willing to work that way, although it's illegal. To work legally and stay longer than three months in Spain, the time limit for a tourist visa, you must have a work permit and residence visa (see page 23), but most employers aren't willing to go through the complicated procedure required to employ you legally. If you're serious about teaching English in Spain and are a non-EU citizen, make sure you have impressive qualifications and that extra something to persuade your prospective employer that you're worth all the paperwork. **Remember that if you originally come to Spain on a tourist visa you must return to your home country and present yourself in person at a Spanish embassy or consulate to obtain a work permit and residence visa.** A useful and informative website, especially for non-EU expatriate English teachers, is ☒ www.expatriatecafe.com.

Qualifications & Courses

The qualifications you need to teach English as a foreign language are a mass of confusing initials. Most people have heard of TEFL, but there's also TESOL and CELTA. To confuse the situation further, TEFL and TESOL aren't in fact qualifications at all, although many people refer to them as if they were. TEFL stands for Teaching English as a Foreign Language and TESOL for Teaching English to Speakers of Other Languages. The two are effectively the same thing and refer to the profession rather than any qualifications.

Qualifications in TEFL or TESOL are offered by numerous organisations. If you plan to teach adults, as is most likely to be the case, the qualification you need is the Certificate in English Language Teaching to Adults (CELTA). Many institutions offer a CELTA course, but the 'gold standard' is the Cambridge CELTA certificate. Cambridge courses are slightly more expensive, but it's worth paying the extra, as the certificate is highly regarded in the industry and some language schools insist on it. Cambridge CELTA courses are designed by individual centres in accordance with specifications produced by the English to Speakers of Other Languages (ESOL) section of the University of Cambridge Examination Board, whose website (🖳 www.cambridge esol.org) has details of locations and a sample syllabus.

To take the CELTA, you must be at least 20 and have a good standard of English and of general education, at least similar to what's expected to enter higher education. Accredited Cambridge courses are available worldwide, so you can obtain the qualification in your home country or in Spain. CELTA courses can be done full- or part-time but they're challenging and time-consuming. A full-time course takes four to five weeks of intensive study and assessed teaching practice, while a part-time course takes from a few months to year or more depending on how much spare time you have. For each course, you must complete 120 hours of teaching (known as 'contact hours') and a further 80 hours or more of assignments and lesson planning. Prices for 2005 are around €1,400 for full- and part-time courses.

Once you've obtained a CELTA, you can undertake more specialised extension courses so that you can teach business English or English to young learners, which will make your services more marketable. Teaching English to young learners is a completely different skill from teaching adults. Lynn Durrant, a CELTA course trainer at International House in Barcelona (see page 216) for more than ten years and a tutor on their Young Learner courses, says: "It's absolutely vital that you're trained specifically to teach young learners. It helps to give you an insight into their behaviour and what they're capable of learning at particular stages."

It's possible to take an online or DVD-based course, such as those offered by the UK company i-to-i (🖳 www.onlinetefl.com) and the US Department of Education-approved Bridge Linguatec Language Services (🖳 www.teflonline.com), whose course takes just 40 hours and cost from $295. The problem with internet courses is that you cannot gain practical experience, which is a major disadvantage when it comes to getting a job. **The more practical experience you have, the better; this will tip the scales in your favour more than any certificate or qualification.**

FINDING A JOB

If you're looking for a job teaching English in a language school in Spain, timing is everything. The main recruiting period is usually from around mid-August with interviews in September for courses starting in late September or early October. The other popular time is January, when some teachers don't return after the Christmas holiday, leaving schools with vacancies they didn't expect to have. Start taking your CV around the schools you're interested in a month or so before you want to start work. Language schools usually prefer you to be living in Spain when you apply, because so many people accept jobs and then return to their home country, never to be seen again.

Jobs are harder to come by in the big cities, as they continue to be favourite destinations for prospective teachers, so it's an employer's market. One former English teacher in Barcelona said that every second person she met seemed to be an English teacher, so it's vital to have as much teaching experience as possible to be able to compete. Rates of pay depend on the area: for example, in a small village with only one school you can sometimes earn more than in a big city, where your skills are less in demand. A good rate is around €12.50 per hour, although many schools pay only around €10 and some as little as €8. Most schools will offer you a temporary contract, so that they don't have to pay you during holidays, especially the long summer holiday, so bear that in mind when you're budgeting. Permanent contracts in language schools are rare.

> A number of language schools operate on a precarious financial basis. Some offer few or no teaching resources to help their staff do their job properly and fail to pay wages on time, if at all. Recently there have been several well publicised language school closures, leaving teachers out of pocket and having to find alternative employment. It's therefore advisable to apply to one of the larger, more established schools with a good reputation.

There are plenty of resources to help you find a job teaching English in Spain, including the following:

● **British Council** – The British Council (🖳 www.britcoun.org/spain) has offices in Madrid (Pº General Martínez Campos 31, 28010 Madrid, ☎ 91 337 3500) and Barcelona (Amigó, 83, 08021 Barcelona, ☎ 93 241 9700) and organises English teaching at schools throughout Spain (listed on the website under 'About Us').

● **Internet** – There are numerous useful websites to look at, including 🖳 www.segundamano.es, a classified advertisements portal. The Barcelona Online site (🖳 www.barcelona-online.com), sponsored by

International House language school (see below), is a useful resource for those looking in the Barcelona area, as are the Barcelona Connect site (💻 www.barcelonaconnect.com), which contains the *Barcelona Connect* magazine, and 💻 www.absolutebarcelona.com, a classified advertisements portal.

- **Language Schools** – You can approach schools directly, and the school that trained you may have a recruitment programme. International House (💻 www.ihmadrid.es/english) has schools all over Spain.

- **Newspapers & Magazines** – The national newspaper *El Pais* has advertisements for teachers under the heading *Trabajo – Idiomas*. In Madrid, *In Madrid*, a free monthly magazine in English, which has an online version (💻 www.in-madrid.com), is a useful resource. In Barcelona, the *La Vanguardia* newspaper is an excellent resource, especially the Sunday edition. Each of the Costas and main islands has local newspapers (listed in **Appendix B**), both English-language and Spanish, where you can find details of local language schools and place an advertisement offering private lessons.

- **Universities** – It's worth checking the notice boards in universities to find students (and possibly teachers) who want private lessons. The city of Valencia is home to one of the largest universities in Spain, so there's no shortage of students who need to learn English to increase their employment possibilities once they graduate.

- **Yellow Pages** – Language schools, academies and institutes are listed in the yellow pages (*paginas amarillas*) under *Escuelas de Idiomas*.

RUNNING A LANGUAGE SCHOOL

Susan Sorrell and Sophie Watts joined forces to start a language school in 2002. They had both trained as TEFL teachers, Sophie in London and Susan in Seville, and between them had many years of experience teaching both English and Spanish. They met when they were both teaching at a language school in Marbella. "We'd both got to the same stage – we were ready to do our own thing," says Sophie. "When you teach in someone else's school, the inevitably repetitive nature of the teaching becomes boring." They decided they wanted the freedom of running their own school and to be a little more innovative in their teaching methods. "We wanted to do things our way," says Sophie, who comes from a family of entrepreneurs in the UK.

Good business practice was second nature to her so she was keen to give it a go. Susan, whose family has lived in Spain for many years, knew the area well and was familiar with the market for language teachers, both English and Spanish. Their language school, The Language House in San Pedro de Alcántara on the Costa del Sol, opened its doors around nine months after they had first discussed their ideas. It was a long, hard road: "We found it difficult to get a loan because we had no assets in Spain or a regular income at that point," explains Sophie. "We also found it very hard to get good advice, despite the fact that, unlike many people trying to start a business out here, we had plenty of good contacts in the area. Advisers tend to assume that you already know things you couldn't possibly know unless you had lived here all your life. So they don't actually offer information; you have to go out and find it out for yourself." It took them two years to discover that their local town hall operates a women's business service which not only runs courses specifically aimed at female entrepreneurs but also has agreements with some local banks to provide businesswomen with short term loans at very low interest rates.

Sophie went on one of the courses and discovered all kinds of useful information and sources of help, which have enabled the two women run their business more efficiently. They were also able to take advantage of the preferential loan facility to expand the school. "We needed a guarantor," explains Sophie, "and luckily we found someone willing to act as one, so it has really helped us to develop the business." Although the course that Sophie went on was in Spanish, the kind of information on offer is invaluable if you're setting up a business, so it's worth finding out whether your local town hall runs something similar. If you don't feel that your Spanish is up to it, see if you can take a friend or colleague to translate for you. If your town hall has a Foreigners' Department, ask what's available. If you speak reasonably good Spanish, approach the department responsible for helping women, the *Delegación de la Mujer*.

Forming a Company

Susan and Sophie didn't want to form a company straight away, but their financial adviser (*asesor fiscal*) suggested that they form a *sociedad civil* (see **Partnership** on page 95). They would be jointly responsible should there be a claim against them but, as the language school wasn't considered high risk, they accepted this. They had to pay 1 per cent of their capital to the tax authorities on forming the partnership and they had to register for *IAE*. They must also both pay personal tax on a self-employed basis, but they legally avoid company tax.

To obtain their opening licence, Susan and Sophie had to go to the town hall and submit the required paperwork (see page 102). They had to show that they were registered with the local tax office for business tax and produce a copy of the rental contract for their premises along with all their personal paperwork. They also had to apply for a health and safety inspection and provide an installation plan, drawn up by an approved architect, showing that they had a toilet, fire extinguishers and a first aid box. Their *gestor* helped them through all the procedures with the town hall.

Employing Staff

To begin with, The Language House had just two members of staff: themselves. Susan teaches English and Spanish and Sophie teaches English. As their business has expanded, they've had to take on staff, although they were nervous of doing so at first. "It's a bit of a minefield," says Sophie. "But we've done everything properly and all our staff are on contracts," continues Susan. They make sure that everyone they take on is registered as unemployed with the National Employment Service (Instituto Nacional de Empleo – see page 72) before offering them a contract. That way, when The Language House employs them, the school is entitled to certain benefits and incentives for providing the jobs (see **Permanent Contracts** on page 111). "In our opinion, staff are what make your school successful," says Sophie, "so we make sure we treat them well by training them properly and then helping them through the early weeks with their lesson plans and materials."

Advertising & Marketing

Most of the Spanish people who want to learn English come to The Language House via word-of-mouth recommendations. English people who want to learn Spanish are more likely to call if they see an advertisement in the newspaper, and they get a lot of business that way. Sophie and Susan are currently considering advertising on English-language radio and feel that they must always keep marketing: "Luckily, having already taught in language schools, we both knew about the seasonality of language teaching," says Susan. "It can be very frustrating, but you have to learn to budget for that. The summer is often a very quiet period, especially August. Even during the rest of the year, you have to be prepared for people who suddenly cancel or drop out of lessons and just disappear."

PRIVATE TEACHING

Teaching on a private basis can be a precarious way of making a living, and it's wise to have another string to your bow until you become established. Whether you're planning to teach English or offer private tutoring of any kind to either children or adults, you must register yourself for self-employed taxation (*autónomo*) and social security (see **Chapter 5**). Remember that, once you're registered, you must pay social security every month, irrespective of the amount you've earned, plus 20 per cent tax on any earnings (see **Chapter 3**).

There are plenty of opportunities for those offering private teaching in Spain. In the big cities, university notice boards are a good place for advertisements, as well as local newspapers and magazines (see **Appendix B**). Private language lessons are often popular with adults, especially when they begin to learn a language and prefer not to make their mistakes in front of a class full of people. If you prefer to teach children, many expatriate parents in Spain are anxious about their children's academic progress, whether they attend a Spanish school or an international school and are happy to have their children tutored in languages or other subjects if they think it will help them.

Art Teaching

If you're a talented artist seeking inspiration from the beautiful light and landscapes of Spain, you could consider giving painting or drawing lessons. Andalusia and Catalonia are the regions that attract most of those offering lessons and potential students. If you're thinking about setting up this type of course, make sure you research the area you're interested in and your potential customer base thoroughly. Budding artists often want traditional Spain, quiet locations and stunning landscapes as opposed to big cities and the hustle and bustle of coastal areas.

Joy Fahey, an artist working in Marbella, is registered as self-employed and offers art courses and workshops in Andalusia (🖳 www. joyfahey.com). She finds that these complement her own painting: "However skilled an artist you are, it's practically impossible to make a living here just by selling your work. So I decided to supplement my income by teaching. I've loved teaching art ever since I studied art therapy many years ago. I think painting is a fantastic release valve for all the stresses and strains of life." Joy has now been teaching in Spain for three years and remembers that her very first class had a solitary student! She has since built that up to over 50 students, although she says that she has a core group of around 20 who keep coming back. She runs two classes per week and has just been joined by another artist who helps with her workshops.

"You need to work hard at advertising," says Joy. "When I started, I advertised in the English-language press and gave out leaflets in what I thought were relevant areas." Now she finds that word of mouth is her most effective form of advertising, but she still works hard to keep the customers coming. The transient nature of the expatriate community means that students come and go for no particular reason and so it's almost impossible to predict her earnings. She has recently advertised in art magazines in the UK and is waiting to see the response. "Make sure you have plenty of money to live on, particularly when you first arrive. Then, once you start earning, get into the habit of saving a little, for the inevitable lean times, which are a fact of life here. Everyone experiences them at some time or another."

INTERNATIONAL SCHOOLS

There's a growing number of international schools in the big cities and coastal areas of Spain. As the expatriate population gets younger, so the need for international schools increases. Coastal areas in particular are seeing a massive influx of young families, arriving to start a new life in Spain and, for most parents, one of their greatest worries is the kind of education their children will receive in Spain. While many expatriate parents opt to have their children (especially younger ones) educated in the Spanish system, others prefer to submit them to the UK or US-style curriculum offered in international schools. In addition, there's a growing demand from Spanish parents who want their children taught in English, especially during their early years of schooling, allowing them the kind of fluency that's impossible to achieve from the English lessons they would receive in a Spanish school. All this means that there's a demand for well qualified, native English-speaking teachers in all subjects.

Curriculum

It's important to check the kind of curriculum that a particular international school operates. For instance, some 'British' schools may closely follow the UK curriculum, offering the same exams as schools in the UK. However, they aren't obliged to do so, and some adapt the curriculum according to the needs of their pupils. Some offer the International Baccalaureate curriculum, others a mixture of the two. One teacher, who has many years' experience and is currently teaching in a top international school in southern Spain, pointed out some unexpected difficulties: "The pupil base of an international school is naturally transient, which means that pupils are arriving and leaving with more frequency than they would in a school in the UK. You're constantly trying to adapt lesson plans to accommodate all levels of ability." Her advice is that you shouldn't assume that, just because a school operates a British curriculum, teaching there will be the same as teaching in the UK. "Always expect the unexpected and be prepared for it. Have plenty of your own resource material available and learn to be laid back, but not to the point of disorganisation. Most important of all, enjoy the experience."

Language

If you teach a subject other than Spanish, it's possible to work in an international school without speaking much Spanish. However, if you want to make the most of your experience in Spain, the recommendation from those who have done it are clear: "Of course you can get away without speaking Spanish in a popular expatriate area," says one teacher. "I know many who have been here for years and only have the basics. All I can say is, they don't realise what they're missing out on."

Qualifications

You must have a degree in your subject and a recognised teaching qualification, e.g. a Postgraduate Certificate in Education (PGCE) in the UK. Members of Council of International Schools require at least two years' teaching experience, but this may vary from school to school, depending on the competition.

Finding Work

If you're interested in this kind of opportunity, the *Times Educational Supplement* (*TES*) is a good place to start, as vacancies for the top international schools are usually advertised there. The *TES* also has a comprehensive website (🖳 www.tesjobs.co.uk), which includes a Working Abroad section and details of new jobs both in the UK and abroad; new vacancies are posted on the website every Friday. There are several other websites where you can find useful information about teaching abroad and contact details of schools in the area you're interested in. The site run by the National Association of British Schools in Spain (NABSS, 💻 www.nabss.org) has alphabetical and geographical listings of all its members, and that of the Council of British Independent Schools in the European Communities (COBISEC, 💻 www.cobisec.org) has a section on Spain and one with vacancies for teachers (although this is throughout the world, not just Spain).

The Council of International Schools, which is a registered charity, has a teacher placement service. You can register your details and qualifications and apply to join the service. Details can be found on the website (💻 www.cois.org/recruitment), but remember that this is a service for member schools around the world and not only in Spain.

Finally, bear in mind that teachers' salaries tend to be significantly lower than in the UK, for example. As one teacher said: "Don't come for the money – indeed, expect to take a wage cut. Come for the experience, the sunshine and the improved lifestyle."

11.

COMPUTING & PUBLISHING

Spain has a shortage of qualified, experienced information technology (IT) professionals to meet the growing demand – especially in the major cities, which dominate the IT market in Spain. If you have IT qualifications – which don't necessarily have to be at degree level – and experience, there are plenty of opportunities in this sector, both in the cities and in the coastal areas. IT tends to be used as an umbrella term covering technical fields, such as systems management and software, and general sectors, such as internet marketing, web design and development, and web-hosting. This chapter looks briefly at the former, including details of salaries, and more closely at the latter because, according to those in the industry, it's a significant growth area – and experts say that the growth will continue for the foreseeable future.

This chapter also explores how the IT sector is developing and changing and the growth of 'lap-top businesses', which can base themselves almost anywhere. This development provides scope for a new breed of entrepreneurs who don't want to be tied to one location. You may even be able to enjoy the lifestyle that Spain has to offer you and your clients but, thanks to the internet, keep your business registered in your home country and so avoid some of the labyrinthine Spanish bureaucracy. Or you may choose to do this as a springboard to basing yourself in Spain permanently.

The IT revolution has enabled writers, editors, proofreaders and other publishing professionals to work anywhere in the world. This chapter looks briefly at the opportunities, most of which are open to people living anywhere in the world and not just in Spain.

INFORMATION TECHNOLOGY IN SPAIN

The information technology sector in Spain is moving so fast that the government, internet providers and many Spanish companies are finding it hard to keep up. Spain was something of a latecomer to the IT revolution, which didn't begin until the mid-'80s. The number of internet users in Spain at the end of 2003 was just under 10 million, compared with 25 million in the UK, whose population is only 50 per cent larger. But, although Spain still lags behind the much of the developed world, it's catching up fast and, thanks to the recent dramatic growth, some analysts predict that it will soon be one of the top internet business markets. The Spanish government knows that it's a key element in the economic growth of the country and has launched various initiatives in the last few years to bridge the gap between Spain and other countries. It has been very active in promoting e-commerce and internet use among the population and plans to spend around €25 million over the next three years providing broadband internet access to towns in rural areas, although a large percentage of the population lives in small towns with narrow streets which make installing the necessary cables difficult.

If you've had experience of either the UK or US markets, you will find that the Spanish market is several years behind what you're used to, but that can be to your advantage in terms of getting a job. Frank Reilly – an IT consultant from the UK who runs an internet consultancy with the same name as its website address (🖳 www.and-m.com) in Valencia, where he has been based for the last six years – compares the sector with that of London at the height of the dot com boom: "Around 2001, the industry in Spain mirrored London in the '90s. There was a lot of excitement about potential growth which was similar to the initial verve in London: people were setting up companies and opening studios everywhere, but it soon turned into disappointment when the majority of them discovered that there just wasn't the revenue there to make a profit. Now I find that much of my work is advising small to medium-size enterprises who want to take their marketing overseas and need to know how to use the internet effectively to help them do that."

Frank tends to have three types of client: Spaniards who want to take their marketing overseas – and these are usually property-related; expatriates starting up small businesses who want to use the internet to promote their products; and a few UK companies wanting to market to Spain. "Spanish companies need more support than the UK companies I deal with," he says. "They need to understand how to use the internet effectively to market their products abroad. It's currently a very under-developed area so there are opportunities. Spanish businesses are not as proactive as they could be and tend not to think through the implications of, say, having their website available in English or other languages. Businesses have been slow to understand the need to adapt their marketing approaches in internet terms in order to keep pace with the rest of the world. However, there's an increasing desire to learn these days, far more so than when I came to Spain six years ago. Spanish companies are becoming more and more aware that the internet is a cost-effective method of marketing."

Frank's advice to those thinking of trying out their IT skills in Spain, apart from learning the local language (see below), is to be financially realistic and learn how to network successfully: "Allow enough money to live on for at least two years. I've been here for over six years and it's only relatively recently that I've felt I'm making some real headway.

That's partly because I've spent time building a good reputation and making the right kind of contacts. The other thing I would advise is that you must register yourself as self-employed and have official status in Spain. There are no short cuts to this and it's worth it just to be taken seriously as a professional."

Frank cautions those who say that if you have access to the internet you can work anywhere: "This definitely has limited application in Spain. Of course, the internet can get you a long way forward in a shorter period of time, but the Spanish business market thrives on personal contact. Spaniards like to meet you, get to know you and trust you before they will deal with you. You will find that almost no one replies to emails or telephone calls, especially from someone they've never met. If you make sure you combine good use of the internet with personal contact, you will be far more successful than if you just sit at your keyboard all day."

A skilled professional in IT systems management with around ten years' experience can command a salary of around €45,000 and a programmer with roughly five years' experience can expect a salary of around €27,000. IT jobs in Spain are listed on a number of websites, including the following:

- 🖳 **www.computrabajo.es** – In Spanish only but gives and idea of what the job situation is like in different areas of Spain;

- 🖳 **www.hays.es** – Available in English, with an extensive IT section including surveys on the sector and an indication of average salaries;

- 🖳 **www.manpower.co.uk** – The Manpower site, in English, with a section called X-Border Connections containing information about jobs available abroad, including IT jobs in Spain.

LANGUAGE

If you choose to work or do business in the IT sector in any of the big cities –whether it's Madrid, Barcelona or Valencia – your first consideration should be your language skills. You must be able to speak fairly fluent Spanish and have a working knowledge of any local languages and dialects. In Madrid, the language situation is relatively straightforward: Castilian Spanish is spoken by everyone. but in Barcelona the main language is Catalan, and in Valencia some people will speak a dialect of Catalan which called *valenciano* (see page 31).

There are some opportunities in the IT sector for those with less than fluent Spanish (see below), but one IT professional based in Barcelona says that jobs in Spanish companies are 'untouchable' without fluent Spanish. Similarly, Frank Reilly, whose business deals with internet-focused marketing and project management, stresses that language is **the** most important consideration, especially if you're planning to work in an area where a regional language is spoken, such as Valencia: "It's a challenge you must meet head on if you're going to stand a chance. Language is probably the biggest obstacle which will prevent you from accessing all kinds of business and job opportunities."

If your Spanish isn't fluent, there may be opportunities with the many large foreign companies that are based in the big cities, especially Barcelona, and who need IT workers for their projects. Some short-term jobs are available and, because of the international nature of the business, Spanish isn't always required. This kind of job could be a good start to gain some experience and make some contacts in the IT sector in Spain. Barcelona is also home to several call centres catering for the European market, where you may find a job which doesn't require any Spanish. In coastal areas, where there are large numbers of expatriate residents who require English-speaking services, you can usually find opportunities in IT if you're a native English speaker with less than fluent Spanish.

SETTING UP

Don Graham, a website designer working in southern Spain, moved from the UK at the end of 2003 to take up a job with a web design company. He'd had plenty of experience in software and web design and development and didn't really research IT jobs in Spain before he arrived. "The good thing about having IT skills is that they're easily transferable," he says. "I was offered a job here unexpectedly and decided to go for it without doing much research because I know I can always get a job. We kept our flat in the UK so that if the Spanish IT sector takes a dip, I can go back there and know I will find work easily."

Don made lots of useful contacts with that first job and gained useful knowledge about the IT sector in southern Spain, but he was hungry for more. "I was constantly watching the press for job advertisements in other web design companies to try to get an idea of how the IT industry was growing and developing and how I might benefit from that. I didn't want to be involved with a one-man band but to be part of a professional operation that provided excellent customer service and was taken seriously within the sector."

Don took plenty of time to make the right kind of contacts and he eventually set up the type of company he wanted to be part of with a former colleague and his girlfriend. "The contacts I'd made were everything and, thanks to them, once we were up and running, the business came in thick and fast – and we found all sorts of other ways to help our business grow just because we had the right contacts. Anyone moving here who wants to make a living should take time to build up an extensive network of contacts in all areas of life. Not only will it help your business, but it will also widen your social sphere, which can, in turn, produce more business contacts."

Don's company, MT-Directo, which was formed in the autumn of 2004, is involved with web design and hosting, corporate image design and database management. "We decided not to limit ourselves to the south of Spain," says Don. "There's so much potential for IT in the rest of the country that we decided to base one of our partners in Barcelona. Not only do we get a Barcelona perspective on the IT sector – and it's one of the top cities to do business in Spain [see page 49] – but it also gives us useful contacts there. We've also opened an office in Madrid, and the company has its registered address there. Again, we wanted to be in touch with the IT sector in the capital city, but we've also found that other businesses take us more seriously because we have a Madrid address. Sadly, many people don't trust businesses on the Costa del Sol because of its bad reputation for fly-by-night or illegal businesses. We're a professional organisation and we didn't want anyone thinking otherwise. It takes a lifetime to build a reputation and five minutes to destroy it."

Laptop Businesses

David Kubiak, an experienced IT professional from the UK, worked in the sector in Barcelona for three years before setting up his own business, RegioNegocios.com, at the beginning of 2003. He used his IT skills and experience and brought together all the services he found distinctly lacking when he was trying to set up his own business. "There's a need for more practical help and advice for foreign entrepreneurs," he says, "so my company offers a full range of services for small business start-ups. We help clients through the required procedures for setting up a Spanish company, either once they're in Spain or via one of our team in the UK, before they arrive. A natural extension of this was opening the business centre that I operate, and it's from there that I've seen an emerging area of internet business."

David discovered that his facilities and services were attracting what have become known as 'laptop businesses'. The owners of these companies come to Spain for the quality of life and bring their business with them, but they're usually offering services to clients in their home country and want the flexibility of operating from both places. They're almost all English-speaking foreigners who need an accessible infrastructure to do business. "They find it virtually impossible as non-residents with limited Spanish language skills to get involved with the usual services, such as contracts on offices or telephone lines," explains David. "In any case, why pay rent on an office when you aren't here half the time and aren't sure when you will be? I can offer them telephone lines, internet access and office space – everything they need, whenever they need it. This way they get the best of both worlds."

Carrie Frais is a woman who has worked hard to get the best of both worlds. She's originally from London, but Barcelona has always been close to her heart. As a journalist she spent two years in the city in 1992 and didn't want to leave, but she decided that there would be more job opportunities in her chosen career – a television and radio reporter – back in London. Ten years later, she returned to turn her new business concept into reality, not only exploiting a gap in the tourist market but operating an entirely internet-based business.

"I'd done a fair bit of indirect market research into what people want from those increasingly popular short breaks abroad," says Carrie. "Most of my ideas were just a gut feeling and I canvassed opinions from friends and colleagues in the media who are often well tuned in to emerging trends. What those friends were saying was that they wanted more independence when booking holidays and an experience to take home with them afterwards. Carrie decided that she would offer something that allowed them to truly delight in Barcelona, but avoid the usual tourist trail.

Her company, IntoBarcelona.com, was born at the beginning of 2003 and offers small groups and individuals a different perspective on Barcelona. She organises *tapas* and wine tours, Catalan cooking courses, which include visiting the famous Boqueria market in the city and choosing the food before cooking it. There are also Spanish lessons and art classes, walking tours and 'pampering' weekends. She has achieved what she set out to do: allow visitors to enjoy the city but also experience something a little different at the same time.

Carrie spent around a year researching the viability of her business ideas during which time she did a business course at the Portobello Business Centre in the UK. "The course was excellent and very reasonably priced because it's subsidised by the EU," says Carrie. "The staff there gave me a plenty of support and mentoring. I also made sure I spoke to as many people as I could who had set up companies and asked them to be honest about the problems and possible pitfalls. Once I got to Barcelona, I took advantage of the good British business networks that are operating there. The British Chamber of Commerce in Barcelona has regular lunches and networking evenings which have proved invaluable." (See **Business Networking Groups** on page 51.)

Carrie's business is unusual in that everything is done via the internet: "The way I've organised the business means that I can operate from the UK and from Barcelona, but I'm taxed in the UK. This makes things far easier in the early days, as I was already registered as self-employed in the UK and am familiar with the system. It has given me some breathing space while I'm getting things going and means that I haven't got bogged down with all the confusing bureaucracy and expense of setting up a Spanish company at a time when I need to dedicate all my time and energy to the business itself." It's legal to run a business in Spain without paying tax there provided you spend fewer than 183 days per year in Spain.

Carrie had to spend a significant amount of money on good website design and marketing, as that's where all her business comes from, but she has saved in other areas, such as renting premises. "I bought a laptop and installed a broadband connection, which is absolutely essential. I have a small office in London and work from home in Barcelona. I would say that starting up this way is probably one of the safest options. Depending on how my business goes, I can choose whether I want to operate from Spain on a more permanent basis or keep things the way they are. At the moment, I prefer to keep the business internet-led as it gives me more flexibility."

JOURNALISM & PUBLISHING

Carrie Frais has made many contacts, both business and social, who are able to live and work in Barcelona thanks to their internet connections. She has many journalist friends, for example, who are based in Spain but report to UK newspapers or magazines. Thanks to the internet, it's possible to write for publications in any part of the world wherever you are.

However, as any journalist knows, contacts are everything, so don't expect to arrive with your laptop and set up business immediately. You will still have to do plenty of research into the kind of publications you might be able to write for in Spain. Both *Benn's Media* and *Willings Press Guide* have media information and entries on newspapers and periodicals all over the world, including Spain, and are a good place to start your research. *Benn's Media* is published by United Business Media International (🖳 www.ubminfo.com) and comes in several volumes. The European volume lists publications in Spain, with brief details about subject areas covered and contact details. It's only available in a print edition, which is fairly expensive, but UK public libraries usually have a copy available for research purposes. *Willings Press Guide* is available on free trial via the internet (🖳 www.mediainfo.co.uk) but costs around £300 to buy (in hard copy or on CD).

If you've been a writer in your home country, try to persuade editors who know your work to use you as their Spanish 'correspondent'. That way you will have some work in the early days, when local contacts and work are likely to be thin on the ground. Whatever happens, make sure that you can support yourself financially for at least a year.

There's a growing number Spanish lifestyle magazines available in the UK (see **Appendix B**), whose readers are usually keen to live and work in Spain themselves. Their hunger for information about all things Spanish and all areas of Spain seems to continue unabated. If you're on the spot and can persuade an editor you've found a different angle on a popular topic, such as house buying or finding a job, it could be the start of a long and happy relationship. There's also no shortage of English-language publications available in both the cities and coastal areas of Spain, where large numbers of expatriates gather (see **Appendix B**). Note, however, that many of these are free publications, which make their money solely from advertising, so they don't usually pay well.

Even if you're working from Spain via the internet for an English-speaking publication, you should be able to speak some Spanish; the more fluent you are, the easier it will be to do your job professionally, as most of your local research will have to be done in Spanish.

Writing for the Internet

A growing number of Spanish companies and government departments have websites in English, and this is another area where your writing skills might be in demand. There's no shortage of internet pages to write for, and the subjects covered are many and various, although not all companies are willing to pay for what they consider to be a 'free' medium and much the same strictures apply here as to journalism and publishing (see above).

A useful website for those wishing make use of the internet for business purposes is The Journolist (💻 www.journolist.com). It's run by John Morrish, who trains journalists for the PMA group, a leading European media and communications company. Useful books are *Researching Online for Dummies*, edited by Reva Basch, which includes a directory of research-related sites and services, and *On the Net* by Misti Jackson, which is aimed specifically at writers.

Other Publishing Possibilities

There are a host of other things that can be done at a distance if you have access to the internet: copywriting, editing, proofreading and of course, writing that novel that you always meant to. If you're thinking (dreaming?) of going down this route, you must be realistic about likely earnings, especially in the early months, as it isn't easy to find work, even if you're qualified and experienced, and work isn't usually well paid. **The chances of your writing a best-seller at your first attempt are remote, and it may be years before you even get anything published.**

There's a wealth of resources available for the aspiring writer who wants to operate from his or her laptop in Spain. Begin your research in your home country by making sure you have up-to-date guides on all the media you might want to write for. The *Writer's Handbook* (Macmillan) and the *Writers' & Artists' Yearbook* (A & C Black), which are updated annually and cost around £15, are comprehensive guides to British and American publishers and literary agents, national and regional newspapers and magazines, useful websites and film and TV companies. There are also details of relevant professional associations and training courses. *The Guardian* newspaper publishes a *Media Guide*, which contains similar contact details. It's published by Guardian Books annually and costs around £18.

12.

HEALTH

If you're a European Union citizen and a health professional, certain EU directives ensure that the qualifications you've gained in your home country will be recognised in Spain. However, recognition procedures can be complicated and long-winded and the experiences of the health professionals who contributed to this chapter varied enormously in this respect.

This chapter looks at the experiences of migrant health professionals, including doctors, nurses, midwives and physiotherapists. It also considers the position of health professionals such as osteopaths and chiropractors, who aren't regulated in Spain. It also covers alternative health practice, investigating ways of setting up a practice outside the mainstream healthcare system.

LANGUAGE & CULTURE

There are a number of issues which health professionals who are thinking of working in Spain should consider carefully before they attempt the practicalities of official recognition and validation of their qualifications. Not only will you have a different language to contend with, but you will also encounter significant cultural differences, which may make it more difficult to practise your profession in Spain than in your home country. Amongst health professionals, midwives seem to be the group that notices the cultural differences between Spain and other European countries most keenly (see page 244). **You cannot afford to underestimate the importance of these differences, even if you're planning to work in an area with a large number of English-speaking expatriates.**

According to EU regulations, member states cannot discriminate against you on the basis of language. However, the European Commission has stated that anyone wanting to pursue their profession in another member state should "possess the linguistic knowledge necessary to do so". According to a recent article in the British Medical Journal, language barriers are one of the main reasons why more doctors don't choose to work in Mediterranean countries such as Spain. **It's highly unlikely that English will be spoken by the majority of your Spanish patients.**

Unless the area you want to work in has a large expatriate population, you will need a fairly advanced command of the language, with the relevant specialist vocabulary. Even if you opt for an area where English is frequently spoken by your patients and colleagues, don't forget that you may still have deal with Spanish health professionals who may not be able to speak English – for example, if you need to refer a patient to another specialist.

Medics Travel is a company that was set up by a doctor, Mark Wilson, to help doctors, nurses, physiotherapists and other health professionals to arrange work opportunities overseas. Its website (💻 www.medics travel.co.uk) contains contact details for professional medical associations in Spain, as well as the main medical schools and their hospitals all over the mainland and the Spanish islands.

RECOGNITION OF QUALIFICATIONS

Until your qualifications are officially recognised by the relevant authority, you cannot practise your profession in Spain. The procedure can take several months, so it's best to set things in motion as soon as possible (see page 28).

There are two categories of EU Directive which affect the recognition and validation process for health professionals: Sectoral Directives and the General Directives.

Sectoral Directives

Professions regulated under the Sectoral Directive system include doctors and specialist doctors (*médicos y médicos especialistas*), general nurses (*enfermeros responsable de cuidados generales*), midwives (*matronas*), dentists (*odontólogos*) and pharmacists (*farmacéuticos*). Qualifications in these professions are automatically recognised, as the required training is similar throughout the EU. Nevertheless, you must still have your qualifications validated and register with the relevant professional body (specified in each of the sections below). In theory, if your profession comes under a Sectoral Directive, the validation process should be simple and quick. In practice, experiences of validation procedures vary wildly. One Scottish dentist had his qualifications authorised without problems in a few weeks, while an experienced community midwife had endless complications and waited 18 months for hers to be validated. As in all matters connected with Spanish bureaucracy, patience is essential.

General Directives

Professions regulated under the General Directive system include physiotherapists (*fisioterapeutas*), opticians (*ópticos*), chiropodists (*podólogos*), psychologists (*psicólogos*), occupational therapists (*terapeutas ocupacionales*) and speech therapists (*logopedas*). The full list can be found on the website of the Ministry for Education, Sport and Culture (see page 241). Recognition and validation under this system is more complicated than under the Sectoral Directive system because these professions aren't automatically recognised. A European Working Party is currently trying to minimise the paperwork and duration of validation periods, but no progress has yet been made in this direction.

If your profession is regulated under the General system, the competent authority will have to examine the kind of training you've had and check that the duration and content is as close as possible to those required for the same profession in Spain. Details of the documents you must provide to apply for recognition and validation under the General system are set out on page 28, but bear in mind that they vary considerably, as the experiences of the professionals included in this chapter show.

DOCTORS

The Spanish health service is very similar in structure to the National Health Service in the UK, but unlike the UK, it's currently suffering a glut of qualified doctors, especially general practitioners (GPs). However, with the ever-growing number of foreign residents in the coastal areas and the islands comes corresponding increase in demand for English-speaking doctors. They tend to work in private health centres and clinics, mainly used by expatriates. Nevertheless, it's still a relatively small market and it isn't easy to become established.

Doctors in Spain are allowed to advertise their services and have to learn to sell themselves, which may feel strange and uncomfortable at first to those used to working for a public health service. "The work can be sporadic," said one GP from the UK who works in a private medical centre on the Costa del Sol and has his own practice further inland. "I advertised for the first six months, but you cannot place an advertisement and then sit back and wait for the patients to flood in. It just doesn't happen like that and you have to understand that this is perfectly normal. The best advertising is word of mouth but it takes time to build up your reputation. You must learn to network, make contacts and be patient. But at the end of the day, you must sell your services just as you would with any other business."

If you're a qualified doctor from the EU who's thinking of working in Spain, your first point of contact should be your professional body in your home country. In the UK, the British Medical Association (BMA) has an International Department which produces a document entitled *Opportunities for Doctors in the European Economic Area* (available to BMA members only) to help doctors who want information about working in Europe. The department also organises seminars with expert speakers who can advise you about getting a job abroad. The *British Medical Journal* is another useful resource and it can be read online, even before it's available in print (🖳 www.bmj.com). It contains articles dating back to 1994, and has a careers section, with articles about working abroad, and an Advice Zone.

It's an advantage to choose an area where you have contacts – either family or friends – and, needless to say, it's almost essential to be able to speak Spanish fluently. Many of the more established language schools offer intensive language courses for health professionals and will organise specialist Spanish conversation groups so that you can make contact and converse with Spanish health professionals.

Qualifications & Registration

If you're a general doctor or a specialist doctor in the EU, your qualifications will be recognised under the EU's Sectoral Directive (see above); the documents you must produce are listed on page 28. General information is available from the EU website – specifically the fact sheets for recognition of medical qualifications in Spain (🖳 http://europa.eu. int/youreurope/index_es.html), which provide details of what's required for Spain and an email link for specific queries.

Your starting point in Spain should be the Ministry for Education, Culture and Sport in Madrid; the department you need is the Subdirección General de Títulos, Convalidaciones y Homologaciones, Paseo del Prado 28 – 4a planta, E-28014 Madrid (☎ 915 065 600). The Spanish Medical Association (Consejo General de Colegios Oficiales de Médicos, C/Villanueva 11, 28001 Madrid, 🖳 www.cgcom.org) is the professional body for doctors. Although the site is only in Spanish, it contains a list of all the medical colleges throughout the country with their contact details. You must become registered with the college (*colegio*) nearest to where you will be practising and must have professional liability insurance, which can be purchased relatively cheaply through the college.

The BMA (see above) can provide information on registration and immigration for most countries as well as hints and advice from doctors who have worked abroad and guidance on returning to work in the UK after a stint abroad.

NURSES

Along with a glut of doctors, Spain has an excess of qualified nurses. According to an article in the *Costa Blanca News* in September 2004, there are around 15,000 qualified nurses in the Valencian Community alone, and a third of those are unemployed, which is why many of them travel abroad to work. The Spanish health service is generally excellent, health professionals are highly trained and the latest technology is available in most major hospitals. Spain has a public health system, and anyone who contributes to the social security system receives free or low cost healthcare. Where it differs from healthcare systems in northern Europe and the US is in terms of aftercare. The Spanish health service assumes that patients have relatives and friends willing to care for them after an operation or when they become elderly or sick, which means that opportunities for nursing Spanish people are limited.

On the other hand, many expatriates, who have left family and friends behind at home, find themselves needing nursing care after an operation or when they become less mobile because of old age or illness – care that they may not be able to obtain in Spain. If you're planning to use your nursing qualifications in Spain, you should therefore look for an area with a large expatriate population – preferably retired people – particularly if your language skills aren't up to working in the Spanish health service. There are nursing agencies in coastal areas, which can place English-speaking nurses to provide post-operative care and ongoing nursing assistance to expatriates. They should interview you and check your qualifications in your home country and arrange recognition of those qualifications in Spain before placing you. Agencies aren't always easy to find, as few advertise. Medical centres and recruitment agencies (see page 73) may have details of local nursing agencies, which may be listed in local newspapers or the English-language press (see **Appendix B**). There are online directories of agencies in certain areas, e.g. ▯ www.go marbella.com on the Costa del Sol and ▯ www.costablancanet guide.com on the Costa Blanca.

The manager of a nursing agency of long standing on the Costa del Sol said that there's considerable demand for qualified and caring nurses: "Caring is the operative word here. It's important to remember that most of our nursing is done in the patient's home and patients are often old and infirm. Our nurses must be flexible and adapt to the patient's needs. Professionalism is vital, but it isn't like working on a hospital ward; we offer a far less clinical service." It's a service that's popular with patients. The agency has been in business for 16 years and has never needed to advertise. The manager advises any nurse thinking of coming to work in Spain to do lots of research and to begin by working as part of a team, rather than going it alone. "You need the support of a medical centre or an agency so that you have other health professionals who can help if you have a problem."

Nursing can be a precarious way to make a living in Spain and you must be prepared to do plenty of networking, advertise your services and generally sell yourself. One nurse who works on the Costa del Sol said that the most important piece of advice for those who might want to do the same is to learn Spanish: "We may be on the Costa del Sol," she said, "and of course you can get by without learning the language, but if you really want to do a good job, you need to be able to communicate with both Spanish patients and Spanish professionals. I do have a few Spanish patients, but I cannot talk to them at the level I'd like to. That's vital in the medical profession and something you take for granted in your home country. I'm working very hard to learn the language. I know I will get far more professional satisfaction when I'm able to communicate with my patients on more than a superficial level."

Qualifications

If you're a nurse or a specialist nurse (which includes midwives) your qualifications will be automatically recognised under the EU's Sectoral Directive system (see page 239). However, the nurses and midwives interviewed for this book all had problems with the recognition process and say that it was difficult and unnecessarily complicated. As one British midwife, who's practising in southern Spain, put it: "We may be used to Spanish doctors and nurses in the UK, but the authorities here have very little experience of English medical practitioners." Problems may arise if you completed your training before the EU Directives were put in place. This happened to one experienced community midwife, who had to go back to her training school to track down a copy of the original course syllabus, which had to be translated and submitted with all her other paperwork.

The Royal College of Nursing (RCN) and the Nursing and Midwifery Council (NMC) in the UK both have international sections which may be able to help with advice about recognition of qualifications. The professional association in Spain is the Spanish Nurses' Association (Organización Colegial de Enfermería, 💻 www.ocenf.org). The website is only in Spanish but includes a list of the *colegios* throughout the country, so that you can contact your nearest one to apply for registration; if you click on *Colegios Provinciales* you can use the map to find the contact details you need.

MIDWIVES

Although Spain currently has an excess of doctors and nurses, it has a shortage of midwives. Community midwives, who look after women throughout their pregnancy, don't exist in Spain. Midwives work exclusively in the labour ward and in a few health centres offering ante-natal care. Pregnancy is generally treated as a medical condition and so obstetric care tends to be medically orientated from day one. Women are referred to an obstetrician, who's usually male, and there's no professionally trained woman who can answer all their questions. Giving birth is generally a more clinical process than in some other European countries, with very few home births and hardly any 'natural' births.

In coastal areas of Spain, the expatriate population is getting younger and more women from other European countries are having babies there. Consequently, there's a demand for the same style of ante- and post-natal care and birthing methods that they've been used to in their home country. Liz Arthur, an experienced midwife who came to the Costa del Sol in 2001, offers her services to both expatriate and Spanish women and has an agreement with a hospital in Marbella, where she has created a birth centre environment, which gives women a choice about where they give birth and a more familiar style of care, whichever type of birth they have.

However, the agreement with the hospital was only achieved after a tremendous amount of hard work on Liz's part and with the help of a Spanish consultant obstetrician and gynaecologist who works with her. Liz says that the fact that he trained in the UK and so understands both the Spanish and the British systems helps tremendously: "It has been an uphill struggle, but it's slowly starting to pay off. My first homebirth in Spain was in a fourth floor flat in Malaga. The patient spoke no English and I spoke very little Spanish, but we got there. She was grateful that my skills enabled her to have the home birth she wanted and I felt privileged to be there. Since that first delivery, I've come a long way. I'm getting positive feedback from both the home and the hospital deliveries I've done with Spanish and expatriate women. I feel at last as if I'm achieving what I set out to do – complement the service that's already here."

Liz's achievements are significant in that they were the result of persistence, hard work and extensive research, without which you won't go far in any business in Spain.

Liz decided to go it alone, but by her own admission, it was tough going. If you're a trained midwife, you may find it easier, certainly at the beginning, to work in a medical centre in an area with a large expatriate population. You will make valuable contacts and have the support network of other health professionals around you. Liz's advice to those thinking of working in Spain is to research, research, research and don't expect Spain, even the tourist areas, to be like your home country with extra sun: "I would urge anyone to make sure their professional standards are of the highest quality. Keep up your registration with your professional body in your home country. In the UK, that requires a certain amount of practical work and post-graduate training, so that you keep up to date with what's new. Finally, wherever you choose to work, you will need to speak Spanish and forget everything you ever took for granted at home. All in all, it's an enormous struggle to work in Spain, especially as a midwife, but I've found it very rewarding."

Qualifications

The qualifications required for midwifery and the registration procedure are the same as for nursing (see **Qualifications** on page 243) – in theory. Liz Arthur describes the frustrations of trying to do things 'by the book': "I had to get a verification certificate from the NMC in the UK. It had to be translated into Spanish by an official translator and then stamped by the town hall closest to the area in Spain that I was planning to practise in. Then I had to go to the Department of Education and Science in Malaga to fill in an application form and everything was sent off to Madrid. The problem was that it took six months for Madrid to approve it, by which time the original verification certificate from the UK was out of date and I had to start the process all over again. I ended up making three applications and the final one had to be stamped by a UK solicitor and then sent to the Foreign Office in London for further validation. Then I could finally register with the *colegio* here in Spain. The whole process took 18 months. It was the proverbial nightmare." Liz's experiences make it clear that validation of qualifications doesn't always go smoothly and that Spanish government departments can be rather arbitrary about their requirements.

PHYSIOTHERAPISTS

Estelle Mitchell, a UK-qualified physiotherapist with more than 26 years' experience, came to work in southern Spain almost by chance after working extensively in both the health service and the private sector in the UK. "I'd had my own private practice on Jersey for ten years, and we were about to take six months off to research various European locations, with a view to working abroad. We came to Spain for a holiday and we never left." Estelle and her husband Bob, who now run their own successful practice, Bodyworks Health Clinic, near Marbella, say that despite the wonderful lifestyle, working as a physiotherapist in Spain has been difficult.

Attitudes to physiotherapists are very different in Spain from those in the UK, for example. They treat on a prescriptive basis, as recommended by a doctor or a surgeon, rather than on a diagnostic basis, and they're usually poorly paid in comparison with the UK.

They knew that there were plenty of potential clients among the English-speaking population in southern Spain and wanted to offer them a 'gold standard': the best facilities and specialists they could. "For me, working in the Spanish health system wasn't an option," says Estelle. "Apart from anything else, you need to speak really fluent Spanish to do that, but more importantly I didn't want to work in that way. I wanted to offer the kind of services I'd been able to offer in the UK. I knew there was a need for it."

Getting the clinic going took just over nine months. "We wanted to do everything properly and legally from the word go, but achieving that hasn't been easy," explains Estelle. "We were going to work from home but discovered that it's impossible because your place of work has to be authorised by the Andalusian government (Junta de Andalucia). So we began the process of licensing the premises we're in now. First, it's hugely important that you have a fluent Spanish speaker to help you contact the Junta de Andalucia; and second, it's vital to have a Spanish lawyer who really knows what he's doing. He or she must be a specialist in this kind of area. Once the premises are registered, any medical staff who work there must also be registered which means you cannot employ anyone on an occasional basis, such as visiting specialists or locums."

Despite all of the problems that she has experienced getting things done properly in Spain (see also below), Estelle's overriding advice to other physiotherapists who want to work there is to do things the same way: "If you value your profession, jump through all the hoops, because then you can hold your head up both in Spain and in your home country. Anything less devalues the profession." She strongly advises less experienced physiotherapists not to try to work here until they've had plenty of varied experience in their home country: "There isn't the same kind of back-up network here, and it would be irresponsible and unprofessional, as you could be seriously compromising your patient's health."

Like other health professionals in Spain, Estelle says it has been a long hard road and only recently, several years down the line, is she finding that all the hard work is paying off: "I'm very busy and, although we used advertising in the early days, now I tend to have more word-of-mouth recommendations. I've managed to build up my own network of health professionals both here and in the UK who I can refer to and who support my services. We work longer hours and for less money here in Spain, but the quality of life and the enjoyment and satisfaction we get from our work is second to none. The only problem is that we haven't had a holiday since we arrived in Spain!"

Qualifications & Insurance

In terms of qualifications, physiotherapists in Spain are regulated under the EU's General Directive system of validation (see page 239), which means that the required paperwork is far more comprehensive than it is for doctors, nurses and midwives.

The Spanish Physiotherapy Association (Asociación Española de Fisioterapeutas) automatically recognises qualified physiotherapists from other EU countries but, as the WCPT website states, "reserves the right to prove individual cases and requires aptitude tests and adaptation periods if necessary." The Ministry of Health in Spain decides on the procedures for these tests and the adaptation period can be up to three months. You must register with the Spanish Physiotherapy Association and there's information on its website

(🖳 www.aefi.net), which is also available in English, although you may experience difficulties accessing the English version.

UK qualified physiotherapists can obtain help and advice about working in Spain from the Overseas Recruitment office of the Chartered Society of Physiotherapy (☎ 020-7306 6666). The Society provides general information sheets about working in particular countries, including Spain, and information about professional liability insurance cover. They can also advise about how to stay abreast of developments in the profession while you're abroad, and they offer a Return to Practice pack to support physiotherapists returning from abroad.

Estelle Mitchell says that getting her qualifications recognised and validated was an experience she wouldn't want to repeat. It took nine months and she had to produce a copy of the original curriculum that she had studied and detail all her work experience. Everything had to be translated into Spanish by an official translator and her documents had to be notarised originals. "Now, thankfully, everything is fully recognised and validated by both the Ministry of Health (Ministerio de Sanidad y Consumo) and with the local Spanish Physiotherapists' Association (Ilustre Colegio Profesional de Fisioterapeutas de Andalucia)."

Estelle is insured through her professional college in Spain and is a member of the Organisation for Chartered Physiotherapists in Private Practice (OCPPP, 🖳 www.physiofirst.org.uk), which also insures her. However, to maintain her registration of OCPPP and the UK regulatory body, the Health Professions Council (HPC), Estelle must do a minimum of 25 hours of postgraduate work per year, all of which must be properly certified. "There's no easy facility for postgraduate education here, but I work hard to do all the work that's required because it's important to me that I keep up my registration and so can maintain my professional standing. One of the other conditions of my UK insurance is that my equipment is serviced regularly, but I've found that difficult too, so I've had to fly an expert over to ensure that the equipment is up to the required standard."

A useful website for physiotherapists is the European region of the World Confederation for Physical Therapy (WCPT, 🖳 www.physio-europe.org). This provides helpful information on migration to all European countries, including Spain, and lists requirements for applying to the competent authority, which in Spain is the Ministry of Health (Ministerio de Sanidad y Consumo).

OSTEOPATHS & CHIROPRACTORS

Osteopaths and chiropractors who want to work in Spain find themselves in something of a grey area, as neither profession is officially recognised by the Spanish government. Moreover, both osteopaths and chiropractors may find it difficult to become established, especially with Spanish patients, who are generally conservative about trying what they consider to be 'alternative' therapies. It may make sense to work in an area where there's a large expatriate population, who are familiar with osteopathic and chiropractic treatments in their home countries.

Osteopaths

The General Osteopathic Council (GOC) in the UK is currently talking to a number of other European countries about recognition procedures, but Spain isn't among them. The Spanish government has said that it will consider recognition, but is waiting to see which other countries approve it. However, although the profession isn't officially recognised in Spain, it isn't illegal and there are many osteopaths practising there, some of whom are listed on the GOC website (🖥 www.osteopathy.org.uk). If you want to practise as an osteopath in Spain, it's worth contacting one or two of those listed, especially those practising in the area that you're considering, although they may not all relish the prospect of your setting up in competition and either decline to offer advice or, worse, give you misleading information.

Chiropractors

Most chiropractors working in Spain are foreigners, as it isn't yet possible to study for a career as a chiropractor there and all the members of the Spanish Chiropractic Association (Asociación Española de Quiropráctica, 🖥 www.quiropractica-aeq.com), which is affiliated to the European Chiropractors' Union (ECU), gained their degrees in foreign universities.

The General Chiropractic Council (GCC) in the UK doesn't list members working abroad in the same way as the GOC, but you can find details of members of the ECU practising in Spain on its website (🖥 www.chiropractic-ecu.org). Try to make contact with one of them and ask his advice.

ALTERNATIVE HEALTHCARE

Alternative healthcare is relatively new to Spain. It's growing in popularity – in some areas more than others – but there's still a long way to go before it achieves the status it enjoys in some other European countries or in the US. Consequently, it's potential growth area, but – like any new market – not without its teething problems.

Alternative therapists of any kind coming to work or set up a practice in Spain face two main problems. The first is that the majority of alternative therapies aren't licensed by the Spanish government. Whilst it isn't illegal to practise alternative therapies, the lack of regulation can lead to bad practice and all practitioners can be tarred with the same brush. Phil Speirs, who publishes *La Chispa* magazine, an alternative living guide to Andalusia, strongly recommends that you bring all your qualifications and plenty of references with you and have them translated into Spanish.

The second problem you may find is that your patient or client base may be restricted to expatriates, especially if you work in a coastal area or on one of the Spanish islands. Many Spanish people are conservative in their attitudes towards healthcare and reluctant to try unorthodox treatments; they want a recommendation from someone they trust who has tried it before they will go as far as making an appointment. As one therapist put it: "It's very much a last resort for a Spanish person to try an alternative therapy. They just don't use alternative treatments in the same way that many northern Europeans do. So most of my business comes from the expatriate community."

Nevertheless, in many coastal areas and some of the major cities there are a growing number of alternative therapists practising acupuncture, homeopathy and massage, as well as offering classes in pilates and yoga. There are also holistic centres, alternative medical centres and yoga retreats in the countryside. (For information about yoga teaching, see page 270). This means that, although there's plenty of potential, there's also plenty of competition for your services, so it's important that you do your market research well. It's also an advantage to be trained to offer more than one type of treatment so that you can offer a variety of services.

Research

There are two useful sources of information about alternative health practices in Andalusia: the Andalucia Com SL website (🖳 www.

andalucia.com – click on 'alternative health') provides a comprehensive guide, and *La Chispa* magazine (Apartado de Correos 281, 29100 Coín, Malaga, 🖥 www.lachispa.net), which is available in yoga schools, alternative healthcare clinics, health food shops and other outlets, contains a wide range of relevant articles and contacts, and advertisements for alternative therapists. The Barcelona Healers and Therapists Network (🖥 www.barcelonahealersandtherapists.net) can provide a list of English-speaking alternative therapists in the Barcelona area.

Make contact with some of the more established alternative health centres in the area that you're interested in. Introduce yourself, let them have details of your qualifications and try to participate in any events they may be organising. Some centres have open days and workshops which are useful sources of contacts and information and will give you an idea of the competition and your likely client base. If you're planning to work on your own, some centres will allow you to use their treatment rooms and equipment for a fee and some have a database of therapists. Ask if they will add your details and put you on their mailing list.

Insurance

It's important to have public liability insurance before you start work. Cover can be hard to obtain, however, owing to the lack of regulation of therapists. Try insurance companies that specialise in cover for expatriates; there are advertisements in the English-language press (see **Appendix B**) and alternative health publications (e.g. *La Chispa* – see above). If your Spanish is up to it, it's worth contacting the Spanish Naturopaths Association (Federación Española de Profesionales en Naturopatía/FENACO, 🖥 www.fenaco.net), which was started more than 20 years ago to help naturopaths, including acupuncturists, homeopaths and osteopaths, who choose to work in Spain or abroad. FENACO attempts to regulate naturopathy and aims for its recognition by the Spanish government; there are branches in many areas of Spain, listed on the website. One of the services offered to members is professional insurance. Some clinics and centres will give discounts to therapists who use their facilities and are members of FENACO, as the organisation is highly regarded.

13.

CHILD CARE

There are a growing number of opportunities in some areas of Spain for expatriates who can offer good quality child care. If you're young, energetic and like children, there's no better way to learn the language than to live with a Spanish family and work as an au pair. This chapter looks at how and where you can find an au pair job in Spain, although this is by no means the only child care avenue open to you as a foreigner and indeed isn't really a way of making a living but may provide a stepping stone to more permanent and better paid work.

There are possibilities for English-speaking nannies, in the cities and coastal areas – and not only among the expatriate population. Spanish parents who need a nanny are often keen to have a native English-speaker caring for their children so that they benefit from hearing English spoken on a daily basis. This chapter explores the best routes to a nanny job in Spain and also looks at the experiences of two women who have set up a child care agency, providing nannies and babysitters to both Spanish and expatriate parents in Barcelona.

There are also an increasing number of English nurseries and day care centres in Spain – especially in areas popular with expatriates – catering for children of all nationalities. This chapter includes the experiences of Julie Salmon, who set up an English nursery near Granada in Andalusia more than a decade ago.

If you think that you might want to work in child care in Spain, it's important to understand that attitudes towards children and the care of children are significantly different from those in most northern European countries, especially the UK. Generally, Spanish children aren't put to bed early in the evening or left in the care of a babysitter while their parents go out to dinner. Children and babies of all ages are involved in every part of Spanish family life, and that includes taking them to a restaurant at 10.30pm and bringing them home in the early hours of the morning. Children are genuinely welcomed everywhere and the relaxed attitude towards their presence means that Spanish parents don't have the same kind of child care needs as parents in some other countries.

Many Spanish working mothers leave their children in the care of other family members, and the thought of paying someone to care for their child – especially someone they don't know well – is anathema. Granny is preferable to a stranger – even one with a long list of admirable qualifications – and what's more Granny doesn't charge! Those who don't have a family member they can call on usually use a nursery or day care centre known as a *guarderia*.

If all this leaves you wondering whether child care in Spain is a possibility worth exploring, take heart. Things are changing, albeit slowly. An increasing number of Spanish parents are keen for their children to learn English and there's a growing and increasingly young expatriate population, who require the kind of child care they've been used to in their home country.

AU PAIRS

If you're a young person, working as an au pair in Spain can be a wonderful way to learn the language and experience Spanish life, although it's rarely a way of making a living long term. There are no particular qualifications for the job, but it obviously helps if you're used to (and like) children, have done some babysitting or have younger brothers and sisters of your own – and of course, don't mind helping around the house. Au pair posts are generally available only to girls aged between 17 and 30. Families sometimes accept young men if their children are all boys, but it's far more difficult for males to find a position.

It will make your settling in period easier if you can speak some Spanish before you arrive and you will usually need to complete the relevant forms and write a simple letter of introduction in Spanish. Once you've settled in, you will be surprised how swiftly your language skills improve thanks to your total immersion in Spanish family life. You will be required to work for around five hours per day (maximum of 30 hours per week), looking after the children and doing light housework and will also be expected to babysit one or two evenings a week (maximum of three). The host family must allow you to attend Spanish classes and religious worship, usually on a Sunday. You should have at least one free day a week, possibly two, usually at the weekend. In return for this you will receive free meals and accommodation, which should include your own room, and receive a small sum of 'pocket money' each week, which is currently around €70, although this should be higher if you're staying in one of the large cities, where the cost of living is higher.

Make sure that you use a reputable introduction agency which understands that the au pair experience should be a mutually beneficial one for the au pair and the host family and screens applicants accordingly. If your placement works well, you will have made friends for life and had a valuable intercultural experience, within the security of a family setting. However, there are always families – in any country – who think that au pairs are simply cheap labour and abuse the system. If you feel that you're being taken advantage of or you're unhappy, a good agency will always help you to find another post. **Never stay in a post where you're unhappy or are being badly treated**. Many EU countries, including Spain, have signed the European Agreement on Au Pair Placement, which will give you an idea of what to expect working as an au pair in Europe. There's detailed information about this on 🖳 www.europa-pages.com/aupair, along with lists of reputable au pair agencies throughout Spain.

Most families need an au pair to help them during the school year, running from September to June, and usually for a minimum of six months. Some agencies offer shorter summer placements during the school holidays. If you're an EU national, all you need is a passport and it's advisable **not** to commit to anything before you arrive in Spain, as it's difficult to obtain a reliable impression of a prospective family, your accommodation and the area in general from abroad. Before you go, check out local agencies in the area you'd like to be in so that you can make contact on arrival. Try to arrive in Spain around a month before you want to start work, to give yourself some breathing space and the chance to familiarise yourself with what's available in the area as well as attend any interviews.

If you're a non-EU national, it's imperative that you obtain a written job offer before leaving your home country. You must have a visa to work as an au pair in Spain and won't be able to get one if you don't have a job offer from a Spanish family. It's advisable to obtain a job offer through a reputable agency, which will usually help you with your visa arrangements. Visa information can be found on page 23.

NANNIES

If you want to work as a nanny as opposed to an au pair, you should be experienced and well qualified. Although no official qualifications are required to care for children in their own home, any reputable nanny agency should insist on a qualification similar to a the National Nursery Examination Board (NNEB) qualification in the UK, which includes two years' full-time training. In addition, you will be expected to produce references from at least two previous employers – which will be checked. Salaries are around €700 to €1,000 per month for a live-out position, depending on the area you're working in.

If you'd like to work in any of the main Spanish cities, you must be able to speak fairly good Spanish. In Barcelona, you will need some knowledge of Catalan as well as Castilian (see page 31). Even if you plan to work with an English-speaking family, you should still make sure that you can speak some Spanish. **As a nanny, you're responsible for young children and, should there be an emergency, your Spanish language skills could save a life.**

There are several ways of finding a job as a nanny. You can approach an agency in your home country, check job opportunities in specialist magazines or via the internet. Be careful if you're searching the internet for jobs, however. Families may advertise privately and it's impossible to know how genuine they are. It's much safer to go through a registered agency. Approach a reputable nanny recruitment agency in your home country that deals with placements in Europe. Often these agencies will also deal with au pair placements and should be members a recognised professional body, which polices the working practices of its members. Relevant organisations are the International Au Pair Association (IAPA, 💻 www.iapa.org) or the Recruitment and Employment Confederation (REC, 💻 www.rec.uk.com), which aims to raise standards in the childcare industry. The agency should have representatives in Spain, so that you have an agency contact when you begin work. It's important to have someone to go to in Spain if you have any problems with your placement.

Specialist magazines which advertise nanny jobs in Spain include *The Lady*, *Nursery World* and *Montessori World*, an online magazine which includes job listings (💻 www.montessori.co.uk).

Setting Up an Agency

Julia Fossi and Julie Stephenson started up a nanny and babysitting agency, called Tender Loving Canguros, in early 2004, partly because there was no local provision for English-speaking child care but plenty of expatriate families who seemed to need it. "We have four children between us and, when we arrived with our families we couldn't speak the language fluently," says Julia. "Although we wanted our children to integrate into Spanish society, we felt rather uncomfortable leaving them with a carer who we couldn't communicate properly with." They therefore started their agency to cater to the needs of expatriate parents in Barcelona, but the two women have also discovered that their English-speaking nannies are popular with Spanish parents. "They're very keen to have an English carer for their children because it means they begin to pick up the basics of English at an early age. Spanish children begin to learn English at school at a much earlier age now; it's obligatory from the age of six, so it's a useful bonus for the parents that use us."

Julie owned a nanny agency in Australia and so has plenty of experience supplying nannies, but she finds Barcelona – and Spain – very different: "You always feel as if you're breaking new ground. While that's very exciting, it can be frustrating and time-consuming too." Despite Julie's experience, it has been a complicated business getting their agency established: "We weren't even sure if we wanted to go down the child care route," says Julia, "but one of the best things we did was to go to one of Barcelona's business networking sessions. The people there gave us lots of ideas and, when we finally came up with the nanny agency idea, we were able to get an objective view and some useful advice from them."

Business networking groups are flourishing in Barcelona (see page 51) and are invaluable both for making contacts and as a professional sounding board. Julie and Julia attended, among others, sessions organised by ENBarcelona. "They're excellent," says Julia, "because most of the people who attend are English speaking and involved in the business community, so they give you an insight into what's going on. What's more, they provide a platform for you to present your ideas because you do a 15-minute presentation about your proposed business, selling yourself and your ideas and you get instant feedback. They're often attended by professional advisers, so you can make useful contacts, which is exactly what we did."

Julia and Julie met an adviser who specialises in business start-ups and advised them about how to proceed with their ideas. He suggested that they should both work on a self-employed basis (*autónomo*) until they were sure how the business would progress, although their long-term plan is to set up a company: "We want the limited liability that a legal company gives you, because we cannot afford to be personally liable should anything go wrong." See page 96 for information about setting up a company in Spain.

Contracts & Marketing

In the early days, the two women found that the services they wanted to offer were unusual in Spain. They spent long hours with their lawyers trying to hammer out the details. "We act as an introduction agency, offering qualified child carers to families; they then sort out the contractual details between themselves," explains Julia. "It got complicated when we needed a contract between ourselves and the parents and the carers, to cover our services to both parties. We had to get hold of a similar contract from the UK and take it to a Spanish civil lawyer, who created an appropriate Spanish contract."

"We've learnt a lot," says Julia, "and we're still learning on a daily basis. We did lots of advertising with flyers to start with. They're cheap and usually fairly effective. We left them at the International Women's Club of Barcelona, which is a high profile organisation here, and also emailed rental and relocation agencies and international schools." Her advice for anyone thinking of doing a similar thing is to learn the language, both Spanish and Catalan: "Here in Barcelona, Catalan is far more important than either of us realised. We could have got more help from the local investment agencies if we'd been able to speak the language and if our promotional literature had been written in Catalan. We arrived here as expatriate wives and didn't have a chance to learn the language beforehand, but if you want to succeed in business, you cannot survive if you cannot communicate."

NURSERIES & DAY CARE CENTRES

Pre-school education isn't obligatory in Spain, but many working parents who cannot rely on the help of family or friends to care for their children turn to nurseries and day care centres. The increase in the number of Spanish women working outside the home means that *centros infantiles* or *guarderias*, as they're known, are springing up all over the country. Nevertheless, in some areas demand for places is high. In the big cities and coastal areas, where there are large numbers of expatriate residents, there are English-language *guarderias* and centres that operate on a bilingual basis. Workplace nurseries, previously unheard of in Spain, are also becoming more common as employers begin to see the benefits of providing on-site child care. Spain is undergoing a big change in its child care policies, so make sure that you're up to date with the latest requirements.

Julie Salmon opened her English nursery, called Toybox, near Granada in 1994. "I'm the only English nursery in Granada," she says, "so I have a certain amount of novelty value." She takes children from the age of 18 months to six years, when they go to school, and runs the school entirely in English: "About 90 per cent of the children are Spanish and their parents are delighted that they're in an English environment and picking up the language naturally at such an early age." She now has around 35 children attending her nursery and an ever-increasing waiting list.

Setting Up

Julie wasn't looking for a business opportunity when she began searching for a nursery place for her son, but what she found was a huge gap in the market. "I didn't mind whether my son went to a Spanish nursery or an English one, but when I began looking around, my heart sank. None of the places I visited was very child-friendly. Either they were terribly overcrowded or they were run like a military establishment, allowing no play or free expression whatsoever." At the time, Julie had no official child care training, but she was determined to do something about the situation. "Although I'd worked with children in the past, I didn't have any of the right qualifications, but I knew that I could do better than what was on offer. So I decided that, to begin with, I'd take on experienced staff who did have the right qualifications while I set about studying to train myself to the required level."

Julie went on to obtain an Honours degree in Childhood and Youth Studies, an Advanced Diploma in Child Development and a Certificate in Health and Social Care. Meanwhile, she began the long process of setting up her nursery and says that, if she had known what was involved, she would never have attempted it. She applied for permission to open her nursery and then spent more than two years waiting for a yes or a no. "During that time, the authorities lost my file somewhere between Seville and Granada and changed the law twice, which affected my application." Julie refused to give up and eventually opened her nursery in 1994, four years after the Spanish educational reforms which had brought about changes in all aspects of education, including the nursery sector.

"When I was setting up, I worked to the UK's OFSTED nursery guidelines and, fortunately, they turned out to be very similar to the new Spanish laws. It was difficult to get specific information in Spain at the time, as the law was in the process of changing but they hadn't got round to implementing the changes in the nursery sector. As it turned out, they were very strict indeed about the requirements for premises, such as the minimum sizes of classroom and the position of toilets and bathrooms. If you have a kitchen and are going to cook on the premises, you must comply with Ministry of Health regulations. The government is really tightening up on health and safety, so make sure you get good advice about the correct procedures."

"Business was very slow to start with – Granada is a tough place to start any business," recalls Julie. "At the end of the first year, the nursery was struggling financially and I decided that it wasn't a viable venture, as I was subsidising everything myself. I informed the parents that I'd decided to close and they were up in arms and even encouraged me to put up my prices so that I could keep operating! Now we have a waiting list and also run an English club in the afternoons called Chatterbox, which allows former pupils to come and keep up the level of English they achieved when they were with us.

"It's far easier now to find help and advice to start a business. Most regional and provincial governments have a department which specialises in women's issues (Instituto de Mujeres). Among other things, these are an excellent source of practical help for women in business, so make use of them," Julie advises. "I was faced with endless closed doors and pushed from pillar to post. These days it's still tough, but at least it's possible."

Staff & Qualifications

Julie advertises for staff in UK publications such as *Nursery World* and the magazine *Montessori International*, which is associated with the Montessori method of teaching. "I go back to the UK when necessary to interview staff," she says. "The main reason I employ staff from the UK is that the whole ethos of the nursery is that it's completely English – a little bit of England in Spain – and the majority of the carers and teachers are native English-speakers. That's how Toybox works and that's what the Spanish parents want. This isn't an area with a large number of expatriates and so there's not much English spoken on a daily basis. I have six staff at the moment: one is Spanish and speaks fluent English, and the rest are English – although most of them speak fluent Spanish so that they can communicate effectively with the parents."

In Spain, there are two types of pre-school: a *jardin de infancia* ('kindergarten') teaches children from birth to three years, and an *escuela de párvulos* ('nursery school') from three to six years. All teaching follows an official curriculum. Teachers must have followed a three-year university teacher training course specialising in pre-school education and have the qualification *Maestro – Especialidad de Educación Infantil* or a foreign equivalent, which enables them to teach all subjects. If you need to obtain this qualification, you must be fluent in Spanish and be able to withstand the rigours of a course which combines academic training and teaching practice. Any recognised qualifications gained in the UK or any other European country are generally recognised in Spain, although the process of official recognition can take some time.

Julie favours the Montessori method of teaching and so tends to employ teachers trained in that method as well as nursery teachers who are qualified under the UK's NVQ system. "We always apply for recognition of UK child care qualifications from Madrid, but it often takes months, if not years, to get a response." Julie and Julia aim to keep their ratio of children to carers as low as possible and to run the centre in a professional way. "We're members of the Association of Infant Centres in Andalusia," explains Julie, "which is a stamp of quality, and parents are welcome to inspect any part of the nursery at any time of the day. We have a good relationship with the parents and are now well and truly part of the community."

Julie's advice to anyone thinking of going down the same road is to take any child care qualifications you have to Spain, get them translated and try to get some experience within the Spanish nursery system: "The best way to do this is to capitalise on the fact that you're a native English-speaker. Spanish parents want their children taught or cared for by a native speaker and they're hard to find outside the main tourist areas. You don't necessarily need to be a fluent Spanish speaker yourself, although you soon will be, working in the Spanish system. Working in the child care environment is a good dry run if you're really determined to open up your own nursery."

14.

LEISURE & TOURISM

There are two areas of Spain's leisure industry that are growing faster than most and offer an array of possibilities for salaried jobs and for setting up businesses. The Spanish government is keen to promote 'active' and 'health tourism' as part of its long-term plan to diversify from Spain's traditional image as a sun, sea and sand holiday destination.

The terrain of the country lends itself well to active tourism with coastlines and mountain ranges which are perfect for all manner of sports and adventure holidays. If you're skilled in a sport of almost any kind and are looking to take advantage of Spain's climate and lifestyle, it's worth researching this increasingly popular sector.

Spanish tourism isn't just about golf and sunbathing on the Costas. There's windsurfing, both in trendy Tarifa to the south and off the coasts of Cantabria in the north, scuba diving off the Costa Brava, mountain biking and hiking on the Costa Blanca and skiing both in the Pyrenees in the north and the Sierra Nevada mountains in the south of the country. The Spanish Tourist Board's website (🖳 www.spain.info) gives details of the many sporting activities that are available in all areas of Spain.

This chapter looks at how to get a job in active or health tourism and in particular at the experiences of Giles Birch and Jonathan Buzzard, two Englishmen who have set up their own ski school in Andalusia, and of Kezia Jacobsen, who is in the process of setting up a health facility on the Costa del Sol.

Another growth area is alternative health (see **Chapter 12**) and yoga. In this chapter we investigate how British men have set up thriving yoga centres in Madrid and Marbella.

Whether you're interested in sports, in active or health tourism, or in yoga teaching, the important ingredients are experience, professionalism and – as ever – finding a gap in the market.

ACTIVE TOURISM

Jonathan Buzzard and his business partner, Giles Birch, set up a ski school, called the Ski Center (🖳 www.sierranevada.co.uk), in the Sierra Nevada mountain range, close to Granada, in 2002. It's a hugely popular ski resort and, surprisingly for many tourists and residents, only a couple of hours from Malaga and the sunny Costa del Sol. "Jonathan and I have plenty of experience both of this particular resort and as instructors," explains Giles. "I'd skied for many years and worked in France before coming to the Sierra Nevada as a Ski Guide in 1995, which was when I met Jonathan. I went on to qualify as a ski instructor with the Spanish Ski School here in the Sierra Nevada and followed that up with a series of training courses with the Spanish Ski Federation [Real Federación Española de Deportes de Invierno – RFEDI]."

There was no shortage of ski schools in the resort, but he and Jonathan identified a need for native English-speaking instructors. "There are around 30 independent ski schools here but, because the majority of visitors (around 80 per cent) are Spanish, fluent English-speaking instructors are thin on the ground. The number of UK and Irish visitors is relatively small, but it's a significant market and so Jonathan and I decided we would offer a really personalised service to our clients. Many of them are residents living on the Costas and in the Algarve in Portugal. They love the fact that it's a very Spanish resort, but at the same time appreciate having instruction in English. We guarantee that any British or American client taking a lesson with us will have either a native English-speaking instructor or at the very least someone who speaks the language fluently. We know they will get more out of their lessons if they can communicate in a relaxed way with their instructor and understand more detailed instructions."

Giles and Jonathan offer both personal one-to-one skiing tuition and a resort orientation service which means that their clients are able to concentrate on the skiing. They both agree that they wouldn't have recognised the gap in the market if they hadn't had years of experience of their market. "You've got to really know what you're doing before you start a business in this kind of area," says Giles, "but there's plenty of potential in active tourism. The government is working very hard to promote it and to create a professional and safe environment. The Ski Center is registered with the government of Andalusia and has been granted status within its active tourism programme. All our instructors must have the correct training and experience."

Qualifications & Experience

Giles suggests that the best way to start in this area is to work in a ski school just as they both did. He says they always look for recognised qualifications when they employ an instructor, along with at least a full season's worth of experience. "Safety is the biggest issue of course and, although we don't have to insist on Spanish Ski Federation qualifications, we're looking for the equivalent from an instructor's home country. The market we cater for is English-speaking so, for example, The British Association of Snowsport Instructors (BASI) qualification would be acceptable." You can find out about BASI courses and job opportunities via its website (⌨ www.basi.org).

Giles began by working for a ski tour operator, and there are plenty of similar companies that specialise in temporary work worldwide, including Spain. They offer jobs as sports and activity teachers for adventure holidays, which is a good place to start building up your experience. The PGL Company is one of the best known companies in this area and you can find information about jobs on its website (🖳 www.pgl.co.uk). Some of the jobs available in 2005 included skiing, windsurfing, canoeing, sailing and surfing instructors. If you're already skilled in any of these sports, but don't have an instructor's qualification, the company will give you full training to the required standard, if you're accepted for a position.

Another source of job advertisements in this sector is the AnyWorkAnywhere website (🖳 www.anyworkanywhere.com). Simply type in the kind of job you want to do and the relevant country and any jobs that meet your criteria are displayed. Most jobs are short-term and run from mid-January until November (except ski jobs, of course) and there are plenty of adventure holiday team member jobs available all over Europe, including Spain. You should be at least 18 years old and be an EU citizen. A useful internet portal with links to all kinds of adventure holiday job sites is 🖳 www.jobs-in-europe.net.

HEALTH TOURISM

Health tourism (sometimes called 'wellness tourism') is growing apace in all areas of Spain, from Galicia in the north to Andalusia in the south. Figures from Spain's Ministry for Industry, Tourism and Trade show that there are 128 health resorts in the country, in addition to the many health and beauty complexes and hotels with spas. There's a growing demand for well qualified staff in both coastal and inland areas from the expatriate community and young Spaniards who want to escape stressful city life for a few days in beautiful natural surroundings.

Kezia Jacobsen ran her own successful beauty business in west London for six years before deciding that her work-life balance had become somewhat uneven: "I was working six days a week and having to catch up with my paperwork on the seventh day. There was no let up," she says. She was familiar with Spain and especially the Costa del Sol area because she had spent some time working there several years before. "When I first started thinking about returning to live and work in Spain, I visited Marbella and found that, since my last visit, it had become more of a city than a tourist resort. The foreign population is far younger, there are more families living here and the international schools are full. It's a vibrant working community and seems to have become the California of Europe. The kind of people that are moving here are demanding the same kind of treatments and therapies that they've been used to in their home countries."

Research

Kezia, originally from India, has travelled extensively in the Far East, researching spas, particularly those in Thailand and Bali, and believes that they're among the best in the world. "I'm passionate about spas in the Far East and, when I decided to open my own spa, I was determined that both aesthetically and practically it would reflect the spas that I'd seen in Thailand and Bali. Spas in the Far East have an amazing sense of service, and use ancient treatments and natural products. Their philosophies are all about well-being and that's what I wanted for my centre.

I aim to treat the mind, body and soul and have a cross between a spa with all its treatments, an ashram yoga centre and a life coaching facility. I've been working on this project and helping to design it for around 18 months now and we hope to open early in 2005." Kezia's day spa, called Shanti-Som Spa, has been built in a beautiful setting with the perfect fusion of outdoor and indoor space. She has big plans to combine holidays with the treatments: "I want people to have a relaxing holiday and be pampered, but I also want them to go away with a whole experience, an education in personal development with all of their senses awakened."

Qualifications

Kezia's advice for anyone who wants to come over to Spain and work in this sector is that they should have plenty of experience and practise in a professional manner: "I have extensive experience myself and I'm always learning new skills to complement my treatments." She herself wouldn't employ anyone unless he had at least three years' experience in this area and all the recognised qualifications.

The main qualifications are those from the British Association of Beauty Therapy and Cosmetology (BABTAC, 🖳 www.babtac.com), whose education and training arm is the Confederation of International Beauty Therapy and Cosmetology (CIBTAC, 🖳 www.cibtac.com). This is the international examination board for the education and training of beauty and holistic therapists worldwide. It has a reputation for high levels of training, and more than 150 schools in 18 countries offer CIBTAC awards. There's also the highly regarded and comprehensive qualification known as CIDESO (Comité International Desthétique et de Cosmétologie, 🖥 www.cidesco.com).

The key to success is professionalism and high standards, whether you simply want a job in the industry or, like Kezia, have plans to start your own business. As with the active tourism business, there's no substitute for long and varied experience in the industry to allow you to see where there might be a gap in the market. It's a case of recognising what the emerging trends are and offering something subtly different, which is what Kezia hopes to do with her Asian-style spa and wellness centre. "I can see the potential," she enthuses, "and my research backs that up with figures, but I know I will still need something to make my spa stand out from all the others."

YOGA

Yoga is relatively new to Spain. It's growing in popularity – in the cities as well as in coastal areas – but there's still a long way to go before it achieve the status it has in some other European countries or in the US. Consequently, it's a potential area for making a living in Spain.

The growing interest in yoga in Spain is partly due to changes in working patterns. Spain may have performed an economic miracle over the last 25 years, but the Spanish are now seeing some of the side effects that many northern Europeans have lived with for years. William Sackville West, who runs City Yoga in Madrid, explains: "Lunches are getting shorter, the siesta is dying out in some areas and the pace of life is becoming far quicker. People are becoming more and more stressed and they're looking for solutions. Yoga is a very popular option to achieve relaxation and it's far more mainstream now than it was, even ten years ago."

William opened City Yoga in the business district of Madrid in January 2003 and three months later 250 people had signed up for classes. Two years on, the centre is still going strong, running as many as 20 classes every day and working at capacity. William attributes its success to the wide range of classes and services he offers and, more importantly, the quality of his teaching staff: "Because the profession isn't regulated, someone can go on a very short training course and call themselves a yoga teacher, which is pretty dangerous for their students. When we're choosing a teacher, we look for someone who has been practising yoga for a long time and who's actually living it rather than just teaching it." City Yoga offers a four-year yoga teacher training course in an effort to maintain high standards in the industry.

Qualifications & Research

Although yoga teaching isn't regulated in Spain, the European Yoga Alliance (🖳 www.euroyoga.yoganet.org), which describes itself as a 'forum for yoga schools and all traditions as well as independent yoga professionals,' works to ensure minimum yoga teaching standards and registers yoga associations, schools and clubs, as well as individual teachers and instructors, that meet those standards. Members of the EYA are therefore more likely to find work and may be favoured by people looking for a yoga teacher.

If you want to teach yoga in Spain, make sure that all your training certificates and qualifications are translated into Spanish and that you can demonstrate your commitment to the practice. Research the area where you intend to work and find out what services are already available. One of the best ways to do this is to work initially within the support network of a yoga centre or an alternative health centre (see page 250). If you participate in the local yoga classes, you can make valuable contacts and begin to get an idea of your market. There are a growing number of 'yoga retreats', especially in the more remote, unspoiled areas of Andalusia, where you can get away from it all with like-minded people. The commercial website 🖳 www.yogadirectory.com has details of many retreats (not all are in exotic locations) and yoga holidays worldwide, including those in Spain, and a useful research and resources section.

There are two useful sources of information about yoga centres in Andalusia: Andalucia Com SL provides a comprehensive guide on its website (🖳 www.andalucia.com – click on 'alternative health'), and *La Chispa* magazine (see page 250) contains a wide range of relevant articles and contacts, and advertisements for yoga teachers. The Barcelona Healers and Therapists Network (🖳 www.barcelonahealersandthera-pists.net) can provide a list of English-language yoga centres in the Barcelona area.

Starting a Business

Many people start by teaching at an existing school and then open their own yoga schools. This is what James Jewell, an experienced yoga teacher from the UK, decided to do when he came to work in southern Spain, in January 2004. Although he had been coming to Spain for many years and knew the area well, he didn't have any business contacts there. "I simply went and presented myself and my qualifications and experience at yoga schools and alternative health centres in the area. It was a bit nerve-wracking at first, but I had to find work to survive. I found the local alternative lifestyle magazine, *La Chispa* (🖳 www.lachispa.net), very helpful and I was lucky because I made some good contacts in the village where I was living. The locals helped me with all kinds of useful information." James has found three locations in the Marbella area where he can hold classes until he's able to teach in the fully equipped yoga studio which is being built in the grounds of his house in Ojen, a small village close to Marbella. "My classes are pretty full already with Spanish, English and international students, but once the studio is completed I aim to hold weekend courses and workshops as well."

William Sackville West decided to concentrate on running the business side of his yoga centre in Madrid, rather than actually teach classes: "I know you're supposed to start small and grow slowly, but I decided from the word go to aim high and create a multidisciplinary space. I'd researched the market well, both in Spain and back in the UK, and knew that there was plenty of potential. However, starting big requires large quantities of money and one of the main problems I found was that, although I had big ideas, banks in Spain are not willing to lend money on the basis of ideas. You can produce the most beautiful business plan in the world but they're only interested in guarantors so that they know they will get their money back if it all folds. The banking system in Spain has improved immensely but it still isn't very sophisticated when you compare it with those of other European countries."

Marketing & Development

Both William in Madrid and James in Marbella never forget that they're working in Spain. William's yoga school caters primarily for the Spanish market and only around 10 per cent of its customers are expatriates, although they hold some classes in English. "You aren't going to survive in business, especially in Madrid, if your client base is only an expatriate one," says William. "We have a youngish, executive crowd of Spanish customers who live locally and work in the nearby business area. We don't want them to feel out of place or uncomfortable, which they might do if we operated solely in English." Although James Jewell works in an area where English is commonly spoken, he feels much the same way: "I hold some classes in English but I try to work in Spanish most of the time. If you don't, you exclude an enormous number of potential students and marginalise yourself and your profession."

William's advice for yoga teachers hoping to work in Spain is to do your research well and learn the language, wherever you plan to work. Most important of all, he says, is that you must be an experienced teacher and practitioner: "It's all about time. You need to have been working and practising yoga for as long as possible and be committed, constant and honest." If you want to make a business out of yoga, high levels of professionalism are required both in your yoga practice and in your attitude to business. The secret of any business, including yoga teaching, is to constantly look at ways in which you can diversify. City Yoga offers all kind of therapies and massage as well as a full yoga programme, including classes for children, and William is currently also working on weekend courses (known as 'retreats'). "Diversity is vitally important," he says, "but we're careful that we don't lose the essence of the centre."

APPENDICES

Appendix A: Useful Addresses

Embassies & Consulates

Embassies are located in the capital Madrid; many countries also have consulates in other cities (British provincial consulates are listed on page 280). Embassies and consulates are listed in the yellow pages under *Embajadas*. Note that some countries have more than one office in Madrid and, before writing or calling in person, you should telephone to confirm that you have the correct office.

Algeria: C/General Oraá, 12, 28006 Madrid (☎ 915 629 705).

Angola: C/Serrano, 64, 28001 Madrid (☎ 914 356 166).

Argentina: C/Pedro de Valdivia, 21, 28006 Madrid (☎ 915 622 800, 💻 www.portalargentino.net).

Australia: Pza Descubridor Diego Ordás, 3, 28003 Madrid (☎ 914 416 025, 💻 www.spain.embassy.gov.au).

Austria: Paseo de la Castellana, 91, 28046 Madrid (☎ 915 565 315, 💻 www.bmm.gv.at/madrid).

Belgium: Paseo de la Castellana, 18, 28046 Madrid (☎ 915 776 300, 💻 www.diplobel.org/spain).

Bolivia: C/Velázquez, 26, 28001 Madrid (☎ 915 780 835, 💻 www.mcei-bolivia.com).

Brazil: C/de Fernando el Santo, 6, 28010 Madrid (☎ 917 004 650).

Bulgaria: C/Travesia de Santa Maria Magdalena, 15, 28016 Madrid (☎ 913 455 761).

Cameroon: C/Rosario Pino, 3, 28020 Madrid (☎ 915 711 160).

Canada: C/Núñez de Balboa, 35, 28001 Madrid (☎ 914 233 250, 💻 www.canada-es.org).

Chile: C/Lagasca, 88, 28001 Madrid (☎ 914 319 160).

China: C/Arturo Soria, 113, 28043 Madrid (☎ 915 194 242, 💻 www.embajadachina.es).

Colombia: C/General Martínez Campos, 48, 28010 Madrid (☎ 917 004 770).

Costa Rica: Paseo de la Castellana, 164, 28046 Madrid (☎ 913 459 622).

Croatia: C/Claudio Coello, 78, 28001 Madrid (☎ 915 776 881).

Cyprus: C/Serrano, 23, 28001 Madrid (☎ 915 783 114).

Czech Republic: Avda. Pío XII, 22-24, 28016 Madrid (☎ 913 531 880).

Cuba: Paseo de la Habana, 194, 28036 Madrid (☎ 913 592 500, 💻 www.ecubamad.com).

Denmark: C/Claudio Coello, 91, 28006 Madrid (☎ 914 318 445, 💻 www.embajadadinamarca.es).

Ecuador: C/Velázquez, 114, 28006 Madrid (☎ 915 627 215/216).

Egypt: C/Velázquez, 69, 28006 Madrid (☎ 915 776 308).

El Salvador: C/General Oraá, 9, 28006 Madrid (☎ 915 628 002, 💻 www.embasalva.com).

Estonia: C/Claudio Coello, 91, 28006 Madrid (☎ 914 261 671, 💻 www.estemb.es).

Finland: Paseo de la Castellana, 15, 28046 Madrid (☎ 913 196 172, 💻 www.finlandia.org).

France: C/Salustiano Olózaga, 9, 28001 Madrid (☎ 914 238 900, 💻 www.ambafrance-es.org).

Gabon: C/General Arrando, 19, 28010 Madrid (☎ 914 138 211).

Germany: C/Fortuny, 8, 28010 Madrid (☎ 915 579 000, 💻 www.embajada-alemania.es).

Greece: Avda. Doctor Arce, 24, 28002 Madrid (☎ 915 644 653).

Guatemala: C/Rafael Salgado, 3, 28036 Madrid (☎ 913 440 347).

Haiti: C/Marqués del Duero, 3, 28001 Madrid (☎ 915 752 624).

Honduras: Paseo de la Castellana, 164, 28046 Madrid (☎ 915 790 251, 💻 www.embahonduras.es).

Hungary: C/Angel de Diego Roldán, 21, 28016 Madrid (☎ 914 137 011, 💻 www.embajada-hungria.es).

India: Avda. Pío XII, 30-32, 28016 Madrid (☎ 902 901 010, 💻 www.embajadaindia.com).

Indonesia: C/Agastia, 65, 28043 Madrid (☎ 914 130 294).

Iran: C/Jerez, 5, 28016 Madrid (☎ 913 450 112).

Iraq: C/Ronda de Sobradiel, 67, 28043 Madrid (☎ 917 591 282).

Ireland: Paseo de la Castellana, 46, 28046 Madrid (☎ 914 364 093).

Israel: C/Velázquez, 150, 28002 Madrid (☎ 917 829 500, 💻 www.embajada-israel.es).

Italy: C/Lagasca, 98, 28006 Madrid (☎ 914 233 300).

Ivory Coast: C/Serrano, 154, 28006 Madrid (☎ 915 626 916).

Japan: C/Serrano, 109, 28006 Madrid (☎ 915 907 600, 💻 www.embajapon.es).

Jordan: Paseo General Martinez Campos, 41, 28010 Madrid (☎ 913 191 100).

Korea: C/González Amigó, 15, 28033 Madrid (☎ 913 532 000).

Kuwait: Paseo de la Castellana, 141, 28046 Madrid (☎ 915 792 467).

Latvia: C/Alfonso XII, 52, 28014 Madrid (☎ 913 691 362).

Lebanon: Paseo de la Castellana, 178, 28046 Madrid (☎ 913 451 368).

Libya: C/Pisuerga, 12, 28002 Madrid (☎ 915 635 753).

Lithuania: C/Fortuny, 19, 28010 Madrid (☎ 917 022 116, 💻 www.emblituania.es).

Luxembourg: C/Claudio Coello, 78, 28001 Madrid (☎ 914 359 164, www.mae.lu/espagne).

Malaysia: Paseo de la Castellana, 91, 28046 Madrid (☎ 915 550 684).

Malta: Paseo de la Castellana, 45, 28046 Madrid (☎ 913 913 061).

Mauritania: C/Velázquez, 90, 28006 Madrid (☎ 915 757 007).

Mexico: Carrera de San Jerónimo, 46, 28014 Madrid (☎ 913 692 814, 💻 www.embamex.es).

Monaco: C/Villanueva, 12, 28001 Madrid (☎ 915 782 048).

Morocco: C/Serrano, 179, 28002 Madrid (☎ 915 631 090, 🖳 www.Maec.gov.ma/madrid).

The Netherlands: Avda. del Comandante Franco, 32, 28016 Madrid (☎ 913 537 500, 🖳 www.embajadapaisesbajos.es).

New Zealand: Plza. de la Lealtad, 2, 28014 Madrid (☎ 915 230 226).

Nicaragua: Paseo de la Castellana, 127, 28046 Madrid (☎ 915 555 510).

Nigeria: C/Segre, 23, 28002 Madrid (☎ 915 630 911).

Norway: Paseo de la Castellana, 31, 28046 Madrid (☎ 913 103 116, 🖳 www.noruega.es).

Pakistan: Avda. Pío XII, 11, 28016 Madrid (☎ 913 458 986, 🖳 www.embajada-pakistan.org).

Panama: C/Claudio Coello, 86, 28006 Madrid (☎ 915 765 001).

Paraguay: Paseo Eduardo Dato, 21, 28010 Madrid (☎ 913 082 746).

Peru: C/Príncipe de Vergara, 36, 28001 Madrid (☎ 914 314 242).

Philippines: C/Eresma, 2, 28002 Madrid (☎ 917 823 830).

Poland: C/Guisando, 23 bis, 28035 Madrid (☎ 913 736 605, 🖳 www.embajada-polonia.org).

Portugal: C/Pinar, 1, 28006 Madrid (☎ 917 824 960, 🖳 www. embajadaportugal-madrid.org).

Romania: Avda. Alfonso XIII, 157, 28016 Madrid (☎ 913 504 436).

Russia: C/Velázquez, 155, 28002 Madrid (☎ 915 622264).

Saudi Arabia: C/Doctor Alvarez Sierra, 3, 28033 Madrid (☎ 913 834 300).

Slovakia: C/Pinar, 20, 28006 Madrid (☎ 915 903 861).

Slovenia: C/Hermanos Bécquer, 7, 28006 Madrid (☎ 914 116 893).

South Africa: C/Claudio Coello, 91, 28006 Madrid (☎ 914 363 780, 🖳 www.sudafrica.com).

Sweden: C/Caracas, 25, 28010 Madrid (☎ 917 022 000, 💻 www. embajadasuecia.es).

Switzerland: C/Núñez de Balboa, 35, 28001 Madrid (☎ 914 363 960, 💻 www.eda.admin.ch/madrid).

Syria: Pza. Platerías Martínez, 1, 28014 Madrid (☎ 914 203 946).

Thailand: C/Joaquín Costa, 29, 28002 Madrid (☎ 915 632 903).

Tunisia: Avda Alfonso XII, 64, 28016 Madrid (☎ 914 473 508).

Turkey: C/Rafael Calvo, 18, 28010 Madrid (☎ 913 198 064, 💻 www.tcmadridbe.org).

United Arab Emirates: C/Capitán Haya, 40, 28020 Madrid (☎ 915 701 001).

United Kingdom: C/de Fernando el Santo, 16, 28010 Madrid (☎ 917 008 200, 💻 www.ukinspain.com).

United States of America: C/Serrano, 75, 28006 Madrid (☎ 915 872 200, 💻 www.embusa.es).

Uruguay: Paseo Pintor Rosales, 32, 28008 Madrid (☎ 917 580 475).

Venezuela: C/Capitán Haya, 1, 28020 Madrid (☎ 915 981 200).

Vietnam: C/ Arturo Soria, 201, 28043 Madrid (☎ 915 102 867, 💻 www.embavietnam-madrid.org).

British Provincial Consulates in Spain

Alicante: British Consulate, Plaza Calvo Sotelo, 1/2, 03001 Alicante (☎ 965 216 190, ✉enquiries@alicante.fco.gov.uk).

Barcelona: British Consulate-General, Edif. Torre de Barcelona, Avda. Diagonal, 477-13, 08036 Barcelona (☎ 933 666 200, ✉ barcelonaconsulate@ukinspain.com).

Bilbao: British Consulate-General, Alamada de Urquijo, 2-8, 48008 Bilbao (☎ 944 157 600, ✉ bilbaoconsulate@ ukinspain.com).

Ibiza: British Vice-Consulate, Avenida de Isidoro Macabich, 45, 07800 Ibiza (☎ 971 301 818).

Madrid: British Consulate-General, Paseo de Recoletos, 7/9, 28004 Madrid (☎ 915 249 700, ✉ madridconsulate@ ukinspain.com).

Malaga: British Consulate, Edif. Eurocom, C/Mauricio Moro Pareto, 2-2º, 29006 Malaga (☎ 952 352 300, ✉ malaga@fco.gov.uk).

Palma de Mallorca: British Consulate, Plaza Mayor, 3D, 07002 Palma de Mallorca (☎ 971 712 445, ✉ consulate@palma.mail. fco.gov.uk).

Menorca: Honorary British Vice-Consulate, Sa Casa Nova, Cami de Biniatap, 30, Es Castell, 07720 Menorca (☎ 971 363 373).

Las Palmas: British Consulate, Edif. Cataluña, Luis Morote, 6-3, 35007 Las Palmas (☎ 928 262 508, ✉ LAPAL-Consular@ fco.gov.uk).

Santa Cruz de Tenerife: British Consulate, Plaza Weyler, 8-1, 38003 Santa Cruz de Tenerife (☎ 922 286 863, ✉ tenerife. enquiries@fco.gov.uk).

Spanish Embassies & Offices Abroad

Australia: Suite 408, Edgecliff Centre, 203 New South Head Road, Edgecliff, NSW 2027 (☎ 02 9362 4212, ✉ buzon. official@sidney.ofcomes.mcx.es).

Canada: Suite 801, 151 Slater Street, Ottawa, Ontario K1P 5H3 (☎ 613 236 0409, ✉ buzon.oficial@ottawa.ofcomes.mcx.es).

UK: 5 Cavendish Square, London W16 0LH (☎ 020-7637 9061, ✉ spanishchamber@compuserve.com).

US: Suite 2029, 350 Fifth Avenue, New York, NY 10118 (☎ 212 967 2170, ✉ info@spainuscc.org).

Contributors

The following is a list of the contact details of contributors to this book, in the same order as the chapters in **Part Two**. In some cases, they asked for their details not to be included or for only certain details to be listed, and we've respected their wishes.

Bars, Hotels & Restaurants

Matthew Loughney, Kitty O'Shea's Bar and Restaurant, Calle de Alcalá 59, Madrid (☎ 915 754 901, 🖳 www.kitty osheas.com).

Steve & Pat Mallen, Bar sin Problemas (Sin's), Avenida Belgica 16, Coveta Fuma Campello, Alicante (☎ 965 638 307).

Emmerson & Yvonne Wade, Ciudad Quesada Guesthouse, Rojales, Nr. Torrevieja, Costa Blanca (☎ 966 716 252, 🖳 www. guesthouseatquesada.com, ✉ emmerson1wade@yahoo.co.uk).

Property

Marion Atkins, Key Property Services SL, Local 7, Zone 4, Urb. San Luis Torrevieja 03184, Alicante (☎ 966 784 403, 🖳 www. keypropertyservices.net).

David Carr Gardening & Garden Design (🖳 www. jardinero ingles.com).

Jane Craggs, Valencia Relocation SL, Urb. El Bosque 421, 46370 Chiva, Valencia (☎ 961 804 206, ✉ rserrano@recol.es).

Jeremy Kaye, Argent Silver SL, Calle Lepanto 10, Bajo B, 03727 Jalón, Alicante (☎ 966 480 093, ✉ jkbuild@terra.es).

Tadeusz Sieracki (🖳 www.javea24hrs.com).

Mark Stucklin, Spanish Property Insight (🖳 www.spanish-propertyinsight.com, ✉ info@spanishpropertyinsight.com).

Retailing

Gerry McKenna, G.T. McKenna, Irish Family Butchers, Centro Commercial Calahonda 2000 Nº3, Calahonda, Mijas Costa, Malaga (☎ 952 930 351).

Teresa Emslie, Ikonia Boutique, Puerto de La Duquesa, Manilva, Malaga (☎ 952 892 970).

Frank Sirett, Elephant Bookshop, Creu dels Molers, 12, 08004 Barcelona (☎ 934 430 594).

Teaching

Joy Fahey, The Joy of Art (Marbella) (☎ 669 050 254, 💻 www. joyfahey.com).

Susan Sorrell & Sophie Watts, The Language House, C/Antonio Machado, Edif. San Juan, 5, 1ºC, 29670 San Pedro de Alcántara, Málaga (☎ 952 853 027, 💻 www.thelanguage house.info).

Computing & Publishing

Carrie Frais, intoBarcelona.com (☎ 620 586 655, ✉ enquiries@ intoBarcelona.com).

Don Graham, MT Director (☎ 902 367 275, 💻 www.mt directo.com).

David Kubiak, Spanish Business Administration, El Centro, Rosellon 369, 08025 Barcelona (☎ 931 830 900, 💻 www.spanish-businessadministration.com).

Frank Reilley, Apt. 94, 46110 Godella, Valencia (☎ 961 310 056, 💻 www.and-M.com).

Health

Elizabeth Arthur (UK & Spanish Registered Midwife) (☎ 690-222 414, ✉ elizabetharthur_1@hotmail.com).

Estelle Mitchell (UK & Spanish Registered Physiotherapist), Bodyworks Health Clinic, Carretera de Cadiz, N-340, Km 165.5, Cancelada 29688, Estepona, Malaga (☎ 952 883 151, 💻 www. marbellaphysio.com).

Child Care

Julie Salmon, Toybox Little School of English, Luna 1, 18193 Monachil, Granada (☎ 958-300 866).

Julie Stephenson & Julia Fossi, Tender Loving Canguros SL (☎ 647-605 989, 💻 www.tlcanguros.com).

Leisure & Tourism

Giles Birch & Jonathan Buzzard, Ski Center (Sierra Nevada) (☎ 646-178 406 (Giles), ☎ 629 540 089 (Jonathan), (🖥 www.sierranevada.co.uk, ✉ skicenter@sierranevada.co.uk).

Kezia Jacobsen, Shanti-Som Day Spa, Marbella. (☎ 952 886 573, ✉ keziaspain@hotmail.com)

James Jewell, Yoga Teacher (☎ 628 442 4388, 🖥 www.yoga mountainyogasea.com, ✉ james@yogamountainyogasea.com).

William Sackville West, City Yoga, Calle Artistas 43, 28020 Madrid (☎ 915 534-751, 🖥 www.city-yoga.com).

APPENDIX B: FURTHER READING

English-Language Newspapers & Magazines

The following is a selection of the many English-language periodicals related to Spain. Unless otherwise stated, addresses and telephone numbers are in Spain.

Lifestyle & Property

Homes Overseas, Blendon Communications, 46 Oxford Street, London W1N 9FJ, UK (☎ 020-7636 6050, 🖳 www.homes overseas.co.uk). Bi-monthly property magazine.

Living Spain, Albany Publishing, 9 High Street, Olney, Bucks MK46 4EB, UK (☎ 01234-710992, 🖳 www.livingspain.co.uk). Bi-monthly lifestyle and property magazine.

A Place in the Sun's Everything Spain, Medway House, Lower Road, Forest Row, East Sussex RH18 5HE, UK (☎ 01342-828 700, 🖳 www.everythingspainmag.co.uk). Previously two separate magazines, now combined, with lifestyle and property articles.

Spain Magazine, The Media Company Publications Ltd, 21 Royal Circus, Edinburgh EH3 6TL (☎ 0131-226 7766, 🖳 www. spainmagazine.info). Monthly magazine about Spanish lifestyle, culture and property.

Spanish Magazine, Merricks Media, 3–4 Riverside Court, Lower Bristol Road, Bath BA2 3DZ, UK (☎ 01225-786857, 🖳 www. merricksmedia.co.uk). Monthly Spanish lifestyle magazine.

Spanish Country Homes, Pérez Galdós 36, 08012 Barcelona (☎ 902 392 396).

Spanish Homes Magazine, The Future Network plc, Beauford Court, 30 Monmouth Street, Bath BA1 2BW (☎ 01225-442244, ✉ shm@futurenet.co.uk). Monthly property magazine.

Villas & . . ., SKR Española, SL, Apartado de Correos 453, 29670 San Pedro Alcántara, Malaga (☎ 952 884 994, 🖳 www. villas.com). Monthly property magazine with articles in English, French, German and Spanish.

Viva España Magazine, Blendon Communications, 207 Providence Square, Mill Street, London, SE1 2EW, UK (☎ 020-7939 9889, 🖥 www. vivaespañamagazine.com). Bi-monthly property and lifestyle magazine.

World of Property, 1 Commercial Road, Eastbourne, East Sussex BN21 3XQ, UK (☎ 01323-726040, 🖥 www.outbound publishing.com). Quarterly property magazine.

Madrid Area

The Broadsheet, Plaza de Canalejas 6, 1° 28014 Madrid (☎ 915 237 480, 🖥 www.tbs.com). Free monthly magazine. Mainly Madrid, but Barcelona and other areas of Spain also covered.

InMadrid, c/ Marqués de Valdeiglesias, 6, 4°A, 28004 Madrid (☎ 915 226 780, 🖥 www.in-madrid.com). Free monthly magazine in English. Also available online.

Madrid Connect, Co & Connect International (🖥 www.madrid connect.com). Free monthly magazine in English, also available online.

Barcelona Area

Barcelona Connect, Go and Connect SL, Apartado de Correos 745, 08080 Barcelona (☎ 902 200 701, 🖥 www.barcelonaconnect.com). Monthly print and online magazine about Barcelona.

Barcelona Metropolitan, Enrique Granados 48, Entlo. 2ª 08008 Barcelona (☎ 934 514 486, 🖥 www.barcelona-metropolitan.com). Free monthly magazine. Also available online.

Catalunya Lifestyle, Golding-Eshuis SL, 25A, Carrer Sant Llorenç 17220 Sant Feliu de Guíxols (☎ 972 327 311, 🖥 www. catalanlife.com). Monthly magazine for foreign residents and visitors, available in print and online versions.

Valencia & Costa Blanca Area

Costa Blanca News, C/ Alicante 9, Polígono Industrial La Cala, Finestrat, Alicante (☎ 965 855 286, 🖥 www.costablanca-news.com). Weekly newspaper published on Fridays.

Valencia Life, Apartado de Correos No. 51, 03720 Benissa, Alicante (⌨ www.valencialife.net). Quarterly magazine.

Malaga & Costa del Sol Area

Absolute Marbella, Office 21, Edif Tembo, C/ Rotary International, 29660 Puerto Banús, Malaga (☎ 902 301 130, ⌨ www.absolutemagazine.com). Glossy fashion and lifestyle magazine in English and Spanish.

Costa del Sol News, CC Las Moriscas Local 10, Avda Juan Lusi Peralta, 29629 Benalmádena Pueblo, Malaga (☎ 952 448 730, ⌨ www.costadelsol news.es). Weekly newspaper published on Fridays.

Essential Marbella, Complejo la Poveda, Bloque 3, 1-A, CN340, km 178.2, 29600 Marbella, Malaga (☎ 952 766 344, ⌨ www. essentialmagazine.com). Free monthly magazine.

Estepona Magazine, Avda. De Andalucía 42, Edificio La Espiga, 1ºB, 29680 Estepona, Malaga (☎ 952 798 208, ⌨ www. esteponamagazine.com). Free monthly magazine about the Estepona area and Spain in general.

Euro Weekly, Avda de la Constitución, Edificio Fiesta, Locales 32 & 33, Arroyo de la Miel, 29630 Benalmadena, Malaga (☎ 952 561 245, ⌨ http://euroweeklynews.com). Weekly free newspaper.

Inland Magazine, Buzon 111, Avda de la Constitución 3, 29120 Alhaurin el Grande, Malaga (☎ 952 596 346, ⌨ www.inland magazine.com). Free monthly magazine for residents and visitors of the inland areas of Malaga province.

La Chispa, Apartado de Correos 281, 29100 Coín, Malaga (⌨ www.lachispa.net). Free bimonthly magazine about alternative living in Andalusia.

Property World, C/España, 1, Edif. Buendia, 1oA, 29640 Fuengirola, Malaga (☎ 952 666 234, ⌨ www.propertyworld-magazine.com). Free monthly magazine.

Sur in English, Diario Sur, Avda. Doctor Marañón, 48, 29009 Malaga (☎ 952 649 600, ⌨ www.surinenglish.com). Free weekly newspaper.

Balearic Islands

The Mallorca Daily Bulletin, San Feliu, 25, Palma de Mallorca, Majorca.

Canary Islands

Island Connections, C/Rodeo Aptos, Royal Palm, Local 236, 38650 Los Cristianos, Tenerife, Canary Islands (☎ 922 750 609, 🖳 www.newscanaries.com). Fortnightly newspaper published in the Canary Islands.

Living Tenerife, Stockford Media SL, Avenida de Santa Cruz 14, 2º Piso, San Isidro 38600 Granadilla de Abona, Tenerife, Canary Islands (☎ 922 394 244 or 922 394 247 or 922 394 249, 🖳 www.livingtenerife.com. Monthly magazine. An annual subscription costs around €35.

The Paper, Oficina C, 2 Fase, Edif. Las Chafiras 'Golf', Las Chafiras, San Miguel de Abona 38369, Tenerife, Canary Islands (☎ 922 735 659, 🖳 www.thepaper.net). Tenerife weekly newspaper.

Tenerife News, Canary Wharf SL, Edif. Siete Fuentes, Calle Siete Funentes 8, 38410 Los Realejos, Santa Cruz de Tenerife, Tenerife, Canary Islands (☎ 922 346 000, 🖳 www.tennews. com). Free fortnightly newspaper.

Appendix C: USEFUL WEBSITES

The following list contains some of the many websites dedicated to Spain as well as websites containing information about a number of countries. Websites about particular aspects of life and work in Spain are mentioned in the relevant chapters.

General Spanish Websites

About Spain (🖳 www.aboutspain.net). Information about specific regions in Spain.

All About Spain (🖳 www.red2000.com). General tourist information about Spain.

Andalucia (🖳 www.andalucia.com). Comprehensive information about the region of Andalusia in English.

Barcelona (🖳 www.xbarcelona.com). Information including job opportunities and useful tips for foreigners living in Barcelona.

Barcelona Online (🖳 www.barcelona-online.com). All kinds of useful living and working information about Barcelona, run by the language school, International House.

BBC (🖳 www.bbc.co.uk/education/spanish/forwork). General information about working in Spain (go to the 'Education/ Learning Languages' section, which takes you to a 'Working in Spain' link).

Escape to Spain (🖳 www.escapetospain.co.uk). General information and a property guide to the Costa Blanca, Costa Brava and Costa del Sol.

Expatica (🖳 www.expatica.com). Excellent information on all aspects of living and working in Spain. Informative articles; Spanish news; job and accommodation search facility.

Fresh Directory (🖳 www.freshdirectory.com). A guide to English-speaking businesses on the Costa del Sol, but also includes extensive up-to-date information about living and working in Spain.

Ideal Spain (🖳 www.idealspain.com). Information about many aspects of living in Spain.

Just Landed (🖥 www.justlanded.com). Information about living and working in Spain.

Madrid Man (🖥 www.madridman.com). A wealth of useful and continually updated information about living and working in Madrid including an 'ask the expert' facility.

Multi Madrid (🖥 www.multimadrid.com). Mainly a tourist website, but contains useful information about the city and includes a virtual Madrid tour online. In English.

Puerta del Sol Blog (🖥 www.puertadelsolblog.com). This site has excellent and extensive links to sites covering all kinds of information about Spain and life in Spain. Includes a link to 100 Spanish newspapers online.

Spain Alive (🖥 www.spainalive.com). Information about specific areas of Spain as well as general information.

Spain Expat (🖥 www.spainexpat.com). Information about living in Spain, including an 'ask the legal expert' facility. The site has particularly good links.

Spain Media (🖥 www.spainmedia.com). Excellent website with good links to newspapers and magazines, both English and Spanish. This site also includes useful articles from *Barcelona Business*, an English-language monthly newspaper which was published from March 1998 to August 2004.

Spain For Visitors (🖥 http://spainforvisitors.com). Good general information about visiting Spain.

Spanish Forum (🖥 www.spanishforum.org). A wealth of useful and continually updated information about all aspects of living and working in Spain, including a free monthly 'e-newsletter'.

Survival Books (🖥 www.survivalbooks.net). Survival Books is the publisher of this book and *The Best Places to Buy a Home in Spain*, *Buying a Home in Spain* and *Living and Working in Spain*. The website includes useful tips for anyone planning to buy a home, live, work, retire or do business in Spain.

Time Out (🖥 www.timeout.com). Reliable information about numerous Spanish cities, including Madrid, Barcelona, Valencia.

TurEspaña – Spanish National Tourist Office (🖳 www.tour spain.co.uk or 🖳 www.spain.info). General tourist information.

Travelling in Spain (🖳 http://travelinginspain.com). Information about Spanish cities with particular emphasis on Madrid.

TuSpain (🖳 www.tuspain.com). General information about Spain with the emphasis on buying property and residential matters.

Typically Spanish (🖳 www.typicallyspanish.com). Information on a wide range of Spanish topics.

Visa Information Online (🖳 www.extranjeros.mir.es). Spanish Interior Ministry website. Information available in English and French in the section entitled 'Orientation for Immigrants'.

Work and Social Affairs Dept. of Spanish Embassy in UK (🖳 www.mtas.es/consejerias/reinounido/working). Excellent information in English about living and working in Spain with useful links.

Making a Living in Spain

Below is a selection of websites with specific information about job-hunting and starting your own business. Area-specific sites are listed under the sub-headings below.

AnyWorkAnywhere (🖳 www.anyworkanywhere.com). Over 30,000 jobs worldwide advertised – a site run by two people who spent five years travelling the world to find work.

Grant Guide (🖳 www.grant-guide.com). Excellent site with information on grants available in all European countries, including Spain. Information available in all EU languages, including English.

INEM (🖳 www.inem.es). The site of the Central Employment/ Unemployment Department (Instituto Naciónal de Empleo). Each region has its own office and all the addresses and telephone numbers are listed on this website (only available in

Spanish). Website details for INEM offices in the areas included in this book can be found below.

Infojobs.com (🖳 www.infojobs.com). In Spanish only but with a good selection of job opportunities in Spain.

Invest in Spain (🖳 www.investinspain.org). Spanish government site primarily for foreign investors but with plenty of useful information about all aspects of business. Available in English.

Jobs in Europe (🖳 www.jobs-in-europe.net). Contains information on 26 countries, including Spain, with links to sites advertising au pair, IT, TEFL and other jobs.

One-Stop Shops for Business Start-Ups (*Ventanillas Unicas Empresariales – VUE*) (🖳 www.ventanillaempresarial.org). Information only in Spanish, but this is an excellent service, so ask a Spanish speaker to translate.

Organisation for Small and Medium-Size Businesses (*Dirección General de Política de la PYME*) (🖳 www.ipyme.org). Spanish only site, but useful information, especially about grants for the creation of some small and medium-size businesses.

Spanish Central Government Tax Agency (*Agencia Estatal de Administración Tributaria*) (🖳 www.aeat.es). Information only available in Spanish.

Spanish Chambers of Commerce in Spain (🖳 www.camaras.org). This central site links into all the Chambers around the country. It's available in Spanish only but if you click on '*buscador de cámaras*', you can choose a regional site, some of which are available in English.

Spanish Credit Insitute (*Instituto de Crédito Oficial*) (🖳 www.ico.es). Website of Spain's state-owned financial agency, attached to the Ministry of the Economy and Finance. This website is available in English and is worth a visit. Click on the section entitled 'Financing Facilities', then on 'Domestic Investment'.

Spanish Institute for Foreign Trade (ICEX) (🖳 www.spainbusiness.com). Lots of useful information about business in Spain in English, including a downloadable *Guide to Business in Spain*.

Spanish Tax Information in English (🖥 www.suma.es). This website also has details of a telephone query service which is available in English, French and German.

UK Inland Revenue Centre for Non-Residents (🖥 www. inlandrevenue.gov.uk/cnr). Information about taxation for expatriates.

UK Trade and Investment (🖥 www.trade.uktradeinvest. gov.uk). Excellent UK government website, primarily for large investors in Spain but contains useful area and sector specific information in the 'Trade' section.

Madrid Area

INEM (🖥 www.comadrid.es). In Spanish only but contains a wealth of information specific to Madrid, about employment, starting a business and opportunities for women.

Madrid Chamber of Commerce (🖥 www.camaramadrid.es). Available in English and gives full information about services to promote business and the economy of Madrid.

Madrid City Council (🖥 www.munimadrid.es). Available in English.

Barcelona Area

Barcelona Activa (🖥 www.barcelonanetactiva.com). Portal for online services for entrepreneurs, run by the local council. The website claims to be in English as well as Spanish and Catalan, but as soon as you leave the home page, it reverts to Spanish. An excellent service nevertheless.

Barcelona Chamber of Commerce (🖥 www.cambrabcn.es). Available in English.

British Chamber of Commerce in Barcelona (🖥 www.british chamberspain.com). Excellent website and extensive services for new entrepreneurs.

Government of Catalonia - Centre for Innovation and Business Development, Barcelona (CIDEM). (⌨ www.catalonia.com). Extensive information about starting a business in Catalonia available in English, French, German and Japanese, as well as Spanish.

INEM (⌨ www.gencat.net). Information only in Catalan.

Servijob.com (⌨ www.servijob.com). Spanish-only site for Barcelona jobs, including classified advertisements from Barcelona's main daily newspaper, *La Vanguardia*.

Valencia & Costa Blanca Area

Alicante Chamber of Commerce (⌨ www.camaralicante.com).

Chambers of Commerce for the Valencian Community (⌨ www.comextcv.com). Available in English with links to other Chambers in the area, some of which are available in English.

Costa Blanca Live (⌨ www.costablancalive.info). Good information and links for the whole Costa Blanca area.

Costa Blanca Netguide (⌨ www.costablanca-netguide.com). Good general and business information about the area.

Costa Blanca World (⌨ www.costablancaworld.com). Includes a section for entrepreneurs called 'Mind Your Own Business'.

INEM (⌨ www.servef.es). Only in Spanish and Valenciano.

Valencian Worldwide Investment and Foreign Trade Agency (IVEX) (⌨ www.ivex.es). Site available in English.

Malaga & Costa del Sol Area

Andalusian Centre for Entrepreneurs (*Centros Andaluces Emprendadores* – *CADE***)** (⌨ www.juntadeandalucia.es/servicioandaluzdeempleo/cade). A useful organisation based in the Technology Park in Malaga. The site is only in Spanish.

Employment Agencies (⌨ www.wemploy.com, ⌨ www. empressolutions.com, ⌨ www.recruitspain.com and ⌨www.

jobtoasterspain.com). English-language agencies on the Costa del Sol.

INEM (🖳 www.juntadeandalucia.es/servicioandaluzdeempleo). Only in Spanish, although an English version was under construction at the end of 2004.

Malaga Chamber of Commerce (🖳 www.camaramalaga.com). Partly in English.

Malaga Technology Park (🖳 www.pta.es). Information about businesses based at the Park and how to establish a business there. Available in English.

Balearic Islands

Balearic Jobs (🖳 www.balearic-jobs.com). Lots of useful information about living and working in the Balearics along with jobs information and useful links.

Chamber of Commerce (🖳 www.cambresbalears.com). Only in Spanish but has links to plenty of other useful sites.

Federation of Small and Medium Size Businesses (🖳 www.pimem.es). Available in English.

INEM (🖳 http://infosoib.caib.es). Information only in Spanish and Catalan, but there are links to other useful sites.

Canary Islands

Canary Islands Business Information System (🖳 www.siecan.org). Available in English.

Canary Islands Special Zone (ZEC) (🖳 www.zec.org). Information about the Canary Islands' low taxation scheme in English, French, German, Italian and Spanish.

Chambers of Commerce (🖳 www.camaralp.es and 🖳 www.camaratenerife.com). These sites are in Spanish only but contain useful links. If you go to the Tenerife Chamber of Commerce website, you can download a census of commercial establishments and general information about all the Canary Islands.

INEM (🖳 www.gobiernodecanarias.org/empleo). Only in Spanish.

Tenerife General Information (🖳 www.etenerife.com). Information about life on Tenerife with useful links.

General Expatriate Information

Americans Abroad (🖳 www.aca.ch). This website offers advice, information and services to Americans abroad.

Australian Department of Foreign Affairs and Trade (🖳 www.dfat.gov.au/travel). Information about political and other matters in countries around the world, plus general travel and health advice and Australian embassy addresses.

Australians Abroad (🖳 www.australiansabroad.com). Information for Australians concerning relocating plus a forum to exchange information and advice.

British Expatriates (🖳 www.britishexpat.com). This website keep British expatriates in touch with events and information about the UK.

British Foreign and Commonwealth Office (🖳 www.fco.gov.uk). Information about political and other matters in countries around the world, plus general travel and health advice and British embassy addresses.

Canadian Department of Foreign Affairs (🖳 www.dfait-maeci.gc.ca). Information about political and other matters in countries around the world, plus general travel and health advice and Canadian embassy addresses. The Department also publishes a useful series of free booklets for Canadians moving abroad.

ExpatBoards (🖳 www.expatboards.com). The mega site for expatriates, with popular discussion boards and special areas for Britons, Americans, expatriate taxes, and other important issues.

Escape Artist (🖳 www.escapeartist.com). An excellent website and probably the most comprehensive, packed with resources, links and directories covering most expatriate destinations. You can also subscribe to the free monthly online expatriate magazine, *Escape from America.*

Expat Exchange (⌨ www.expatexchange.com). Reportedly the largest online community for English-speaking expatriates, providing a series of articles on relocation and also a question and answer facility through its expatriate network.

Expat Forum (⌨ www.expatforum.com). Provides interesting cost of living comparisons as well as seven EU country-specific forums, including Spain.

Expat World (⌨ www.expatworld.net). 'The newsletter of international living.' Contains a wealth of information for American and British expatriates, including a subscription newsletter.

Expatriate Experts (⌨ www.expatexpert.com). A website run by expatriate expert Robin Pascoe, providing invaluable advice and support.

Expats International (⌨ www.expats2000.com). The international job centre for expatriates and those wishing to recruit them.

Family Life Abroad (⌨ www.familylifeabroad.com). A wealth of information and articles on coping with family life abroad.

Foreign Wives' Club (⌨ www.foreignwivesclub.com). An online community for women in bicultural marriages.

New Zealand Ministry of Foreign Affairs and Trade (⌨ www. mft.govt.nz). Information about political and other matters in countries around the world, plus general travel and health advice and New Zealand embassy addresses.

Real Post Reports (⌨ www.realpostreports.com). Provides relocation services, recommended reading lists and plenty of interesting 'real-life' stories written by expatriates in just about every city in the world.

SaveWealth Travel (⌨ www.savewealth.com/travel/ warnings). Travel information.

Southern Cross Group (⌨ www.southern-cross-group.org). A website for Australians and New Zealanders providing information and the exchange of tips.

Third Culture Kids (💻 www.tckworld.com). A website designed for expatriate children living abroad.

Trade Partners (💻 www.tradepartners.gov.uk). A government-sponsored website whose main aim is to provide trade and investment information on just about every country in the world. Even if you aren't planning to do business abroad, the information is comprehensive and up to date.

The Travel Doctor (💻 www.tmvc.com.au). Contains a country-by-country vaccination guide.

Travel Documents (💻 www.traveldocs.com). Useful information about travel, specific countries and documents needed to travel.

Travel for Kids (💻 www.travelforkids.com). Advice on travelling with children around the world.

US Government Trade (💻 www.usatrade.gov). A huge website providing a wealth of information principally for Americans planning to trade and invest abroad, but useful for anyone planning a move abroad.

US State Government (💻 www.state.gov/travel). US Government website.

Women of the World (💻 www.wow-net.org). A website designed for female expatriates anywhere in the world.

World Health Organization (💻 www.who.int).

World Travel Guide (💻 www.wtgonline.com). A general website for world travellers and expatriates.

Worldwise Directory (💻 www.suzylamplugh.org/worldwise). This website run by the Suzy Lamplugh charity for personal safety, provides a useful directory of countries with practical information and special emphasis on safety, particularly for women.

APPENDIX D: WEIGHTS & MEASURES

Spain uses the metric system of measurement. Those who are more familiar with the imperial system of measurement will find the tables on the following pages useful. Some comparisons shown are only approximate, but are close enough for most everyday uses. In addition to the variety of measurement systems used, clothes sizes often vary considerably with the manufacturer. The following websites allow you to make instant conversions between different measurement systems: 💻 www.omnis.demon.co.uk and 💻 www.unit-conversion.info.

Women's Clothes

Continental	34	36	38	40	42	44	46	48	50	52
UK	8	10	12	14	16	18	20	22	24	26
US	6	8	10	12	14	16	18	20	22	24

Pullovers

	Women's						Men's					
Continental	40	42	44	46	48	50	44	46	48	50	52	54
UK	34	36	38	40	42	44	34	36	38	40	42	44
US	34	36	38	40	42	44	sm		med		lar	xl

Men's Shirts

Continental	36	37	38	39	40	41	42	43	44	46
UK/US	14	14	15	15	16	16	17	17	18	-

Men's Underwear

Continental	5	6	7	8	9	10
UK	34	36	38	40	42	44
US	sm		med		lar	xl

Note: sm = small, med = medium, lar = large, xl = extra large

Children's Clothes

Continental	92	104	116	128	140	152
UK	16/18	20/22	24/26	28/30	32/34	36/38
US	2	4	6	8	10	12

Children's Shoes

Continental	18 19 20 21 22 23 24 25 26 27 28 29 30 31 32
UK/US	2 3 4 4 5 6 7 7 8 9 10 11 11 12 13
Continental	33 34 35 36 37 38
UK/US	1 2 2 3 4 5

Shoes (Women's and Men's)

Continental	35	36	37	37	38	39	40	41	42	42	43	44
UK	2	3	3	4	4	5	6	7	7	8	9	9
US	4	5	5	6	6	7	8	9	9	10	10	11

Weight

Imperial	Metric	Metric	Imperial
1oz	28.35g	1g	0.035oz
1lb*	454g	100g	3.5oz
1cwt	50.8kg	250g	9oz
1 ton	1,016kg	500g	18oz
2,205lb	1 tonne	1kg	2.2lb

Length

Imperial	Metric	Metric	Imperial
1in	2.54cm	1cm	0.39in
1ft	30.48cm	1m	3ft 3.25in
1yd	91.44cm	1km	0.62mi
1mi	1.6km	8km	5mi

Capacity

Imperial	Metric	Metric	Imperial
1 UK pint	0.57 litre	1 litre	1.75 UK pints
1 US pint	0.47 litre	1 litre	2.13 US pints
1 UK gallon	4.54 litres	1 litre	0.22 UK gallon
1 US gallon	3.78 litres	1 litre	0.26 US gallon

Note: An American 'cup' = around 250ml or 0.25 litre.

Area

Imperial	Metric	Metric	Imperial
1 sq. in	0.45 sq. cm	1 sq. cm	0.15 sq. in
1 sq. ft	0.09 sq. m	1 sq. m	10.76 sq. ft
1 sq. yd	0.84 sq. m	1 sq. m	1.2 sq. yds
1 acre	0.4 hectares	1 hectare	2.47 acres
1 sq. mile	2.56 sq. km	1 sq. km	0.39 sq. mile

Temperature

°Celsius	°Fahrenheit	
0	32	(freezing point of water)
5	41	
10	50	
15	59	
20	68	
25	77	
30	86	
35	95	
40	104	
50	122	

Notes: The boiling point of water is 100°C / 212°F.

Normal body temperature (if you're alive and well) is 37°C / 98.6°F.

Temperature Conversion

Celsius to Fahrenheit: multiply by 9, divide by 5 and add 32. (For a quick and approximate conversion, double the Celsius temperature and add 30.)

Fahrenheit to Celsius: subtract 32, multiply by 5 and divide by 9. (For a quick and approximate conversion, subtract 30 from the Fahrenheit temperature and divide by 2.)

Oven Temperatures

Gas	Electric	
	°F	°C
-	225–250	110–120
1	275	140
2	300	150
3	325	160
4	350	180
5	375	190
6	400	200
7	425	220
8	450	230
9	475	240

Air Pressure

PSI	Bar
10	0.5
20	1.4
30	2
40	2.8

Power

Kilowatts	Horsepower	Horsepower	Kilowatts
1	1.34	1	0.75

APPENDIX E: MAPS

The map opposite shows the 17 autonomous regions and 50 provinces of Spain (listed below). The maps on the following pages show airports with scheduled services from the UK and Ireland (see **Appendix F**), high speed train (AVE) routes, and motorways and other major roads.

Galicia	26. Barcelona
1. Coruña	27. Tarragona
2. Lugo	**Extremadura**
3. Pontevedra	28. Cáceres
4. Orense	29. Badajoz
Asturias	**Castilla La Mancha**
5. Asturias	30. Guadalajara
Castilla y León	31. Toledo
6. León	32. Cuenca
7. Palencia	33. Ciudad Real
8. Burgos	34. Albacete
9. Zamora	**Madrid**
10. Valladolid	35. Madrid
11. Soria	**Comunidad Valenciana**
12. Salamanca	36. Castellón
13. Avila	37. Valencia
14. Segovia	38. Alicante
Cantabria	**Andalucía**
15. Cantabria	39. Huelva
La Rioja	40. Seville
16. La Rioja	41. Córdoba
País Vasco	42. Jaén
17. Vizcaya	43. Cádiz
18. Guipúzcoa	44. Málaga
19. Alava	45. Granada
Navarra	46. Almeria
20. Navarra	**Murcia**
Aragón	47. Murcia
21. Huesca	**Baleares**
22. Zaragossa	48. Baleares
23. Teruel	**Canarias**
Cataluña	49. Santa Cruz de Tenerife
24. Lérida (Lleida)	50. Las Palmas de Gran Canaria
25. Gerona (Girona)	

REGIONS & PROVINCES

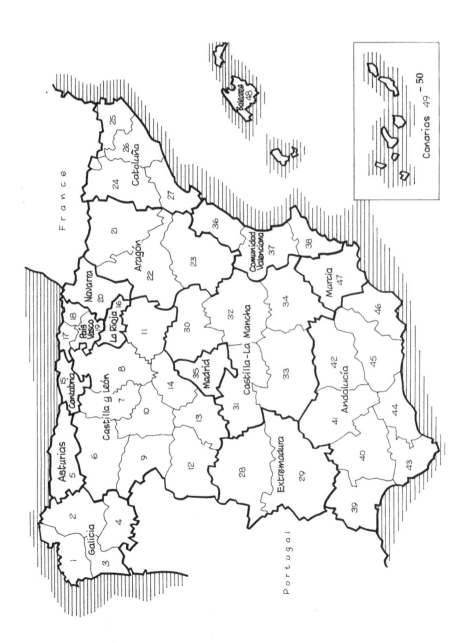

AIRPORTS

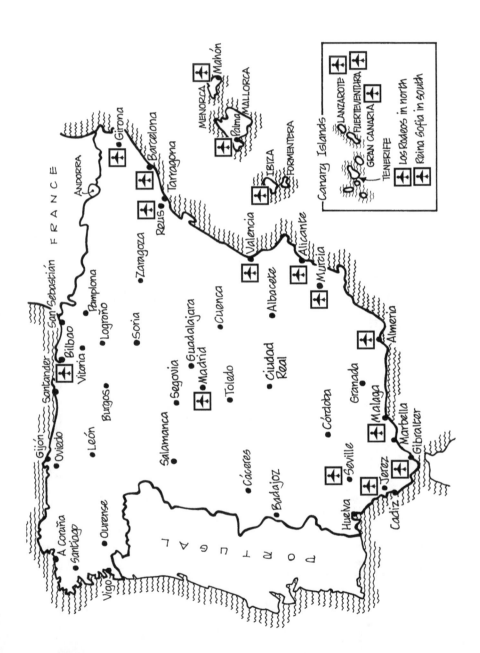

AVE NETWORK

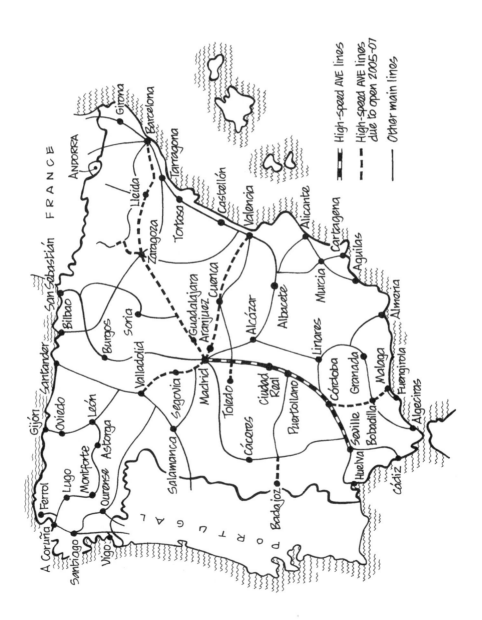

Motorways & Major Roads

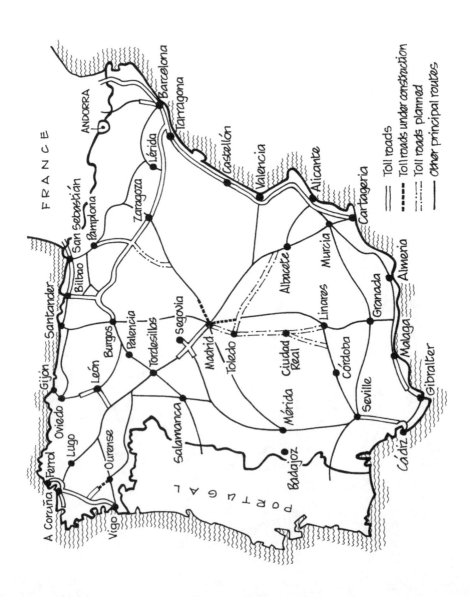

APPENDIX F: AIRLINE SERVICES

The tables on the following pages indicate scheduled flights from UK and Irish airports to Spain. Details were current in September 2004. Airlines are coded as shown below (note that these aren't all official airline codes). Telephone numbers in italics are Irish numbers; those in plain type are UK numbers.

Code	Airline	Telephone	Website
AE	Air Europa	0870-240 1501	www.aireuropa.com
AL	Aer Lingus	*0813-365 000*	www.aerlingus.com
AS	Air Scotland	0141-222 2363	www.airscotland.com
BA	British Airways	0845-773 3377	www.britishairways.com
BG	Budgetair	*01-611 4777*	www.budgetair.ie
BI	BMIbaby (British Midland)	0870-264 2229	www.bmibaby.com
BM	British Midland	0870-607 0555	www.flybmi.com
CJ	City Jet	*01-8700 300*	www.cityjet.com
EA	Excel Airways	08709-989898	www.excelairways.com
EJ	EasyJet	0871-750 0100	www.easyjet.com
FB	Flybe	0871-700 0535	www.flybe.com
FS	Flyglobespan	0870-556 1522	www.flyglobespan.com
GB	GB Airways (British Airways)	08708-509850	www.gbairways.com
IB	Iberia	0845-650 9000	www.iberia.com
J2	Jet 2	0870-737 8282	www.jet2.com
ML	MyTravelLite (Airtours)	0870-156 4564	www.mytravellite.com
MO	Monarch	0870-040 5040	www.monarch-airlines.com
RA	Ryanair	0871-246 0000	www.ryanair.com

	Belfast City (028-9093 9093)	Birmingham (0870-733 5511)	Bristol (0870-121 2747)	Cardiff (01446-711111)	Cork (021-431 3131)	Dublin (01-814 1111)	East Midlands (0871-919 9000)	Edinburgh (0870-040 0007)	Exeter (01392-367433)	Glasgow Prestwick (0870-040 0008)	Leeds/Bradford (0113-250 9696)
Alicante	BM EJ	ML	EJ	BI	AL	AL BG	BI EJ	AS BI FS	FB	AS BM EA FS	BM J2
Almeria		ML									
Barcelona		BA	EJ			AL IB	BI EJ	FS		BA FS	J2
Fuerteventura										EA	
Girona						RA		AS		AS RA	
Ibiza							BI BM				
Lanzarote		ML								EA	
Las Palmas		ML							BR	BR	
Madrid		BA IB	EJ			AL IB		BA IB		AE BA	
Mahon										EA	
Malaga	EJ	ML	EJ	BI	AL	AL BG CJ RA	BI EJ	AS FS	FB	AS EA FS	J2
Murcia			ML			RA	BI				J2
Palma	BM FS	ML	EJ	BI	AL	BI	BI	AS BM FS		AS BI EA FS	BM J2
Reus						RA					
Tenerife		ML								EA FS	
Valencia						AL					

	Liverpool (0870-750 8484)	London Gatwick (0870-0002 468)	London Heathrow (0870-000 0123)	London Luton (01582-405100)	London Stansted (0870-000 0303)	Manchester (0161-489 3000)	Newcastle (0870-122 1488)	Southampton (0870-122 1488)	Teesside (01325-332811)
Alicante	EJ	BA EJ/IB MO	BM GB IB	EJ MO	EJ	BI EA MO	AS EJ	FB	BI
Almeria		BA EA			RA	EA			
Barcelona	EJ	BA EJ	BA IB	EJ	EJ	BI MO	EJ		
Fuerteventura		EA				EA			
Gibraltar		GB		MO		MO			
Girona		GB	IB	RA	RA		AS		
Ibiza		EA EJ GB			EJ	BI EA			
Jerez					RA				
Lanzarote		EA GB			EA	EA	EA		
Las Palmas		EA GB				EA			
Madrid	EJ	AE BA EJ/IB	BA BM IB	EJ		BA BM			
Mahon		EA GB		MO		EA MO			
Malaga	EJ	BA EA/EJ GB MO	BA IB	EJ MO	EJ	BI EA MO	EA EJ MO	FB	BI
Murcia		GB			RA	BI ML		FB	
Palma	BR EJ	AE EA GB	BM	EJ MO	EJ	BI EA MO	AS EA EJ		BI
Reus				RA	RA				
Seville		GB	IB						
Tenerife		EA GB		MO	EA	EA ML MO	EA		
Valencia		GB	IB			IB			

INDEX

V

W

Y

LIVING AND WORKING SERIES

Living and Working books are essential reading for anyone planning to spend time abroad, including holiday-home owners, retirees, visitors, business people, migrants, students and even extra-terrestrials! They're packed with important and useful information designed to help you **avoid costly mistakes and save both time and money.** Topics covered include how to:

- Find a job with a good salary & conditions
- Obtain a residence permit
- Avoid and overcome problems
- Find your dream home
- Get the best education for your family
- Make the best use of public transport
- Endure local motoring habits
- Obtain the best health treatment
- Stretch your money further
- Make the most of your leisure time
- Enjoy the local sporting life
- Find the best shopping bargains
- Insure yourself against most eventualities
- Use post office and telephone services
- Do numerous other things not listed above

Living and Working books are the most comprehensive and up-to-date source of practical information available about everyday life abroad. They aren't, however, boring text books, but interesting and entertaining guides written in a highly readable style.

Discover what it's really like to live and work abroad!

Order your copies today by phone, fax, post or email from: Survival Books, PO Box 3780, YEOVIL, BA21 5WX, United Kingdom (☎/▤ +44 (0)1935-700060, ✉ sales@survivalbooks.net, 🖥 www.survivalbooks.net).

BUYING A HOME SERIES

Buying a Home books, including *Buying, Selling & Letting Property*, are essential reading for anyone planning to purchase property abroad. They're packed with vital information to guide you through the property purchase jungle and help you **avoid the sort of disasters that can turn your dream home into a nightmare!** Topics covered include:

- Avoiding problems
- Choosing the region
- Finding the right home and location
- Estate agents
- Finance, mortgages and taxes
- Home security
- Utilities, heating and air-conditioning
- Moving house and settling in
- Renting and letting
- Permits and visas
- Travelling and communications
- Health and insurance
- Renting a car and driving
- Retirement and starting a business
- And much, much more!

Buying a Home books are the most comprehensive and up-to-date source of information available about buying property abroad. Whether you want a detached house, townhouse or apartment, a holiday or a permanent home, these books will help make your dreams come true.

Save yourself time, trouble and money!

Order your copies today by phone, fax, post or email from: Survival Books, PO Box 3780, YEOVIL, BA21 5WX, United Kingdom (☎/▤ +44 (0)1935-700060, ✉ sales@survivalbooks.net, ▣ www.survivalbooks.net).

OTHER SURVIVAL BOOKS

The Alien's Guides: The Alien's Guides to Britain and France provide an 'alternative' look at life in these popular countries and will help you to appreciate the peculiarities (in both senses) of the British and French.

The Best Places to Buy a Home in France/Spain: The most comprehensive homebuying guides to France or Spain, containing detailed profiles of the most popular regions, with guides to property prices, amenities and services, employment and planned developments.

Buying, Selling and Letting Property: The most comprehensive and up-to-date source of information available for those intending to buy, sell or let a property in the UK.

Foreigners in France/Spain: Triumphs & Disasters: Real-life experiences of people who have emigrated to France and Spain, recounted in their own words – warts and all!

Lifelines: Essential guides to specific regions of France and Spain, containing everything you need to know about local life. Titles in the series currently include the Costa Blanca, Costa del Sol, Dordogne/Lot, Normandy and Poitou-Charentes; Brittany Lifeline is to be published in summer 2005.

Renovating & Maintaining Your French Home: The ultimate guide to renovating and maintaining your dream home in France: what to do and what not to do, how to do it and, most importantly, how much it will cost.

Retiring Abroad: The most comprehensive and up-to-date source of practical information available about retiring to a foreign country, containing profiles of the 20 most popular retirement destinations.

Broaden your horizons with Survival Books!

Order your copies today by phone, fax, post or email from: Survival Books, PO Box 3780, YEOVIL, BA21 5WX, United Kingdom (☎/🖷 +44 (0)1935-700060, ✉ sales@survivalbooks.net, 🖥 www.survivalbooks.net).

Qty.	Title	Price (incl. p&p)			Total
		UK	Europe	World	
	The Alien's Guide to Britain	£6.95	£8.95	£12.45	
	The Alien's Guide to France	£6.95	£8.95	£12.45	
	The Best Places to Buy a Home in France	£13.95	£15.95	£19.45	
	The Best Places to Buy a Home in Spain	£13.95	£15.95	£19.45	
	Buying a Home Abroad	£13.95	£15.95	£19.45	
	Buying a Home in Florida	£13.95	£15.95	£19.45	
	Buying a Home in France	£13.95	£15.95	£19.45	
	Buying a Home in Greece & Cyprus	£13.95	£15.95	£19.45	
	Buying a Home in Ireland	£11.95	£13.95	£17.45	
	Buying a Home in Italy	£13.95	£15.95	£19.45	
	Buying a Home in Portugal	£13.95	£15.95	£19.45	
	Buying a Home in South Africa	£13.95	£15.95	£19.45	
	Buying a Home in Spain	£13.95	£15.95	£19.45	
	Buying, Letting & Selling Property	£11.95	£13.95	£17.45	
	Foreigners in France: Triumphs & Disasters	£11.95	£13.95	£17.45	
	Foreigners in Spain: Triumphs & Disasters	£11.95	£13.95	£17.45	
	Costa Blanca Lifeline	£11.95	£13.95	£17.45	
	Costa del Sol Lifeline	£11.95	£13.95	£17.45	
	Dordogne/Lot Lifeline	£11.95	£13.95	£17.45	
	Poitou-Charentes Lifeline	£11.95	£13.95	£17.45	
	Living & Working Abroad	£14.95	£16.95	£20.45	
	Living & Working in America	£14.95	£16.95	£20.45	
	Living & Working in Australia	£14.95	£16.95	£20.45	
	Living & Working in Britain	£14.95	£16.95	£20.45	
	Living & Working in Canada	£16.95	£18.95	£22.45	
	Living & Working in the European Union	£16.95	£18.95	£22.45	
	Living & Working in the Far East	£16.95	£18.95	£22.45	
	Living & Working in France	£14.95	£16.95	£20.45	
	Living & Working in Germany	£16.95	£18.95	£22.45	
	Total carried forward (see over)				

ORDER FORM

Qty.	Title	Price (incl. p&p)			Total
		UK	Europe	World	
	L&W in the Gulf States & Saudi Arabia	£16.95	£18.95	£22.45	
	L&W in Holland, Belgium & Luxembourg	£14.95	£16.95	£20.45	
	Living & Working in Ireland	£14.95	£16.95	£20.45	
	Living & Working in Italy	£16.95	£18.95	£22.45	
	Living & Working in London	£13.95	£15.95	£19.45	
	Living & Working in New Zealand	£14.95	£16.95	£20.45	
	Living & Working in Spain	£14.95	£16.95	£20.45	
	Living & Working in Switzerland	£16.95	£18.95	£22.45	
	Normandy Lifeline	£11.95	£13.95	£17.45	
	Renovating & Maintaining Your French Home	£16.95	£18.95	£22.45	
	Retiring Abroad	£14.95	£16.95	£20.45	

Total brought forward — **Grand Total**

Order your copies today by phone, fax, post or email from: Survival Books, PO Box 3780, YEOVIL, BA21 5WX, United Kingdom (☎/🖨 +44 (0)1935-700060, ✉ sales@ survivalbooks.net, 💻 www.survivalbooks.net). If you aren't entirely satisfied, simply return them to us within 14 days for a full and unconditional refund.

I enclose a cheque for the grand total/Please charge my Amex/Delta/Maestro (Switch)/MasterCard/Visa card as follows. (delete as applicable)

Card No. _ _ _ _   _ _ _ _   _ _ _ _   _ _ _ _   Security Code* _ _ _

Expiry date _____ Issue number (Maestro/Switch only) _____

Signature _____ Tel. No. _____

NAME _____

ADDRESS _____

_____

_____

* The security code is the last three digits on the signature strip.